T0209614

WHAT DOES THE RULING CLASS DO
WHEN IT RULES?

RADICAL THINKERS } V

SET 1 ($12/£6/$14CAN)

MINIMA MORALIA
Reflections on a Damaged Life
THEODOR ADORNO
ISBN-13: 978 1 84467 051 2

FOR MARX
LOUIS ALTHUSSER
ISBN-13: 978 1 84467 052 9

THE SYSTEM OF OBJECTS
JEAN BAUDRILLARD
ISBN-13: 978 1 84467 053 6

LIBERALISM AND DEMOCRACY
NORBERTO BOBBIO
ISBN-13: 978 1 84467 062 8

THE POLITICS OF FRIENDSHIP
JACQUES DERRIDA
ISBN-13: 978 1 84467 054 3

THE FUNCTION OF CRITICISM
TERRY EAGLETON
ISBN-13: 978 1 84467 055 0

SIGNS TAKEN FOR WONDERS
On the Sociology of Literary Forms
FRANCO MORETTI
ISBN-13: 978 1 84467 056 7

THE RETURN OF THE POLITICAL
CHANTAL MOUFFE
ISBN-13: 978 1 84467 057 4

SEXUALITY IN THE FIELD OF VISION
JACQUELINE ROSE
ISBN-13: 978 1 84467 058 1

THE INFORMATION BOMB
PAUL VIRILIO
ISBN-13: 978 1 84467 059 8

CULTURE AND MATERIALISM
RAYMOND WILLIAMS
ISBN-13: 978 1 84467 060 4

THE METASTASES OF ENJOYMENT
On Women and Causality
SLAVOJ ŽIŽEK
ISBN-13: 978 1 84467 061 1

SET 2 ($12.95/£6.99/$17CAN)

AESTHETICS AND POLITICS
THEODOR ADORNO, WALTER BENJAMIN, ERNST BLOCH, BERTOLT BRECHT, GEORG LUKÁCS
ISBN-13: 978 1 84467 570 8

INFANCY AND HISTORY
On the Destruction of Experience
GIORGIO AGAMBEN
ISBN-13: 978 1 84467 571 5

POLITICS AND HISTORY
Montesquieu, Rousseau, Marx
LOUIS ALTHUSSER
ISBN-13: 978 1 84467 572 2

FRAGMENTS
JEAN BAUDRILLARD
ISBN-13: 978 1 84467 573 9

LOGICS OF DISINTEGRATION
Poststructuralist Thought and the Claims of Critical Theory
PETER DEWS
ISBN-13: 978 1 84467 574 6

LATE MARXISM
Adorno, Or, The Persistence of the Dialectic
FREDRIC JAMESON
ISBN-13: 978 1 84467 575 3

EMANCIPATION(S)
ERNESTO LACLAU
ISBN-13: 978 1 84467 576 0

THE POLITICAL DESCARTES
Reason, Ideology and the Bourgeois Project
ANTONIO NEGRI
ISBN-13: 978 1 84467 582 1

ON THE SHORES OF POLITICS
JACQUES RANCIÈRE
ISBN-13: 978 1 84467 577 7

STRATEGY OF DECEPTION
PAUL VIRILIO
ISBN-13: 978 1 84467 578 4

POLITICS OF MODERNISM
Against the New Conformists
RAYMOND WILLIAMS
ISBN-13: 978 1 84467 580 7

THE INDIVISIBLE REMAINDER
On Schelling and Related Matters
SLAVOJ ŽIŽEK
ISBN-13: 978 1 84467 581 4

WHAT DOES THE RULING CLASS DO WHEN IT RULES?

STATE APPARATUSES AND STATE POWER UNDER FEUDALISM, CAPITALISM AND SOCIALISM

Göran Therborn

VERSO

London • New York

First published by NLB 1978; copyright © Göran Therborn 1978
This edition published by Verso 2008; copyright © Göran Therborn 2008
All rights reserved

3 5 7 9 10 8 6 4 2

Verso
UK: 6 Meard Street, London W1F 0EG
USA: 20 Jay Street, Suite 1010, New York, NY 11201
www.versobooks.com

Verso is the imprint of New Left Books

ISBN-13: 978-1-84467-210-3

British Library Cataloguing in Publication Data
A catalogue record for this book is available from the British Library

Library of Congress Cataloging-in-Publication Data
A catalog record for this book is available from the Library of Congress

Printed in the United States of America

Contents

Part Two

State Power – On the Dialectics of Class Rule

Part Three

Taking State Power from Advanced Capitalism: Some Reflections on Socialism and Democracy

Science and Politics – A Foreword

Two concerns are intimately interwoven in this book: one of empirical social theory and one of the practice of revolutionary politics in the advanced capitalist countries. The first essay, dealing with the state apparatus, owes its conception to the 22nd Congress of the French Communist Party, at which the concept of the dictatorship of the proletariat was deleted from the statutes. But it goes beyond the framework of the political debate that accompanied and followed that event. Entering the field of organization theory, it seeks to elucidate the forms of state organization characteristic of feudal society, the classical and modern Western world, and the contemporary regimes of Eastern Europe.

The experiences of twentieth-century dictatorship may provide good reasons for abandonment of the bewildering distinctions between democratic and dictatorial dictatorship called for by classical Marxist-Leninist discourse. However, the concept of the dictatorship of the proletariat was central to the thought of Marx and Lenin, and designates, together with its corollaries, a crucial object that cannot be discarded in a facile manner. Above all, it points to the organization of the state as a decisive manifestation of definite social relations of class domination. To empirical social theory this raises the question: how does the very organization of the state apparatus express and reproduce class relations? To practical revolutionary politics it poses the problem: how should a socialist state in the West be organized so as to reproduce the domination of the proletariat and allied classes and strata of the working population, and so as to further the development of a classless society? Such difficulties can hardly be overcome by reference to conceptual analyses made by Lenin, however penetrating they may have been. Nor is it helpful simply to give up the terminology of Marx and Lenin without fully confronting the underlying problematic.

To a certain degree, the origins and development of the second essay are opposite in character. It grew out of dissatisfaction with the academic debate raging within Anglo-Saxon political science and sociology – a debate about whether pluralism or a power elite should be seen as the dominant force of modern western politics. A first version was presented two years ago at the annual conference of the British Sociological Association. Further elaboration was inspired by current political discussion of the mass base of bourgeois rule. How has the tiny bourgeois class, or the even smaller leading fraction of it, been able to rule in democratic forms marked by legal freedom of opinion-making and equal and universal suffrage? This problem has been posed, yet hardly answered by (among others) Louis Althusser, Christine Buci-Glucksmann and supporters of the traditional Gramscian focus on hegemony. In attempting to provide the initial elements of a solution, I have presented an overview of the political modalities of class rule. The analysis undertaken here is also related to an essay which is not included in this volume: 'The Rule of Capital and the Rise of Democracy'.[1]

The political conjuncture in which this book has been written is significantly characterized by the fact that advances towards socialism have again become a concrete possibility in certain developed capitalist societies: in particular, France and Italy. The strategic debates and programmes appearing in these and other countries have fired the keen but largely stereotyped interest of the mass media in something called 'Eurocommunism'. The third text contains some reflections on the way in which the present political constellation has arisen, and especially on the content, problems and prospects of the democratic-socialist strategy.

This work is a collection of essays rather than a book divided into chapters. But the three parts should be read in the light of one another. For example, the concept of organizational technology developed in the first essay bears upon the operation of the processes of state mediation conceptualized in the second. The mechanisms of reproduction, formats of ruling class representation and processes of mediation are not only inter-related to one another in the exercise of state power; they are also operative in the reproduction of the state apparatus – a task which is central to the maintenance of state

---

[1] *New Left Review* No. 103 (1977).

power. The strategic problems raised in the last essay are largely based upon the provisional findings of the two preceding ones.

The range of topics discussed – from the state of medieval feudalism to that of the contemporary USSR, from Max Weber's sociology of bureaucracy and classes to Western Communist strategy – will no doubt appear to many as foolhardy, and perhaps even fatal. However, in one important sense, the investigation has a rather limited scope: it is intended neither as a ready-made historical analysis nor as a compilation of recipes for revolution, but as a framework for empirical analysis and serious political discussion. For both political and scientific reasons, I have tried to keep one eye constantly open to problems of empirical investigation and corroboration. Regardless of the value of this particular attempt, the present domination of research by non-empirical theory and narrow empiricism obliges historians and empirical social scientists to adopt as their own the words of Danton and Lenin: 'Audacity, audacity, still more audacity!'

This volume advances a number of positions which will arouse scientific as well as political controversy. But it is written for readers of diverse experience and opinion, for political comrades of different organizations and academic colleagues belonging to various disciplines and schools – in fact, for everybody interested in social analysis and politics. It draws heavily on existing theory, research and politics, both non-Marxist and Marxist. As far as possible, I have tried to come forward with positive alternatives, rather than purely negative polemics.

The terms 'empirical social theory' and 'social science' are neither cautious paraphrases nor synonyms for historical materialism, although, as I have argued in my *Science, Class and Society*, the latter is the basic, although not the only science of society.[2] Arising out of a break with German philosophy, Marxism defined itself as an empirical science of society and social history committed to a revolutionary standpoint. But since the classical age of Lenin, Kautsky and their contemporaries, Marxist theory in Europe has been mainly philosophical in character and subject to the domination of professional philosophers. Consequently, the relation of *philosophy* and politics has been more central to modern European Marxists than that of *science* and politics.

This paradoxical evolution of Marxism – from philosophy to

[2] NLB, London 1976.

science and then back to philosophy – is described by Perry Anderson, with characteristic erudition and brilliance, in *Considerations on Western Marxism*.[3] However, our understanding of the contemporary history and future prospects of Marxist theory may be assisted by a few supplementary observations. It is true, of course, that since about 1920 the basic determinant of the trajectory of European Marxism has been the defeat and retrenchment of the revolutionary labour movement in the West, coupled with a dearly-bought victory in the East that was defended by authoritarian means. But the philosophical turn of Western Marxism was not simply the child of revolutionary defeat. It was also, and perhaps primarily, born out of a profound crisis of traditional *bourgeois* culture and society – a crisis which was generated by the holocaust of World War I and dramatically revealed by the alternative of the October Revolution. The inability of the categories of aesthetics, *Historismus* and classical bourgeois philosophy to grapple with the new world of war and revolution was a crucial reason why intellectuals like Lukács, Korsch, Marcuse and Gramsci turned to Marxism. (After the experience of Fascism, a fresh generation of philosophers, which included Althusser, Sartre and Della Volpe, also became disillusioned with bourgeois idealism.)

Philosophy is not inherently a retreat from politics; indeed, premodern political theory consisted entirely of political philosophy. Although Western Marxism has typically been concerned with epistemology, it has also produced much straightforward political philosophy: from *History and Class Consciousness* to the recent works of Althusser and younger writers such as Etienne Balibar, Christine Buci-Glucksmann and Giuseppe Vacca. Another reason for the philosophical complexion of Western Marxism was probably the shift in the centre of gravity of Marxist theoretical research towards countries where philosophy has been, or still is, the dominant idiom of social and political theory. Although philosophy was a major form of discourse on society in Wilhelmine and Weimar Germany, this phenomenon has above all concerned the Latin countries. Among the thirteen leading figures of Western Marxism listed by Anderson (pp. 25–6) seven are from the Latin countries, compared to one out of eleven of the foremost representatives of classical Marxism after the two founders.

[3] NLB, London 1976.

The circumstance that many Marxist theoreticians of recent decades have been philosophers is thus not only a sign of defeat and retrenchment, but also one of victory and advance. More worrying is the relative stagnation in the fields of economic and political theory. Here again Anderson's lists disclose an interesting pattern, even if the criteria on which they are based are not beyond discussion. Of the eleven most prominent classical Marxists, eight sprang from two particular intellectual cultures: those of Russia and German Austria. (The figure rises to nine if we include Luxemburg, who was born in Austrian Galicia and received her political formation both in the labour movement of Russian-occupied Poland and in the German SPD.) We cannot examine here the reasons for the extraordinary Marxist vitality of these two intelligentsias, however fascinating such a study would be. But the fact that philosophical discourse did not occupy a dominant position within these two cultures does tend to confirm the pattern that has been suggested.[4] By contrast, none of those who appear in the post-classical list came from that background. On the one hand Stalinism, on the other the defeat and capitalist integration of Austrian Socialism explain the caesura.

It is of course necessary to stress, as does Anderson, that the philosophical advances of Western Marxism suffer from severe limitations, not only with respect to the objectives of historical materialism but also in relation to bourgeois social theory. For the existence of philosophy as a pervasive idiom of Latin and (to a lesser extent) German social thought does not signify that philosophy incorporated the most advanced bourgeois contributions to social theory. Philosophical Western Marxism largely left untouched the powerful and impressive tradition of German historiography, as well as the new discipline of sociology, which, although long academically insecure and peripheral in Europe, represented in the works of Durkheim and Weber an intellectually vanguard force.

It should not be thought, however, that Marxism was preserved in Europe after the 1920s only as philosophy. Developing outside the political-theoretical centre of activity was an important and sophisticated historiography – represented in Britain by Hill, Hobsbawm, Thompson and others, and in the East by Kuczynski,

---

[4] The later, highly specialized analytical philosophy of the Vienna Circle had a very limited social range.

Porshnev et al. – as well as individual contributions to economic theory and economic history such as those of Dobb and Sweezy. Nor should we ignore the important role of Communist Party training manuals and mass agitational pamphlets in the maintenance of a Marxist tradition. Even though such material was certainly lacking in intellectual stimulation, it helped to reproduce a milieu in which politically pertinent theory and research could develop once the parameters of the situation had changed. It was to this tradition, in at first its most dogmatic forms, that the newly-radicalized generation of the late sixties turned when the flood of semi-anarchist spontaneism had run its course. To be sure, central contributions have been made by individuals of other milieux: Perry Anderson himself; Olin Wright and Wallerstein in the United States; Cardoso in Latin America; the able representative of the Trotskyist tradition, Ernest Mandel; and many others. Still, it should not be forgotten that the mainstream of the current resurgence of Marxist theory and research is flowing out of the Communist tradition.

Despite all these qualifications, it is undeniable that Marxist theory has for long been dominated by philosophy. But that dominance is now coming to an *end*. This appears likely not so much because the upheavals and crises which have shaken advanced capitalist societies since the late sixties are bringing about a reunion of theory and political practice, or at least are making the two of greater relevance to each other – for that is being effected by political philosophy itself. There is another, more important factor. Today, the disciplines of sociology, politics and economics have largely displaced philosophy as the major form of discourse on society, though this is still a rather slow process in the Latin countries. The vast university expansion of the last decade has primarily affected social science faculties. Thus, the present generation is revolting not so much against bourgeois philosophy – which was the case of Lukács, Gramsci and their contemporaries – as against bourgeois disciplines of social science. Like that earlier generation, they will bring their peculiar intellectual training with them into the realm of Marxism.

On the whole, I think that this will be a very important and positive change – one which, side by side with Marxist philosophy, will enrich both the theory and practice of Marxism. But it too poses certain problems and difficulties. Further progress is hampered by the disjuncture which has arisen between the development of socialist politics (above all in the Latin countries) and that of social science (above all in the Anglo-Saxon world). The new social-scientific Marxism is thus in danger of becoming an esoteric academic discipline, as divorced from the problems and concerns of the labour movement as the most abstruse philosophy. Nevertheless, political events in France, Italy, Portugal and Spain have already had significant repercussions in other developed countries; while, as the pathbreaking works of Nicos Poulantzas may suffice to indicate, a flourishing scientific Marxism exists today in the Latin countries. Within the domain of science, a further problem affects the relation between theory and empirical practice. For example, the recent revitalization of Marxist economics appears to have resulted in, on the one hand, highly formal theory influenced by Sraffa's critique of marginalism, and, on the other, theoretically unstable empirical investigations. A similar division can be observed in the political field. Finally, science is no guarantee against errors and mistakes, such as may be found among even its greatest geniuses.

The new turn in Marxist theory calls for consideration of the relation between science and politics. Although this little preface cannot serve as substitute for such an undertaking, we may perhaps suggest a few remarks.

There are at least two important differences between scientific and political practice. First, the former is committed above all to the search for truth, while the latter is geared to realization of a desirable state of society. On this basis, characteristic anti-ideologies arise among both types of practitioner. Science tends to breed either cynical aloofness from the 'demagogy' and violence of politics, or a kind of rationalistic elitism, according to which all political problems would be soluble if only the 'experts' could come together and win acceptance of their conclusions. Among political activists, the distinct practice of science tends to be either dismissed as an irrelevant luxury or regarded as an object which should be bent for apologetic or denunciatory purposes. Secondly, the skill of the political practitioner concerns above all the handling of personal relations so as to win other people's confidence and support; whereas the scientific commitment to objective truth is impersonal in character. (Indeed, the pursuit of scientific activity – in archives and laboratories, at the computer and the writing-desk – tends to generate isolation from everyday social relations.) The former practice may thus lead to intellectual opportunism, and the latter to abstract rigidity.

However, there are also points of contact, and even deep affinity, between science and politics, particularly revolutionary politics. I am not referring here to the correct and noble dictum of Lassalle, which was taken over by Gramsci as the motto for his paper *L'Ordine Nuovo* – 'To tell the truth is revolutionary.' The essential point is rather the following: if you want to change something fundamentally and in a definite direction, you have to know how it works; if you want only to sit on it, then no such problems arise.

Provided that their practice is of a responsible and revolutionary nature, the cadre and the scientist have at least two important traits in common. First, they are marked by a profound *realism*, in several respects. Theoretical formulations must always be judged not only in terms of their internal consistency or continuity with the past, but also on the basis of their capacity to grasp the complex and fluid structure of reality. Realism involves acknowledgment of the facts, even where their existence is unwelcome. History may be reconsidered and reinterpreted, but it cannot be remade. Similarly, the future has to be built on the foundation of the past and present, not merely constructed in thought out of ideals. The cadre and the scientist are thus anti-apologetic as well as anti-utopian.

Secondly, in contrast to the soft pliability of programmes and the hard crust of dogma, the practice of the good cadre and scientist is guided by *specificity*. Neither can stop at the bald conclusion that things do or do not exist, or that positions are correct or incorrect. For they exist or are correct in definite quantities, forms and contextual patterns, and at precise points in time; and they disappear or become incorrect in definite quantities, forms and contextual patterns, and at precise points in time.

A number of friends have read and commented upon various parts of the manuscript, and I should like to take this opportunity to offer them my thanks. I am especially grateful to Erik Olin Wright, who has taken the time to go very carefully through the first two essays. From participants in his seminar on the state, held at Madison, Wisconsin in spring 1977, I have received valuable criticisms of an earlier version of the text on the state apparatus. The great helpfulness and generous intellectual encouragement shown by the NLB collective have been a very important support in my endeavour. They have also helped me with my incurable Scandinavianisms.

This work deals mainly with the history and politics of other societies than my own, and I am therefore very interested in contact with comrades and colleagues who have more direct experience of the topics discussed. I may be reached through: Sociologiska institutionen, 220 05 Lund 5, Sweden.

Lund, August 1977.

The Dictatorship
of the Proletariat
and the Class Character
of the State Apparatus

I

The Problem and the Questions

The Dictatorship of the Proletariat: The Words and the Concept

'A Marxist is solely someone who *extends* the recognition of the class struggle to the recognition of *the dictatorship of the proletariat* . . . This is the touchstone on which the *real* understanding and recognition of Marxism should be tested!'[1] Lenin's words are absolutely unequivocal. But what use should be made of them now that the term 'dictatorship of the proletariat' has been deleted from the programmes and statutes of most Communist parties of the advanced capitalist countries?

There are a number of options open. It is possible to ignore Lenin's thesis, with a brief reference to changes in the world since his time. This is tantamount to a statement of the contemporary irrelevance of the theory of the state developed by Lenin and Marx.[2] Recent party congresses may then be taken as a starting-point for elaboration of post-Marxian and post-Leninist theories of the 'democratic state'. If this course is followed, perhaps it will turn out that Social Democracy was right after all, or at least that it is right today, sixty years after the October Revolution. Alternatively, Lenin can be invoked as an authority with which to condemn modern 'deviations' and 'betrayals' in a moral or sectarian stand. Such a reiteration of the orthodox Leninist position[3] would keep alive an

---

[1] V. I. Lenin, 'The State and Revolution', *Collected Works*, Moscow 1964, vol. 25, p. 412. Emphasis in the original.

[2] For a lucid analysis of the development of Marx's theory of the state, see E. Balibar, 'La rectification du *Manifeste Communiste*', in his *Cinq études du matérialisme historique*, Paris 1974.

[3] Étienne Balibar has made an important contribution to discussion of this question in *On the Dictatorship of the Proletariat*, NLB, London 1977.

important heritage, but it would also restrict efforts to come to grips with the present problems of the western labour movement.

There is, however, at least one other possibility – to treat Marx and Lenin not as historical authorities whose function is to be rhetorically venerated or scholastically quoted, but as guides to contemporary scientific and political analysis. Beyond oratory or dogma, what then really matters is the content of their theories, not the forms of their expression. For it is, in fact, possible to concede the two main arguments advanced by the French Communist Party (in particular) for the abandonment of the term 'the dictatorship of the proletariat', and at the same time to retain and employ – scientifically and politically – the real knowledge contained in the Marxist-Leninist concept designated by this formula.

Two principal arguments have been put forward against the latter. One is the ring of the word 'dictatorship'. This objection should not be dismissed, in a crudely intellectualist manner, as opportunism. The harsh experience of Fascism has taught the European working class, in every concrete way, the difference between democratic and dictatorial regimes of bourgeois class rule. As the Communists slowly learned in the thirties, it is not immaterial which of these forms of the dictatorship of the bourgeoisie is dominant. Moreover, restrictions and violations of proletarian democracy in the socialist states teach us that there are also significantly different forms of proletarian dictatorship. Both experiences call for specification of the various types of class rule and class dictatorship. The second argument concerns 'the proletariat'. The PCF, among others, contends that the category is too narrow a designation for the broad social bloc of workers and employees that party strategy seeks to constitute into the base of a new, socialist state.[4] More specifically, it has been argued that the leading role of the working class within this bloc should not be ensured by the coercion implied in the term 'the dictatorship of the proletariat'.[5] In effect, this objection raises the problem of class alliances. There is no doubt that

[4] Both arguments are presented in Georges Marchais' report to the 22nd Congress of the French Communist Party, which is published in full in *Le Socialisme pour la France*, Paris 1976. An extract from this speech is appended to Balibar, op. cit., 1977. Similar arguments have been advanced by members of the Italian Communist Party; see, for example, L. Gruppi, 'Sur le rapport démocratie socialisme', *Dialectiques* no. 17, Paris 1977.

[5] Gruppi, op. cit., pp. 47–8.

these can genuinely be posed within the framework of the dictatorship of the proletariat – as Lenin's policy towards the peasantry in Soviet Russia proves. On the other hand, the successes, errors and failures of socialist practice, from the Soviet Union to Chile, certainly underline the crucial importance of broad and enduring social alliances and majorities for revolutionary politics. This second argument is consequently not without validity either.

Historical developments make necessary much greater refinement and specification of the notion of the dictatorship of the proletariat. It is possible, indeed, that these may justify programmatic abandonment of the term itself. However, neither historical experience nor contemporary official arguments affect the basic issues focussed by the concept. 'The question of the dictatorship of the proletariat,' Lenin wrote, 'is a question of the relation of the proletarian state to the bourgeois state, of proletarian democracy to bourgeois democracy.' He continued, 'the formula "dictatorship of the proletariat" is merely a more historically concrete and scientifically exact formulation of the proletariat's task of "smashing" the bourgeois state machine . . .'[6] In their preface to the 1872 edition of the *Communist Manifesto*, Marx and Engels had added: 'One thing especially was proved by the [Paris] Commune, viz., that the working class cannot simply lay hold of the ready-made state machinery and wield it for its own purposes.'

The concept of the dictatorship of the proletariat, then, refers to two fundamental theses. First, the idea that *the very form of organization of the state is a materialization of a particular mode of class rule*. Secondly, in consequence of the first, that *the socialist state of the working class must have a specific form of organization*. The term 'the dictatorship of the proletariat' is used by Marx, Engels and Lenin as synonymous both with 'rule of the proletariat' and with the particular form of state that expresses this rule.

If the above points are correct, then it follows that a strategy for socialism or for a transitional stage of 'advanced democracy' must dismantle the governmental, administrative, judicial and repressive apparatuses of the existing bourgeois state. In other words, the working class needs not only an economic programme of nationalizations and social services, but also a political programme of changes

---

[6] V. I. Lenin, 'The Proletarian Revolution and the Renegade Kautsky', *Collected Works*, vol. 28, pp. 232–3.

in the organization of the state that will bring about a popular democracy.

This is, of course, not the place to contribute to such a programme, which must be formed through discussion in the revolutionary workers' movement of each country. But the elaboration of a strategic programme must be based on scientific Marxist analyses. These must provide answers to questions such as the following: wherein lies the bourgeois class character, not of current government policies, but of the way in which contemporary capitalist states are organized? What forms would have to be taken by a state that reproduces the power of the working class and its allies?[7]

Marxists have devoted unbelievably little systematic attention to these problems since the time of Lenin. Let us recall some of the most important theoretical contributions made recently in Western Europe to analysis of the state. Nicos Poulantzas has produced a number of complex, and in many ways path-breaking, studies of classes and the capitalist state. But nowhere does he directly investigate the forms of state organization. In *Political Power and Social Classes*, he stresses relative autonomy from the economy as the distinctive characteristic of the capitalist state.[8] Only with extreme brevity does he refer to its system of organization – namely, a 'bureaucratism', 'which expresses above all the political impact of bourgeois *ideology* on the state'.[9] Here as well as later[10], Poulantzas focuses more on the bureaucracy as a specific social category than on bureaucracy as a bourgeois form of state organization. In this respect, he displays a basic affinity with his otherwise very different opponent, Ralph Miliband.

Miliband's work *The State in Capitalist Society* (London 1969) is the most ambitious empirical investigation of modern advanced capitalist states yet undertaken by a Marxist; but it too almost com-

---

[7] These problems are brushed aside by Balibar as unimportant 'institutional' aspects; see op. cit., pp. 111–12.

[8] This is also the basis of Poulantzas's rather superficial characterization of the absolutist state as capitalist; see *Political Power and Social Classes*. NLB 1973, pp. 161–7.

[9] Poulantzas, op. cit., p. 332.

[10] Poulantzas, *Classes in Contemporary Capitalism*, NLB 1975, esp. pp. 183–9. For a brief treatment of the organization of the state apparatuses, see ibid., esp. pp. 28ff. On the other hand, in his analyses of fascism (*Fascism and Dictatorship*, NLB 1975) and of other dictatorships (*The Crisis of the Dictatorships*, NLB 1976) Poulantzas has cast much light on the state apparatuses.

pletely bypasses the problem of organization. In an approach reminiscent of Poulantzas's view of 'bureaucratism', the author seeks to define the class character of the state primarily by reference to the bourgeois ideological orientation of its personnel. In a more recent work *Marxism and Politics* (Oxford 1977), Miliband's discussion of the state assigns a central place to the varying degrees of its 'relative autonomy'.

Theorizations of 'state monopoly capitalism', such as the massive treatise by Paul Boccara and others[11], virtually exclude questions of the state apparatus from their overwhelmingly economic analysis. By contrast, such problems are at the heart of the major strategic and programmatic discussion developing in the French, Italian and Spanish labour movements. However, these so-called Euro-communist contributions have been primarily concerned with the bearing of ideology on the state and with a number of specific, yet crucial, questions concerning government apparatuses, parliament, regional decentralization, and popular rank-and-file assemblies. The administrative and repressive apparatuses have been tackled mainly in the context of concrete and limited proposals for reform.[12]

In Santiago Carrillo's recent book '*Eurocomunismo' y Estado* (Barcelona 1977), which is the true 'Eurocommunist' counterpoint to *State and Revolution*, many crucial problems of the class character of the state apparatus are rather contemptuously brushed aside. Thus: 'This conception of the state and of the struggle to democratize it presupposes the renunciation, in its classical form, of the idea of a *workers' and peasants' state*; that is, a state which, mounted according to a new plan, brings workers and peasants from their factories and fields to staff its offices and sends into their place functionaries who up to that point used to work in the offices.' (p. 97) The Spanish CP leader is, of course, right to expose the obscuring and utopian features of this 'classical idea'. But what is a socialist state – a state of transition to classless society – if not a strenuous effort to dismantle the barriers between the workers in their fac-

---

[11] *Traité d'économie marxiste et d'économie politique. Le capitalisme d'état*, Paris 1971, 2 vols.

[12] See *Programme commun du parti communiste et du parti socialiste*, Paris 1972, pp. 160–2; J. Fabre–F. Hincker–L. Sève, *Les communistes et l'état*, Paris 1977, pp. 177ff.; and 'Per la riforma del amministrazione publica', of which I have consulted the German translation published in the collection *Sozialismus für Italien*, Hamburg/West Berlin 1977.

tories and the functionaries in their offices? Would a democratically governed state lead to classless society if it were administered in a bureaucratic or technocratic manner? Carrillo's failure to confront this problem is further underlined by his cavalier assumption that the executives of existing capitalist corporations could be incorporated as such into the new post-capitalist society (p. 104). For Carrillo, the transformation of the state apparatus is mainly a problem of obtaining hegemony within the ideological apparatuses. Nor does the sympathetic critic of 'Eurocommunism', Fernando Claudin, concern himself with these questions in a book *Eurocomunismo y Socialismo* (Madrid 1977) which appeared simultaneously with that of Carrillo.

A Socialist intellectual, Norberto Bobbio, initiated a highly valuable discussion in Italy in 1975–76 by posing two provocative questions: Is there such a thing as a Marxist doctrine of the state? What are the alternatives to representative democracy? Many of the best minds of the PCI contributed answers. Although Bobbio had also invoked Max Weber and the phenomenon of bureaucracy, the debate revolved mainly around the subject of representative democracy. Major articles on the constitution of a non-authoritarian state – variously termed 'mass democracy' (Ingrao) and 'mixed democracy' (Occhetto) – sought to relate parliamentary representation to direct democracy at the base. But the question of the overall class character of the state was hardly raised.[13]

The 22nd Congress of the French Communist Party did much to stimulate debate on the very concept which it abandoned: the dictatorship of the proletariat. Thus, at round-tables organized by journals such as *Dialectiques* (nos. 17 and 18–19) and *La Nouvelle Critique* (nos. 93, 96 and 101), a number of participants touched upon questions and difficulties of great import – even though they were unable to go into them very deeply in their necessarily brief contributions. The same may be said of Althusser's booklet *22ème Congrès* (Paris 1977), which, more than Balibar's above-mentioned book on the dictatorship of the proletariat, tries to come to grips with the concrete political problems now facing the revolutionary labour movement in the West. The collective work edited by Nicos

---

[13] The interventions are published in a book *Il marxismo e lo stato*, Rome 1976. The one which most closely touches problems of the non-governmental apparatuses of the state is: Giorgio Ruffolo, 'Eguaglianza e democrazia nel progetto socialista'.

Poulantzas, *La crise de l'état,* includes a few illuminating observations on experiences of the French state apparatus. The PCF has recently put out a book of both analytical and programmatic value which deals directly with political and administrative questions of the state – *Les communistes et l'état.* However, it suffers from an unclear distinction between state power and state apparatus – which leads the authors largely to subsume the latter under the former in their analysis and programme. 'The essence of this transformation does not lie in an internal modification of the state, however indispensable that may be, but in the reversal of the relation between state and workers.'[14] What is doubtful here is the word 'but'. For if the internal organization of the state bears a class character, then a reversal of the relationship between state and workers directly depends, among other things, upon an 'internal modification' of the former.

Although the Swedish CP is a long way from political power, even a brief overview of recent 'Eurocommunist' writings on the state should mention a book by a leading Swedish Communist, Jorn Svensson, *Du skåll ta ledningen och makten.* (Thou shalt take power and leadership.)[15] In programmatic form, this work lucidly brings out the different class character of the socialist and capitalist states.

On the academic level, a lively Marxist discussion on the state has arisen in West Germany. However, although it is often of high intellectual calibre, it has contributed little to clarification of the character of the state apparatus. Like Poulantzas, most West German authors regard separation and relative autonomy from the economy as the essential characteristic of the capitalist state. Even in the best works, problems of state power, state apparatus, structural dynamics and class struggle are often jumbled together under the notion of 'structural selectivity'.[16] Three particular traditions

---

[14] Fabre–Hincker–Sève, op. cit., p. 150. Emphasis omitted.

[15] Stockholm 1975. The title refers to a line from Brecht: 'Du musst die Führung übernehmen' (*Lob des Lernens*).

[16] In their criticism of narrowly instrumentalist conceptions of the state, West German academic Marxists sometimes simply dismiss the problematic of *The State and Revolution*; see, for example, C. Offe–V. Ronge, 'Thesen zur Begründung des Konzepts des "kapitalistischen Staates" und zur materialistische Politikforschung', in Altvater, Basso, Mattick, Offe et. al., *Rahmenbedingungen und Schranken staatlichen Handelns. Zehn Thesen,* Frankfurt 1976, p. 54. In an interesting critical review of a number of different analyses, Offe rashly concludes that it is possible to demonstrate empirically the class content of a state's policy only after it has been overthrown by revolution; see 'Klassenherrschaft und

lie as a dead weight upon this discussion. One is the focus on political legitimation inherited from Weber and the Frankfurt School[17]; another is a functionalist economistic orientation which concentrates analyses of the state on its functions in the reproduction of capital.[18] While these two trends allow consideration of important and substantial problems – though at the price of neglecting political analysis proper – the interpretation of Marx's thought in terms of the 'logic of capital' has led several writers into intensive preoccupation with a philosophical problem largely of their own making – namely, the attempt to 'derive' the 'logical' possibility and necessity of the state from the concepts of commodity and capital.[19]

At least one Marxist study of the socialist state deals directly with the question of the class character of its apparatuses: Charles Bettelheim's *Les luttes de classe en URSS* (Paris 1974, 1977) – of which only the first two volumes, dealing with the period up to 1930, have appeared so far. This is an important work, which should be taken seriously even by those who fundamentally disagree with the author's ideas about the 'capitalist' character of the Soviet Union

---

politisches System. Zur Selektivität politischer Institutionen', in his *Struktur-probleme des kapitalistischen Staates*, Frankfurt 1972. The organizational question is not dismissed altogether in the important work by Joachim Hirsch, *Staats-apparat und Reproduktion des Kapitals*, Frankfurt 1974. But he subsumes the problem of the state apparatus under that of the functionality of its *Besonderung* (separation from civil society) to the reproduction of capital, and devotes no real analysis to it as a crystallization of class power; see esp. pp. 226ff.

A general overview of the achievements of West German Marxist study of the state may be gained from V. Brandes (ed.), *Handbuch 5.Staat*, Frankfurt 1977.

[17] For a good sample of its recent exercises, see R. Ebbinghausen (ed.), *Bürgerlicher Staat und politische Legitimation*, Frankfurt 1976.

[18] An example is the recent work on the West German state by Projekt Klassen-analyse, a very productive and intellectually solid collective, *Der Staat der BRD*, Hamburg/West Berlin 1977. It contains virtually no political analysis proper, of the government, of the repressive, judiciary and administrative apparatuses of the state and their traverse by and insertion in the class struggle.

[19] The central text of this debate is S. V. Flatow–F. Huisken, 'Zum Problem der Ableitung des bürgerlichen Staates', *Probleme des Klassenkampfes*, no. 7, 1973. For a presentation of the later adventures, or misadventures, of this peculiar dialectic, see B. Blanke–H. Kastendiek–U. Jürgens, 'Zur neueren marxistischen Diskussion über die Analyse von Form und Funktion des bürgerlichen Staates', *Probleme des Klassenkampfes*, no. 14/15, 1974. It should be added that this philosophy of the state bears a certain relation to the more substantive problem of the inevitable restriction of state reformist intervention by the economic laws of capitalism. A recent contribution to this discussion is the essay 'Staat, Akkumula-tion des Kapitals und soziale Bewegung', by Elmar Altvater et al., in Altvater, Basso et al., op. cit.

today. However, Bettelheim starts out in the first volume with a fatal theoretical flaw. Instead of basing his analysis on a systematic, comparative conception of the capitalist and socialist states, he confronts the real history of the USSR with an ideal variant. This is quite acceptable as a starting-point for a critical historical study. But, first, the procedure does not permit any conclusions to be drawn as to the class nature of the actual, 'deviant' Soviet state. Secondly, whereas feudal and capitalist states have exhibited a wide historical range of variations, aberrations and impurities, the above-mentioned approach tends arbitrarily to predefine the socialist state as a single form. Future volumes will show how Bettelheim handles these difficulties. The second volume is much less guided by a Maoist bias; but it focuses mainly on the economic and ideological spheres, and relatively little on the state.[20] So far at least, we have to say that Bettelheim has left the basic theoretical problems unanswered.

An outstanding exception among recent Marxist works on the state is Perry Anderson's great study of the feudal state. In support of his thesis that the Absolutist state had a feudal character, Anderson compares it with the later, capitalist states in respect of military organization, administration, diplomacy and sources of revenue.[21] This is done very convincingly, with profound historical erudition and a sharp analytical edge. The implications of Anderson's work will be extremely useful in the course of the present study, even though he himself does not elaborate, or even state very explicitly, the theoretical rationale of his analysis.

The current discussion of the dictatorship of the proletariat has arisen primarily in Western Europe, and the rapid survey we have made has been confined to contributions by West European Marxists. It should at least be mentioned that there exist other Marxist theorists, whose work is equally, if not more, significant. As far as I know, however, they have not solved the initial questions either. One valuable contribution – of which I have been able to consult only the first two volumes (of four) in German translation – is a collective Soviet handbook entitled *The General Marxist-Leninist Theory of the State and Law*.[22] Its strength lies above all in

---

[20] Jean Elleinstein's *Histoire de l'URSS* (4 vols., Paris 1973–5) is mainly a narrative history. It is noteworthy as the first attempt by a politically prominent Communist scholar to engage in serious study of the Soviet Union.

[21] P. Anderson, *Lineages of the Absolutist State*, NLB, London 1975, pp. 29ff.

[22] *Marxist-leninistische allgemeine Theorie des Staates und des Rechts*, Berlin 1974, 4 vols. to appear.

the sections on law, and it is concerned more with problems of categorization and description than with strictly theoretical analysis.

In his *Leninism and the Transition from Capitalism to Socialism* – an educational work of some political interest – Konstantin Zarodov motivates his simple assertion that the establishment of the dictatorship of the proletariat is one of the 'principal laws' of socialist transition by referring to the necessity of a 'power supported by force' with which to defeat the exploiters. Zarodov expresses very well that conception from which most West European Communist parties are now eager to distance themselves. But beneath both positions very important problems remain unanalysed.[23]

As for the Chinese, I know of no large-scale study or precise formulation of the organizational characteristics of the proletarian state. Their main emphasis has been on ideological factors, especially the struggle within the party between 'two lines' – one representing the proletariat, the other the bourgeoisie. As these lines are given no precise definition or empirical connection with class forces, they have involved above all the following opposition: the current leadership exercises the dictatorship of the proletariat, whereas former leaders (Liu Shao-chi, Lin Piao, Chen Po-ta or the 'gang of four') are denounced, after their fall, as agents of a bourgeois and fascist dictatorship. However, both in theory and in practice, the Chinese have also affirmed a number of concrete characteristics specific to proletarian state and party functionaries: egalitarian remuneration and consumption habits; participation in manual labour; ideological training; and accountability to mass criticism. These are fully in keeping with Lenin's April Theses and are of importance in the abolition of the separateness of the state apparatus.[24]

From a strict Trotskyist position, it seems impossible to pose the

[23] K. Zarodov, *O leninismo e a passagem do capitalismo ao socialismo*, Lisbon 1976, 3 vols. (booklets), vol. 2, p. 41. Zarodov's text is used in the formation of cadres in the Portuguese Communist Party – a party which, at its 1974 Extraordinary Congress, deleted the concept of the dictatorship of the proletariat from its programme.

[24] I originally intended to refer here to Chang Chun-chiao's 'All-round Dictatorship against the Bourgeoisie' (*Peking Review* No. 14, 1975, also published in pamphlet form) as a recent authoritative Chinese statement. But now that he has been denounced as one of 'the gang of four' seeking to restore capitalism, that should be left for the record and replaced by a pamphlet by Hua Kuo-feng, *Continue the Revolution under the Dictatorship of the Proletariat to the End*, Peking 1977. The basic Chinese works are, of course, those of Mao Tse-tung – for example, the essays 'On the Correct Handling of Contradictions among the People'; 'On the Ten Great Relationships', contained in the famous little red

problem of the class character of the state organization; it is defined out of existence by the use of certain categories. Thus, although Trotsky consistently characterized the USSR as a workers' state, the only argument he ever gave was the fact that it had its roots in, and continued to defend, a nationalized economy. Once the nature of a state is defined by the economic base and content of state policies, then the problem of the class character of the state apparatus is replaced by the ambiguous notion of bureaucracy.[25] It must be added, however, that Trotskyist studies of the 'bureaucracy' of their Stalinist and post-Stalinist enemies, above all the great works of Isaac Deutscher, have manifested a remarkable analytical sobriety, which stands in stark contrast to the sweeping vituperation of Maoist exposures of the 'capitalist' USSR.

The highly developed Marxism of Latin America has produced a number of absorbing works on the state; but again, it has devoted little analysis to the state apparatus. Sometimes, important issues are treated in too cavalier a fashion, even in otherwise penetrating contributions. For instance, Octavio Ianni quite straightforwardly characterizes the populist regimes of Perón and Vargas as petty-bourgeois, at the same time as he stresses that one of their hallmarks was the promotion of trade unions that were effectively controlled by the state.[26]

The North American Marxist, Erik Olin Wright, has undertaken a careful and systematic comparison of Lenin's conception of bureaucracy with that of the great bourgeois sociologist, Max Weber. Wright ends his excellent essay by explicitly raising the problem dealt with in the present study: 'What is needed is . . . a theoretical orientation . . . that provides a systematic understanding of the relationship of social structure to the internal organizational processes of the state.'[27]

---

book of the Cultural Revolution, *Quotations from Chairman Mao Tse-tung*. So far, five very carefully (and politically) edited volumes of Mao's writings have been published.

[25] For Trotsky's views on bureaucracy and the Soviet Union, see *The Revolution Betrayed*, New York 1972.

[26] O. Ianni, *A formacão do Estado Populista*, São Paulo, 1973. Among recent important Latin American contributions, at least the following should be mentioned: F. H. Candoso, *O modelo político brasileiro*, São Paulo 1975; J. F. Leal, *La burguesia y el estado mexicano*, Mexico 1972; and idem, *Êstado, burocracia y sindicatos*, Mexico 1975.

[27] E. Wright, 'Bureaucracy and the State', Chapter four in *Classes, Crisis and State*, NLB, London 1978.

Finally, we should not forget an outstanding Asian contribution to the debate – a practical one. For at least a decade the Vietnamese struggle was at the centre of the world revolutionary movement against imperialism. Today, liberated Vietnam is being developed explicitly according to the concept of the dictatorship of the proletariat. Even if the experience of the European labour movement leads us to accept the arguments against the particular formulation, the heroic combat of the Vietnamese people should serve as a reminder of the importance of the content of the concept, and of the urgent need to clarify it.

An Analytical Model

Our critical look at previous analyses is not meant to suggest that Marxists have generally ignored the class character of the state apparatus. Indeed, we shall draw extensively upon past experiences, observations and reflections.[28] However, although there has been no shortage of implications, passing remarks, quotations from classic texts, and ideological polemics, almost no systematic theoretical analysis has been devoted to the problem. In the present theoretical and political conjuncture, I think it appropriate to bend the stick in the other direction: to attempt to develop a formal, comparative analytical model of the class character of the state apparatus, which may serve as a tool both for scientific investigation of the historical types of state, and for a programmatic debate about why and how the state apparatuses of the advanced capitalist countries should be 'smashed'.

In my opinion, such a model should start not from the functionalist problematic of the role of the state in the reproduction of capital, but from the relations between antagonistic classes, as determined by the forces and relations of production. Poulantzas has already developed the idea that the state should be regarded neither as a specific institution nor as an instrument, but as a relation – a materialized concentration of the class relations of a given society. These remarks apply also to its two distinct aspects: state power and the state apparatus. State power is a relation between social class forces expressed in the content of state policies. The class character of these policies may be seen in their direct effects upon the forces

---

[28] There are a number of solid non-Marxist works pertinent to an investigation into the class character of the state apparatus. I shall refer below to those of which I have made direct use.

and relations of production, upon the ideological superstructure, and upon the state apparatus. These points will be elaborated in the second essay of this volume.

State power is exercised through the state apparatus, or more precisely, through a system of state apparatuses. The separate existence of the state is part of a specific division of labour within society. Its internal organization thus reflects in a particular way the social division of labour and the prevailing social class relations, contributing to their reproduction in the ever-ongoing social process. In the historical course of the class struggle, the state apparatuses come to crystallize determinate social relations and thus assume a material existence, efficacy and inertia which are to a certain extent independent of current state policies and class relations. It follows that, although the variance between state power and the state apparatus is limited by the fact that they express the class relations of the same society, at any given moment significant disjunctures appear between the two. The possibilities of variance are substantially increased by the coexistence within a particular state system of several apparatuses, in which different sets of class relations may have crystallized.

These disjunctures have a fundamentally destabilizing effect. For example, a bourgeois revolution, involving the distribution of land to individual peasants, is inherently unstable if it is accomplished by a predominantly proletarian state apparatus of the kind created in Russia after October. Conversely, the nationalization of the 'commanding heights' of the economy is unstable as an expression of working class power, if it is carried out by a bourgeois state apparatus. Thus, the two aspects of the state are analytically distinct, and disjunctures between them affect the mode of the class struggle and confront the revolutionary class with specific tasks vis-à-vis the organization of the state.

What will be presented here is neither a historical study nor a set of categorical definitions, but a theoretical model for concrete analysis and programmatic discussion. The aim is to show that different types of class relations and of class power generate corresponding forms of state organization, and to elucidate the way in which the class character of the state apparatus is determined and revealed. The model, then, is *explanatory*, rather than descriptive of ideal types; and it is based on the *comparative* study of feudal, capitalist and socialist states.

Like any text which is inspired by Marxism, the present work is subject to exegetic criticism. Yet it does not set out to repeat and reformulate what Marx, Engels and Lenin said but to build upon their foundation. The model should be judged primarily on 'pragmatic' grounds, rather than by the criterion of strict correspondence with Marxist–Leninist social theory. Does it enable new knowledge to be produced? Does it throw fresh light on the relevant phenomena, without obscuring what has already been clarified? These are the most important questions that the reader will have to ask himself or herself.

As an analytical model, the one we shall attempt to construct is open also to both logical and empirical refutation. Its logical coherence depends on the existence of a real causal relation between the forms of state organization and the particular class relations to which they are linked in the model. It may be empirically disproved if the forms of state organization mentioned cannot be identified with the class of the model, or with any other; or if the variations of state organization are more readily explicable by variables other than class struggle and class power. Medieval France and Germany, the France of the Great Revolution, and revolutionary Russia appear to constitute the first crucial empirical tests.

In order to make the text easier to read, the theory will be presented rather discursively. Empirical references will be used mainly for indicative and illustrative purposes, and it is not claimed that they provide a genuine verification. This applies especially to the discussion of the institutions and practices of contemporary states that claim to be socialist. Although I personally believe that it is correct to characterize them as in varying degrees socialist, the references in the text in no way preclude empirical investigation of their nature. They are intended to supply concrete illustrations and to highlight critical aspects that have to be made the subject of further examination and reflection.

Finally, the tentative and approximative character of this essay should be underlined at the outset.

Before we conclude this lengthy introduction, we need to supplement the general conceptualization of the state with two further specifications. Since we are interested in the state as an organization, we must have a grasp of what formal organization involves. Secondly, we will have to examine briefly the characteristic features of feudal, capitalist and socialist class relations, since we will claim that it is these that generate the specific forms of state organization.

A New Approach to the Study of Organizations

As an apparatus, or system of apparatuses, the state is a type of formal organization. It is distinguished by its specific functions: coercive defence, political governance (by supreme rule-making), administrative management (by rule-application), and judicial regulation of a given social formation. However, it should be possible to analyse the state apparatus in essentially the same terms as other organizations or apparatuses.

An abundant literature already exists on organizations and organizational analysis.[29] Although Marxists must take some of this into account, nearly all of it suffers from a fundamental flaw: it does not consider organizations as part of the ongoing historical process of (simple and expanded) social reproduction and revolution. From Weber's conception of rational bureaucracy to modern functionalism, systems approaches and notions of forms of compliance, the conceptualization and analysis produced by organizational theory have generally been situated within a *subjectivist problematic*. They have focussed on the organizational subject – its goals, its decision-making or 'adaptive' behaviour, its modes of legitimation and enforcement of compliance – that is to say, on the creators or leaders of the organization and on their problems. Of course, this is not an unimportant area of investigation, and researchers have not been unaware of the fact that these variables are affected by a wider extra-organizational setting. To some extent they have even understood the ways in which this influence is exerted. However, there remains in all these approaches a basic dichotomy between the organizational subject and its 'setting' – a dichotomy which hinders deeper consideration of the processes of social reproduction and change. This is a more fundamental weakness than the customary lack of a class analysis of organizational structures, because it is in and through these processes that classes and the class struggle operate.

In order to understand the class character of the state apparatus, then, we must begin to develop a new approach to study of the organization. We should view it not as a goal-oriented subject in an environment, but as a formally bounded system of structured processes within a global system of societal processes. This difference

[29] For a survey of the principal contemporary approaches, see J. March (ed.), *Handbook of Organizations*, Chicago 1965; A. Etzioni (ed.), *A Sociological Reader on Complex Organizations*, London 1970; or O. Grusky–G. Miller (eds.), *The Sociology of Organizations*, New York 1970.

of approach is expressed in the following diagram, albeit in a rather simplistic manner:

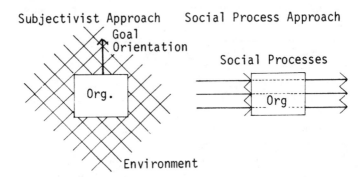

The approach must be a formal one if it is to be applicable to diverse types of organization. At the same time, it will be of little value if it produces merely a system of empty descriptive generalities, or a set of definitions that reformulate existing knowledge. The schema must make possible a number of specifications and distinctions, and serve as a guide to empirical research. It should not assume, but rather allow us to discover, the class character of particular organizations.

Systems approaches to the study of organizations and politics usually operate as a variant of the subjectivist problematic. Utilizing highly abstract concepts, they typically analyse the organization as a self-maintaining system. Nevertheless, certain ideas developed by systems theory can be taken over and put to different use. Thus, if we conceive of organizations as processes formally structured by specific mechanisms of input, transformation and output, we can relate them directly to the ever advancing social processes of reproduction and change, which provide the inputs and receive the outputs. The class character of an organization may then be determined by the way in which the input, transformation and output processes are traversed and shaped by the class struggle.

What, then, is the formal content of the inputs, transformation and outputs of an organization? We can answer this question by generalizing and extending the four factors involved in productive organizations – work materials, personnel, energy and technology –

in such a way as to yield the following schema: 1. The *tasks* of the organization; 2. The different kinds of *personnel*; 3. The *material resources* necessary to sustain the transformations carried out in the organization and its personnel; 4. The *organizational technology*, i.e., the technique of getting things done, which is applied in the handling of tasks, the patterning of the personnel, and the use of incoming material resources. Every organization has formal procedures that regulate the inputs, transformation and outputs of these factors, and if the basic theses of historical materialism are valid, these procedures will be produced by the class struggle and constitute crystallizations of class relations.

We are now able to outline what happens when a given technology is applied within an organization. The working materials are worked upon (or to put it in other terms, the incoming tasks are handled); the persons are patterned as incumbents of a structure of positions; and the energy is utilized. As outputs, the factors take the form of external activities of the organization: output of decisions and policies; behaviour of its personnel towards other individuals; outflow of material resources. The outputs and personal behaviour should be distinguished according to whether they relate to other organizations of the same type. A state, for instance, relates to foreign states in other ways than it does to the society of which it is part, or to different organizations of that society.

One further specification needs to be made. The problem of the class character of the state apparatus does not refer to the effects of state policies – which involve the analytically distinct, though empirically closely related question of state power – but to their form and intrinsic content.

The highly abstract schema can now be made somewhat more concrete by the identification of no fewer than nine (or, with the output specifications, eleven) variables.

Input mechanisms:
1. Principles regulating the type of task dealt with by the state;
2. Criteria of personnel recruitment to the state apparatuses;
3. Modes of securing state revenue;
Processes of transformation:
4. Modes of decision-making and handling of tasks;
5. Patterning of organizational positions and of relations among their incumbents;

6. Modes of allocation and utilization of material resources;
Output mechanisms:
7. Patterning of decisions and practices of the state
   a. towards other states
   b. towards the society of which it is part;
8. Patterning of relations of the state personnel
   a. with the personnel of other states
   b. with other members of the same society;
9. Modes of outflow of material resources from the state.

As expressions of class relations, these variables will have a strong tendency to vary together as a cluster. However, the above list should be supplemented by a specification of the key variable and, if possible, of their critical limits of variation. This is especially important from the point of view of the dialectical distinction between qualitative and quantitative change.

Technology differs from the other variables of the organization system in that it is not part of the same input-transformation-output process. Although technology enters the organization from the prevailing state of the social forces and relations of production, its functioning is, in a sense, purely internal to the organizational process. Within this process, the technological input is not transformed, but rather *applied* in the transformation of the other inputs: in the handling of tasks, the patterning of personnel, and the utilization of energy. Nor is technology really an output of productive or other organizations. The kind of technology employed has significant *effects* upon the organization's environment, because of its implication in the character of transformation processes and of the output of transformed inputs.

For these reasons, technology should be treated separately as a special variable. For these reasons, too, it should be considered as the strategic variable of the organization system – in this case, the state apparatus. Of all the factors involved, technology has the broadest reach: it is applied in the process of transformation and affects the regulation of all the other inputs and outputs. It is thus in the light of the regulation of these other factors that the highly abstract concept of organizational technology will become somewhat more concrete.

It should be stressed that technology here refers to *organizational* technology, which directly involves institutionalized social relations of command and compliance, leadership and execution. We shall expand on these points later. Organizational technology is invested in material means of production and communication; but it is not reducible to them. It is analogous to the forces of production – a concept which refers basically to 'die Art und Weise der Arbeit' (the methods of labour), the different ways in which productivity is ensured.[30]

The analysis would become even more complex if we took into account the fact that the state apparatus is, in reality, a set of apparatuses. Corresponding to the four principal functions of the state, four types of apparatus can be distinguished: the governmental apparatus (i.e. the rule-making legislative and executive bodies, both central and local), the administration, the judiciary, and the repressive apparatus (police, military, etc.). In practice, these types are not always clearly differentiated, but where they are, each one of them normally comprises a number of apparatuses.[31]

Although the state is, in a fundamental sense, always one, the level of integration of its apparatuses varies considerably, and it should not be taken for granted that they share a common class character. For the state is the concentrated expression of a highly complex set of class relations, which are refracted in disjunctures of varying profundity between the different apparatuses. Within limits imposed by the general nature of the state, it is especially probable that the class character of its diverse apparatuses will vary with the link between the tasks of the apparatus and the concerns of classes rooted in the mode of production. It may thus be expected that, allowing for a possible period of revolutionary 'smashing', the army of capitalist states would retain feudal traits longer than, say, the fiscal apparatus; that the agricultural apparatuses would have a more pronounced petty-bourgeois and small bourgeois character; or that the welfare apparatus, whilst remaining bourgeois, would be

[30] Cf. G. Therborn, *Science, Class and Society*, NLB 1976, pp. 362ff.
[31] What Althusser has called the ideological apparatuses of the state should more precisely be analysed as part of the ideological superstructure. The family, for example, evidently cannot be considered as part of the state, whereas an ideological apparatus like the school system is organizationally patterned by the *administrative* apparatus of the state. It also seems more fruitful to treat the judiciary and the police-army as distinct apparatuses. Miliband's amalgamation of them (in *The State in Capitalist Society*, London 1969) makes it more difficult to analyse both the special function of the feudal judiciary and the relative independence of the courts in capitalist society.

affected by its close relationship with the working class. In the rest of this text, however, the state apparatus will be generally treated as a single whole.

Modes of Production and Types of Class Relations

According to the Marxian metaphor of base and superstructure, the character of the state depends upon the particular combination of relations and forces of production that constitutes the economic base of society. As I have elaborated at some length in my *Science, Class and Society*, the relations of production, which determine the class content of human social relations, involve three aspects: the distribution of the means of production, the goal of production, and the structure of the social relations that link the immediate producers to one another and to the appropriators of the fruits of their surplus labour. Before we proceed any further, we must specify those class relations that are characteristic of the feudal, capitalist and socialist modes of production.

Feudal class relations and feudal class rule: The principal means of production are here distributed among individual landlords, who basically owe their property to inheritance, to their original military eminence, or to other services rendered to a superior lord. Although the immediate producers are thereby collectively separated from the means of production, their labour is not immediately directed and supervised by the landlords. Their class subjection to the owners of the means of production, as indeed relations among the feudal aristocrats, is based rather on non-economic mechanisms: differences in military capability, non-economic manners and resources, and kinship. The unequal relation is one of degree rather than kind: the supreme lord is no more a god than are his peasants beasts of toil. Under this system, production is oriented essentially towards noble consumption.

From these basic features of the relations of production, certain political and ideological characteristics of feudal class rule can be seen to follow. Expansion typically involved conquest of foreign lands and subjection of the immediate producers tied to them. The combination of the individual mode of appropriation with a rigorous kinship system made of marriage an important economic and political affair. The nature of relations between the producers and their lords, and the orientation of production gave an important place to breeding, manners, qualitative personal relationships, ritual and ceremonial consumption, as attributes of the ruling aristocracy. These became still more significant as the development of the means of repression made obsolete the knightly army and the military role of the nobility.

Capitalist class relations and bourgeois rule: the direct producers are here separated from the means of production not as a collective, but as individuals without capital. The means of production take the form of commodities appropriated by any individuals who have the exchange values necessary to purchase them. Relations within and between the bourgeoisie and the proletariat are market relations of exchange and competition. The basic relation of exploitation between the two classes combines a market bond – that links buyers and sellers of the commodity labour-power – with the process of extraction of surplus value. This appropriation of the labour product is conducted under conditions of direct control by the capitalists over the use of labour-power, where the goal of production is the accumulation of capital.

These social relations entail at least two important general characteristics of bourgeois class rule. One is the combination of personal freedom and equality (expressed in exchange and competition on the market) with the lack of freedom and equality inherent in the domination of capital over labour. The second essential feature is the separation of mental from manual labour, and the hierarchical subordination of the latter to the former.[32] In contrast to the unity of tasks realized under the feudal and handicraft systems, the direct management and supervision of production by capital is necessitated by the very dynamics of capital accumulation. The intrinsic importance of specialized, quantifiable knowledge gives rise to the separation within the capitalist enterprise of mental from manual labour – and more generally of conception from execution. The former tasks are reserved for the owners and representatives of capital.

The principles of capitalist organization of the work process were

---

[32] This does not mean that a kind of subordination of manual to mental labour is theoretically inconceivable outside capitalism. However, the prolific writings on the 'post-capitalist', 'post-industrial' society by Daniel Bell and *tutti quanti* do not put forward a convincing case that this is an essential feature of the present epoch. After all, science and the university have hardly replaced capital accumulation and private enterprise as the main determinants of social relations in advanced Western societies.

formulated with unsurpassed candour and explicitness by Frederick Taylor, architect of the so-called Taylor system of 'scientific management': 'The managers assume . . . the burden of gathering together all of the traditional knowledge which in the past has been possessed by the workmen and then of classifying, tabulating and reducing this knowledge to rules, laws and formulae . . . All possible brainwork should be removed from the shop and centered in the planning or lay-out department'.[33]

It should be noted that this subordination is quite distinct from the pre-capitalist, feudal or mandarin, *contempt* for manual labour. What the bourgeoisie sets against it is not possession of general 'culture', good breeding or manners, but specific mental activities – mental *labour*.[34]

The proletariat as the ruling class: The dictatorship of the proletariat – that is, its class rule – is transitional by its very nature. This is not to say that it inevitably leads to classless communist society: a given proletarian dictatorship may develop into a new form of class rule or relapse into an old one. What is meant by describing it as inherently transitional is that it is a contradiction in terms. The proletariat has no other class to exploit; but how is it then defined as a ruling class after the overthrow of the bourgeoisie?

The working class becomes the ruling class by destruction of the power of the bourgeoisie and construction and defence of a socialist mode of production. However, it continues to occupy a distinct position in the production process; differences between 'town' and 'country' (i.e., between industrial proletariat and peasantry) still exist, as does, most importantly, the division between mental and manual labour; petty-commodity production usually persists alongside socialist production.

The basis of this transitional mode of production, in which the working class remains a distinct ruling class, is the following: although the means of production are in the hands of the collectivity led by the direct producers, and although they are oriented towards

[33] F. Taylor, *The Principles of Scientific Management*, New York 1967, p. 111; and 'Shop Management' in idem, *Scientific Management*, New York 1947, pp. 98–9. Both quotations are taken from Harry Braverman's excellent book *Labour and Monopoly Capital*, New York 1974.

[34] For a Marxist tribute to the mental, managerial labour of the 'hard men in top hats who organized and presided over these vast transformations of the human landscape – material and spiritual', see E. J. Hobsbawm, *The Age of Capital 1848–75*, London 1975, pp. 56–7.

the creation of use-values for society as a whole, nevertheless the direct producers remain separated from management in a dual relationship of *collective* supremacy and leadership, and *individual* subordination to managerial expertise. The class rule of the proletariat is consequently troubled by a deep-rooted contradiction. The lingering hierarchy of specialization continues to confront the collective supremacy of labour – the directive capacity, solidarity, egalitarianism and organization of a previously (and, in non-socialist countries, still) exploited and downtrodden class. After the overthrow of capitalism, the class struggle concerns fundamentally the efforts of the proletariat to abolish itself as a distinct class, and thus to avoid subjection to a new or old form of class exploitation.

It follows from the peculiar nature of post-capitalist society that the non-proletarian forces need not be bourgeois – need not, that is, be seeking to restore the capitalist mode of production. The enemies of the working class in power are all those forces that oppose its self-abolition as a class.

Dynamics, Temporalities and Contradictions

The dynamic of our analytical model of the state apparatus is provided by the developmental logic of the class struggle and of the various modes of production. The state apparatus feeds back into society a contribution to the regeneration of the class relations that formed it. It does this by reproducing the state-society relationship inscribed within it, and by structuring the way in which the things done by the state are actually performed. With the development of the modes of production and their articulation within the social formation, the relations of size and strength among the different classes undergo change. Both the state apparatus and the class relations that formed it are reproduced or transformed by the interventions of the state – by that state power which is the central focus of the class struggle and its changing relationship of forces.

In the historical development of this social dynamic, a number of temporalities affect the organization of the state. These will have to be examined more closely in a future analysis. Of particular importance are trend and conjunctural temporalities, both of the mode of production and of the concrete social formation.

The principal conjunctural variations of the mode of production are evidently periods of expansion and of stagnation or crisis. As far as trends are concerned, a distinction can be drawn between competitive and monopoly capitalism. In a similar way, a socialist society that is faced with the tasks of industrialization should probably be differentiated from socialism that develops on an already existing industrial foundation; the strength of the working class and its relations with other classes and strata are crucially affected by the level of economic development. In the case of feudalism, there is perhaps another definite distinction between the classical, medieval period and the era of the rise of mercantile capital. Mercantile capital not only coexisted with feudalism within the social formation; it also entered into the reproduction of the feudal mode of exploitation itself, connecting the economic units of the latter with one another.

Particular social formations are part of a wider international system, and are modified by profound changes elsewhere within it. Here we should mention the impact on feudal societies and states of the first bourgeois revolution and of the decisive defeat of subsequent revolutions from below in 1848; the response of capitalist states to the first successful proletarian revolution; and the effect of independent socialist revolutions upon existing socialist societies. The principal conjunctural variations affecting the social formation are war and peace, victory and defeat.

The state-society relationship, the concrete class character of the state apparatus, the peculiar strengths and weaknesses of the individual apparatuses – all these are significantly affected by their location in every dimension of historico-social time. The interrelation of the different temporalities poses special problems. For example, many of the controversies over the notion of state monopoly capitalism would be more fruitful and conclusive if they directly confronted this interrelation. Both supporters and opponents of the theory discuss state monopoly capitalism as the outcome of a trend, representing a new phase in the development of capitalism. But the features emphasized by its proponents – including the 'fusion' of state and monopoly capital into a 'single mechanism' – seem to have spread most extensively in the advanced capitalist countries during the two world wars – that is to say, as conjunctural phenomena. Clearly, it becomes necessary to consider the continuity and discontinuity of the wartime and post-war periods. The fact that the effects of these temporalities are on the whole disregarded in the exposition that follows further underlines the very general and preliminary nature of this contribution to analysis of the class character of the state apparatus. We are still only at the beginning of a Marxist study of the state.

The state apparatus is part of a complex social totality in constant process. Uneven development and internal contradiction of its parts form the basis of change within this totality, defining the location and topography of the social battlefield. The structure and modifications of the state apparatus are overdetermined by the relations and forces of production – by their mutual reinforcement or contradiction. The latter affect the entire organization of the state by directly structuring the existence and inter-relations of classes as well as the relationship between state and economy. Moreover, the state personnel is also impregnated with the social phenomena of ideological qualification-subjection. But the state apparatus also manifests a specifically political dialectic, which, like the ideological one, is overdetermined by that of the economic base.

A state apparatus operates simultaneously as an expression of class *domination* (that is, as a particular form of the class division of labour in society) and as the *execution* of the supreme rule-making, rule-applying, rule-adjudicating, rule-enforcing and rule-defending tasks of society. The two aspects constitute an intrinsic unity: execution of these tasks is class domination, and class political domination is the execution of these tasks. But the forces of execution may also enter into contradiction with the relations of domination in the state apparatus. Thus, both military and administrative developments rendered feudal cavalry and vassalage inadequate; and the late feudal state had to enlist non-noble mercenary armies and functionaries in order to execute the repressive and administrative tasks of feudal domination. The growth of new apparatuses of the bourgeois state – related to social services and state planning – has necessitated forms of organization which conflict with the classical bureaucracy. The socialist state, for its part, has to face the contradiction between collective class domination and non-proletarian, expert execution.

There is, then, a dynamic specific to the state apparatus. The new tasks and problems confronting the state basically derive from the changing social totality in which it operates. But the successful organization of class domination in the state apparatus itself generates new problems of government, administration, judicature and repression – problems which call into question the existing organizational forms of domination. This contradiction between domination and execution, which may take many, diverse forms, has to be resolved one way or the other, and it thus becomes an internal force for change within the state apparatus. This contradiction is in turn just one aspect of the general political dialectic of domination-execution, which is grounded in the fact that the state is a unification of a fundamentally divided class society. It is invested at one and the same time with the exercise of ruling class domination and the common tasks of society. The essay on state power will discuss these points further.

After these lengthy preliminary remarks, we must now look at the class character of various types of state, and suggest provisional answers to some of the questions that have arisen. Since the present text is a contribution to a debate that has been largely confined to Europe, these answers will refer mainly to the history and contemporary situation of that continent. Further specifications of a similar kind would be needed in order to deal adequately with the states of Africa, Asia and Latin America.

II

(Provisional) Answers

Inputs into the State

Technologies of Organization

The feudal polity was primarily a military institution, equipped for war and armed peace. Initially, its most distinctive technology of rule took the material form of the expensively armoured knight. However, by the fourteenth century, English longbowmen and Swiss pikemen were already rendering the cavalry obsolete.[35] What then was the basic technology of the feudal state – the feudal technique of rule?

Feudal class relations were, as we have noted, characterized by a general hierarchy of rights and privileges, the holders of which were bound to one another by ties of personal loyalty. In a society where the vast majority of the population were kept in ignorance of almost everything outside the field of everyday work (except the other worlds of heaven and hell), the higher, aristocratic positions provided self-confidence, a relatively broad outlook, and, as the generations went by, a rounded upbringing and manners capable of ensuring obedience and respect.

This *general noble authority*, held together by hierarchical bonds of *personal loyalty* and classically expressed in a code of honour and fidelity, constituted the fundamental technology of feudal rule. It could function with reasonable efficiency in a social formation which

[35] S. Finer, 'State and Nation-Building in Europe: The Role of the Military', in C. Tilly (ed.), *The Formation of National States in Europe*, Princeton 1975, pp. 103ff. Cf. O. Hintze, 'Wesen und Verbreitung des Feudalismus', *Gesammelte Abhandlungen*, vol. 1, *Staat und Verfassung*, Leipzig 1941, pp. 84–5.

was largely governed by customary law, and which was circumscribed by rudimentary means of communication and slow-
changing forces of production and destruction. On the basis of an
amateur general authority, and with no special competence or
training, the feudal nobleman could adjudicate disputes according
to existing laws and customs, apply royal decrees, maintain the
obedience of his peasants and retainers, and lead armies and diplo-
matic missions. The efficacy of this mode of state organization is
illustrated by the figure of the justice of the peace, who, recruited
from the local squirearchy, continued to dominate the British
system of rural administration and judicature until as late as the
second half of the nineteenth century.[36]

Of all the complex transmutations of the feudal state, only two
very important developments will be mentioned here. First, the
king showed a marked tendency to convert the independent
authority of the aristocracy into a delegated royal one, and to rule by
means of non-noble or *parvenu* retainers. These efforts met with
varying success, but no feudal state was ever reduced to a simple
royal retinue. Such an outcome would, indeed, have signified the
emergence of a non-feudal state.

Secondly, the rise of mercantile capital involved, in the ages of the
Renaissance and Absolutist monarchies, the permeation of the
system of feudal rule by commodity relations. The noble landowner,
administering the state on his enfiefed land, was supplemented and
replaced by, for instance, the tax farmer, who retained as profit part
of the state taxes which he extracted. The military service of noblemen who had been allotted tax-exempt land gave way to mercenary
condottieri – entrepreneur-commanders who raised armies in return
for the spoils of war. On the basis of their newly-acquired wealth,
the tax farmer and the *condottiere* assumed positions of command
which were marked by a general amateur authority and a contractual
relationship to the head of state similar to those of the medieval
nobleman.[37] The pattern which developed in the leading Absolutist
state of late-feudal Europe – France – ultimately, as de Tocqueville

---

[36] The *administrative* duties of the feudal justices of the peace were eventually
transferred to elected county councils when they were set up in 1888. (D. Thom-
son, *England in the Nineteenth Century*, London 1950, p. 179.) Max Weber paid
some attention to the extraordinary longevity and vitality of this feudal institution: *Economy and Society*, New York 1968, III, pp. 1059ff.

[37] Cf. Anderson, *Lineages of the Absolutist State*.

observed in his writings on the revolution, undermined the position of the ruling aristocracy: not so much because of the influx of commoners into the state, but because the aristocrats were increasingly isolated from their local power base as a parasitic court nobility.[38]

In most countries, feudal forms of rule survived in a number of state apparatuses – particularly local rural administration, the upper reaches of diplomacy, and the army – for a considerable period after the bourgeois revolution. However, they were confronted with national states newly established by the bourgeois revolution; with the creation of a free labour market; the general extension of commodity relations to all means of production; and the unprecedented economic pace of industrial capitalism. All these processes broke down the feudal polities, or defeated them on the battlefields of Jena and Austerlitz. Even the revenge of Leipzig and Waterloo could not halt the trend for long. (In fact, the most formidable enemy of the revolutionary French bourgeois state was another bourgeois state: Britain.)

The new political technology that emerged comprised at least two important novel elements: 1) *bureaucracy* – that fitting object of the most famous analysis of the greatest social scientist since the classical economists, Max Weber; and 2) *parliamentary politics* – the force shaping the legislative and supreme executive apparatuses of the new representative state.

Max Weber's presentation of modern bureaucracy stressed its foundation upon *specialized knowledge* (*Fachwissen*). In order to grasp the class character of Weberian bureaucracy, we must first identify the kind of specialization and knowledge involved in the phenomenon.

The bureaucratic ideal type is actually an amalgamation of several distinct modes of organization, run by professionals utilizing a highly specific technology. First of all, the knowledge of the bureaucrat is of a particular intellectual variety: it refers to rules, especially legal ones. In Weber's clear formulation, the efficiency of the bureaucracy turns upon its treatment of issues according to *calculable rules*, and 'without regard to individual persons'. The 'specific nature' and 'special virtue' (*die eigentlich beherrschende*

---

[38] A. de Tocqueville, *The Ancien Regime and the French Revolution*, London 1971, Part 2, Ch. 1.

Bedeutung) of bureaucracy can be attributed to its application of this principle.[39]

In the ideal type of rational bureaucracy, this kind of knowledge is connected with the unproblematic combination of specialization, hierarchy and knowledge. The speed and predictability with which given rules are applied, is enhanced by specialization, whilst uniformity is increased if complicated cases are referred upwards in a hierarchical order. The impersonal *formal rationality* of capitalist bureaucracy takes as given both the content and the enforcement of the rules to be applied.

Weber's sociology of *Herrschaft* is, as I have noted elsewhere[40], essentially a sociology from above, which focusses almost exclusively on how domination is justified and administered. There is, however, a basis in reality for the presuppositions of the operational code of the capitalist state. The market sets the rules of bourgeois society and provides the economic constraint for their enforcement, even if ideological socialization proper, and in the last instance coercive violence, are also always necessary. The social dynamic is located in the realm of private enterprise and capital accumulation, and it is the common public needs of these that are ensured by the 'calculable rules' of the state.

However, the differences between the capitalist state and the bureaucratic enterprise should not be neglected. The entrepreneur has to confront the risks and uncertainties of a fluctuating competitive market and cannot work only according to fixed, calculable rules. Bureaucracy is above all an organization for legal regulation of the market and of the problems it engenders; but it is not suited for active intervention on the market. Weber's analysis naturally focussed on the post-Jena Prussian-German *Rechtsstaat*, or legal bureaucracy, under which specialized knowledge and strict hierarchy fitted with each other. In 20th-century monopoly capitalism, a new technology of bourgeois state organization has arisen.

Before we turn to these later phenomena, we must briefly consider the other political technique of competitive capitalism: namely, parliamentary politics. The bourgeois revolution split into two the feudal unity of government, legislation, administration, and judicature, each regulated by a specific technology. Government

---

[39] Weber, op. cit., III, pp. 974, 975; H. Gerth–C. Wright Mills (eds.), *From Max Weber*, New York 1958, pp. 215, 216.

[40] Therborn, *Science, Class and Society*, pp. 297 ff.

and legislature now had to represent the nation, not the hierarchical orders of the realm. The king, his retainers, the aristocrats and the spokesmen of the other estates were superseded by politicians owing their position to personal abilities (although it was understood that to possess any political ability at all, the individuals concerned had to be members of the ruling class, its allies or clientele). The parliamentary politician governed above all by skilful mediation between fellow MPs of his class, each with his idiosyncracies and immediate economic and social preoccupations: by playing them off against one another, creating heteroclite and shifting coalitions, and by persuading and cajoling with a peculiar kind of abstract oratory. Famous examples of such a figure are Guizot and Thiers, Disraeli and Giolitti, and, an apparently older type of statesman, Bismarck.

The further development of capitalism has brought to the fore two new techniques of bourgeois rule. To the extent that the popular masses could not be excluded from the politics of the 'legal nation', nor be kept isolated and encapsulated by local bosses and notables, the classical form of parliamentary politics was no longer an adequate instrument. It had to be supplemented or replaced by an original politics able to take hold of these new, partly-emancipated masses and keep them in a position of subordination. This new kind of bourgeois leadership may be termed *plebiscitary politics*. By means of mass appeals, the politician's message, and above all his image and attractive personal qualities, are conveyed to the people through public posters, mass-circulation newspapers, loud-speakers, and the television screen. Pioneered by Louis Bonaparte in the middle of the nineteenth century, this type of politics has been taken up and massively developed during the present century. Except in the Fascist regimes, however, it has supplemented rather than replaced parliamentary politics. The French Fourth Republic, the parliamentary factionalism of Italian Christian Democracy, and, outside Europe, the functioning of the US Congress and the parliamentary style of the dominant Japanese Liberal Democratic party all bear eloquent witness to the continuing importance of the traditional skills: manipulation of agendas and procedures, horse-trading, formation of unstable coalitions on a clique basis, and monitoring of confidence votes.

Classical parliamentary politics developed out of the bourgeois 'public' of salons and clubs, and, with its internal rituals and particular rhetoric, served to insulate the legislative apparatus both from the stable ceremony of the court and noble house, and from the experience and life-styles of the working classes. It is for this reason that it constitutes an enduring and central component of bourgeois political technology.

In the twentieth century and particularly the last few decades, a new mode of organizing the bourgeois state has developed alongside the legal bureaucracy. Like the latter, it is characterized by specialization, impersonality and stratified monopolization of intellectual knowledge by professionals. But it does not rely to the same degree upon calculable rules and fixed hierarchies. We may term this form *managerial technocracy*. Its rationality is substantive rather than formal; and, instead of juridical knowledge, it promotes technical and scientific expertise, applied with discretion and consideration of actual effects, rather than with calculable legal precision. The stable hierarchy is broken up by *ad hoc* committees, working parties, and special enquiries. Weber's assumption of a fit between competence and position on the administrative ladder no longer holds when what is at stake is not so much uniformity of regulation as effectiveness of state intervention. In the internal control system, cost-benefit analysis and budgetary policy have overtaken legal reviews in importance.

The new technology has emerged above all in connection with the increasingly social character of the productive forces and the rising challenge of the working class. These two processes also appear to be the most basic determinants of the growing state interventions on the market through countercyclical policies, state enterprises, and 'planning' for economic growth, technological development and environmental effect.

As we shall see below, the private-public distinction is a central feature of the bourgeois polity. However, it is becoming more and more blurred. Whereas, in the age of competitive capitalism, the legal state bureaucracy and private entrepreneurs occupied clearly demarcated functions, the present-day state goes far beyond mere regulatory activity to intervene massively *on* the market, affecting the supply and demand of commodities and money. In this respect, the state managerial technocracy is very similar to that of the modern giant capitalist corporation. Unlike the private entrepreneur, the latter is not confined to skilful adaptation to the vicissitudes of the market; it can act upon its parameters and engage in planning and prediction. Internal budget systems and operations analyses now move back and forth between the state and the corporations, as do management personnel.

The most important example of such managerial-technocratic administration is the system that has developed since the time of the New Deal in the United States – a country which never had a strong bureaucracy of the classical kind. In France, it first assumed importance with the postwar rise of planning – described by a well-informed liberal writer, Andrew Shonfield, as 'an act of voluntary collusion between senior civil servants and the senior managers of big business'.[41] One advanced case, which is little known in the wider world, is that of post-war Norway. The country has been largely administered by means of a sophisticated national budgeting system, evolved by economists working within the econometric tradition of Ragnar Frisch.[42]

In the present discussion, we have dealt only with administrative technology. But a similar trend can probably be discovered in the military sphere, where the new forces of repression and destruction have generated novel forms of military rule. The army bureaucrat, charged with application of the rules of strategy in a strict hierarchy of command, has been supplemented with staffs of weapons specialists, war economy planners, intelligence officers, and directors of subversive operations.

Managerial technology supplements, and in some cases overshadows, legal bureaucracy; but it does not replace it. The two coexist within the modern bourgeois state, often in uneasy relationships of conflicting competence, procedure and status.[43] Italy presents a particularly striking contrast between a highly archaic bureaucracy and a dynamic technocracy rooted in the economic sector of the state and represented by managers such as Mattei and Cefis.[44] The

[41] A. Shonfield, *Modern Capitalism*, London 1965, p. 128.

[42] J. Higley–K. E. Brofoss–K. Groholt, 'Top Civil Servants and the National Budget in Norway', in M. Dogan (ed.), *The Mandarins of Western Europe*, New York 1975, pp. 252–74.

[43] Writing with a conservative conception of bourgeois administrative law, the West German jurist Ernst Forsthoff has advanced some sombre reflections on the problem of the compatibility of classical bureaucracy and managerial technocracy: *Rechtsstaat im Wandel*, Stuttgart 1964; *Der Staat der Industriegesellschaft*, Munich 1971.

[44] S. Passigli, 'The Ordinary and Special Bureaucracies in Italy', in Dogan, op. cit., pp. 226–37. A fascinating insight into Italian state enterprise management is provided by an excellent piece of investigative journalism: E. Scalfari–G. Turani, *Razza padrona*, Milan 1974.

combination of the two techniques has not overcome the intrinsic divisions of the bourgeois state or its incapacity to engage in comprehensive planning.[45] Moreover, the new technology of rule has generated problems of its own. When the higher education system is no longer completely reliable (as has been the case since the upheavals of the late sixties) some state technocrats will cease to regard application of their knowledge and execution of their tasks as automatically synonymous with the maintenance of capitalist domination. However, in their technocratic myopia, state managers may miscalculate the political impact of their measures. Thus, the French Barre Plan aroused a general strike in May 1977 which was supported by forces ranging from the very respectable CGC to the Communist-led CGT.

From his own class standpoint, Max Weber was convinced that bureaucracy was the most efficient form of organization, surpassed only by that of the capitalist entrepreneur within the specific market sphere.[46] Lenin, in *State and Revolution*, seemed to think that no special political technology was necessary in the socialist state: the running of the state had been simplified to the point where it could be subsumed under the functions of accounting and control practised by 'the armed workers, by the whole armed population'. The later development of the USSR and the other socialist countries pointed in rather a different direction, and has often been depicted in terms of the rise of bureaucracy. Were Weber and all his bourgeois successors perhaps right after all?

Now, however the Stalinist form of authoritarian organization should be grasped, the type of administrator which it produced was certainly not that of the specialized bureaucrat, stably perched on a rung of the hierarchical ladder and impersonally applying calculable rules. The peculiar Stalinist technology of rule cannot be examined here. But we shall argue that one of its central components was an authoritarian and brutal variant of a genuinely working-class technique of organization – one which long predates Stalin and which constitutes the specific technology of the proletariat as the ruling class, that is, of the socialist state.

This mode of organization is as old as the labour movement itself; but it was Lenin who made one of the most important single contri-

[45] Cf. Hirsch, op. cit., pp. 231 ff.
[46] Weber, op. cit., I, p. 225.

butions to the new technology with his theory and practice of the formation of professional working class revolutionaries.[47] He thus helped to demonstrate the unquestionable incorrectness of Weber's position.

In its trade unions and parties the proletariat has developed an unprecedented political form – that of *collective mass organization*. This differs from both the feudal manor and the capitalist enterprise; from the various state machines and the churches; and from the conspiratorial group and the bourgeois political club. The central figure is not the priest shepherding his flock towards salvation, nor the feudal seigneur, capitalist manager-technocrat or rule-applying bureaucrat, but *the organizer*. His principal ability is that of ideological and practical mobilization for common goals. He also has a special kind of knowledge which has as its object class organization and class struggle; or, to put it more generally, social organization and the social struggle of which he is himself part. Such scientific knowledge of the class struggle was of course made possible by the historical union of Marxism and the labour movement.

Now, two points should be emphasized from the outset. First, the labour movement is organized in a fundamentally different way from a state bureaucracy or a capitalist firm. Secondly, however, there are different labour movements and different kinds of labour organizer. This diversity has given rise to, and provides an objective basis for, criticism of labour organizers on the grounds of conservatism, authoritarianism, sectarianism, adventurism, incompetence, privileged position, and so on. But they should not for all that be confused with officials of a bourgeois state or managers of a corporation. The so-called trade-union bureaucrat is little guided by precise rules in carrying out his job: in recruiting members, running the union, or bargaining with the employers. Even if indirectly, he must somehow gain collective acceptance of his decisions and of the results of negotiation; he cannot simply issue orders with calculable precision.[48]

[47] Lenin's theory and practice of the party are often obscured by myths concocted out of superficial or unremittingly hostile readings of *What is to be Done?* For some references to the working-class character of Lenin's conceptions, see *Science, Class and Society*, op. cit., p. 327n.

[48] Sune Sunesson, a Swedish student of trade unions and a colleague of mine, has already presented similar considerations.

In the communist movement this working-class organizer is called a *cadre*. The distinctive political technology of the socialist state may accordingly be termed *cadre administration* or *cadre leadership*. But it is inherent in the contradictory character of socialism that this working-class form of organization coexists unpeacefully with both bureaucracy and technocracy.

Organizing a proletarian revolution and the socialist transformation of society is not the kind of task that can be handled primarily by the speedy and precise application of calculable rules. The overall goal is given to the individual cadre in the form of the party line, but the class struggle cannot be worked out with the same exactitude as market transactions. The party line changes often, mainly by a shift in the emphasis on existing rules and directives, and all the time these have to be applied to the concrete and changing situation in which the cadre works. As an organizer of men, he cannot carry out his instructions 'without regard to the individual'. On the contrary, his ability to get things done depends greatly on his capacity to take into account the individuals with whom he has to work, and to establish a personal relationship with them. The means to enforce rules can be determined in advance even less than their content; it is largely a matter of inspiration, persuasion, intimidation, example and leadership.

The cadre is also a specialist in the mobilization of the masses. A handsome tribute has been paid to the efficiency of cadre administration and leadership, not only by those non-proletarian movements of national liberation that have tried to use them, but also by the imperialist specialists of counter-insurgency who have sought to imitate them again and again, though with little success.

The important difference between the capitalist bureaucrat and the East European cadre has been clearly expressed and critically examined in the remarkable work of Bálint Balla. Writing in Weberian language and from a left-Hegelian point of view, he says: 'While bureaucracy is characterized by reliability, continuity, efficacy, precise application of prevailing instructions – yet also by pedantry, formalism, red tape and Veblen's "trained incapacity" – cadre administration is marked on the one hand by flexible, immediate, "line-oriented" dynamism, by superiority over formalities and pragmatic ability to adjust to changing situations, yet on the other hand by diffuse unreliability and dilettantism, amorphous aversion to responsibility, rigid authoritarianism, rule-resistant incompetence and emotional paternalism' (sic).[49]

An American China scholar, Franz Schurman, has tried to differentiate the cadre from the manager and bureaucrat in terms of their characteristic 'leadership styles'. For this purpose, he uses two dimensions: orientation to stability or change, and mode of organizational integration, human or technical. Like the manager and unlike the bureaucrat, the cadre is 'change-oriented'; but he alone leads by means of *human* organization – by welding men together for solidary achievement of certain goals.[50] Schurman's categories seem much too general and do not specify the kind of change and human organization involved. But he undoubtedly catches an important aspect of the cadre's particularity. Schurman's distinction between the cadre and both the manager and the bureaucrat is especially valuable, because the Stalinist critique of bureaucracy, which was directed primarily against its routinism, formalism and slowness, rather than its insulated hierarchy, could also be levelled by managerial technocrats.

What differentiates the cadre from the manager seems to be two features in particular. First, cadre leadership is based primarily not upon universalistic intellectual knowledge – of engineering, sales, administration, and so on – but on *commitment* to the aims and 'line' of the organization and on experience of its struggles. (By contrast, feudalism rested upon *personal* loyalty to a superior.) Secondly, the cadre does not normally have at his disposal the kind of chain of command which is constituent both of bureaucracy and management and of the feudal hierarchy. The cadre typically has to *lead* rather than command. This is so because he is not (only) above the collective, but (first of all) a part of it. The characteristic problem of the working-class organizer is to unify a collective and to keep it united in solidarity and commitment.

In the socialist countries, this type of cadre leadership is to be found most clearly in the relationship of the party secretary and party committee to, on the one hand, the productive, administrative or military unit in which they operate, and, on the other, the ordinary party members and popular masses with whom they are concerned

---

[49] B. Balla, *Kaderverwaltung*, Stuttgart 1972, pp. 203–4.

[50] F. Schurman, *Ideology and Organization in Communist China*, Berkeley 1970, pp. 162 ff, 235–6.

in the waging of mass economic, political or ideological campaigns. There may be manipulation, cajoling, intimidation, as well as persuasion and inspiration; but in both cases the mode of activation is not that of command. The principle of democratic centralism does provide a command structure; but at the two levels we are discussing, not even the Stalinist party functionary could carry out his tasks just by issuing orders according to the statutes of 'democratic centralism'.

What makes the cadre part of the collective is above all an ideological bond of solidarity, sustained by links of common organizational practice. In contrast to the manager or bureaucrat, the labour organizer does not organize the jobs upon which other people depend for a living. This line of demarcation is crossed when only a cash nexus links a group of people with their representative. Thus, many US business union leaders should probably be regarded as salesmen (managers of a kind) rather than as trade-union cadres.

The parliamentary politician and plebiscitary leader do not operate with a chain of command either. But they are not thereby collective organizers. The former is basically a middleman between individuals and groups; while the latter inspires a personal following which is typically much looser than a collective organization, and which, possessing only a rudimentary internal structure, has little capacity for endurance and sustained joint effort. Moreover, the bourgeois politician, of either type, usually owes his leadership position to diffuse personal abilities rather than to commitment to a precise political line.

Bourgeois Catholic and Fascist parties and unions, as well as modern bourgeois mass parties in general, have tried to imitate forms of labour organization in their struggle against the working class. But, in its state apparatuses, the bourgeoisie has generally ruled through bureaucrats, managers and parliamentary or plebiscitary politicians. The 1793–94 Jacobin government of revolutionary France seems to exhibit certain similarities with an authoritarian cadre state. However, to portray the CPSU of the twenties and thirties as an example of 'the Jacobin model', as does the Italian historian, Giuliano Procacci, in his penetrating book on the Soviet party, is in my opinion misleading.[51]

Procacci focusses on the militarization of the party during the

[51] G. Procacci, *Il partito nell' Unione Sovietica*, Bari 1974, pp. 124 ff.

civil war and on the combination of centralized direction and mass enthusiasm. But the analogy with Jacobinism provides little insight into the enduring, pervasive and well-structured presence of ruling Communist parties at all levels of state and society – not only at peaks of crisis, but also during decades of peace. Indeed, analogical references to different historical and social contexts are always rather suspect.

Let us recall some general traits of Jacobin history. The movement originated as a parliamentary club – the *Club Breton* – at the National Assembly of Versailles in 1789. When the latter moved to Paris, the club was housed in a Jacobin convent of the Dominican order (which gave it its name), functioning as a parliamentary party and pressure group. It soon received the affiliation of a large number of clubs from all over France, which had previously existed as intellectual societies of the local petty bourgeoisie or as masonic lodges. Though bound together by increasing revolutionary zeal and by extensive correspondence, this system of clubs never formed a united party in the modern sense of the term. (The famous, or infamous, Jacobin centralization affected primarily the state apparatus, and was in any case largely a conjunctural phenomenon, since a separation of powers was integral to the Jacobin political conception.) From the fall of the Gironde in June 1793 until Thermidor of the following year, this network formed the political backbone of the government. But this brief period was one of external war against a formidable coalition of all the forces of European reaction. The revolutionary government was led not by the Jacobin Club in Paris, but by two parliamentary committees invested with extraordinary powers by the Convention in a time of mortal danger: the Committee of Public Safety and the Committee of General Security. The direct cause of the fall of Robespierre and the radical Jacobins was a conflict between the two committees combined with a parliamentary conspiracy in the Convention. Indeed, on the very eve of the Ninth of Thermidor, Robespierre had been enthusiastically applauded at the Jacobin Club.[52]

We have argued that cadre organization is a genuinely working

[52] The standard work on the Jacobins still seems to be Crane Brinton's magnificent sociological history: *The Jacobins*, New York 1930. On the Committee of Public Safety there is above all R. Palmer, *Twelve Who Ruled*, Princeton 1941. For a general narrative overview, see A. Soboul, *The French Revolution 1878-1799*, Vol. 2, NLB, London 1974, Chapters 3 and 4.

class form of organization. This is tantamount to saying that it belongs to class society. In a classless communist society, Stalin's dictum of 1935, 'Cadres decide everything'[53] is replaced by: 'The masses decide everything'. An advance towards that goal necessitates both a fight against bureaucracy and technocracy and a process of self-abolition of cadres.

Organizational technology may be summarized as a combination of two variables. It involves, first, a *directive dynamic*: a mode of orientation and a basis of leadership; and secondly, a *mode of activation* of the members of the organization, whereby their contribution to its orientation is ensured. Both derive from the social relations of the prevailing type of society: from class relations. We may express this by means of the chart on pages 64–5.

The chart should not be seen as anything more ambitious than a kind of summary of the preceding argument. Two notes of caution may be necessary. The historical coexistence and interaction of different modes of production implies that several organizational technologies interpenetrate, under the domination of one of them, within a single state. Secondly, the empty boxes on the chart indicate the great number of possible 'aberrations' and 'deviations' from the modal types. This is further emphasized by the fact that no exhaustive logic underlies the combination system. There may be other directive dynamics and other modes of activation than the ones listed. Our aim has not been to present a theory of organizations, but to define the contours of the most important types of state organization in modern history: feudal, capitalist, and socialist. The empty boxes also conceal the coexistence of different technologies. Thus, the late feudal states contained elements of bureaucracy and sometimes even of parliamentary politics (as is illustrated by the Swedish eighteenth-century Age of Freedom); bureaucracy and parliamentary politics are normal aspects of monopoly capitalist states; and socialist states are also bureaucratic and technocratic, and, if 'Eurocommunism' leads to socialism, will embrace aspects of parliamentary politics as well. As a comparison, the communist form of organization of society has been added, although it does not involve the existence of a separate state.

Now that we have completed this first general survey, we shall try

---

[53] J. Stalin, *Problems of Leninism*, Moscow 1941, p. 543. The occasion was an address to graduates of a very special apparatus of the state: the Red Army Academies.

to specify the fundamental input and output mechanisms and processes of transformation with regard to the tasks, personnel and material resources of the three main types of state. In order to facilitate an overall view, we present a summary of our findings in a chart at the end.

Tasks

At a very general and abstract level, the tasks of the state may be defined as internal and external defence of a social formation, and supreme rule-making, rule-application and rule-adjudication. The concrete content of these functions is so varied that an exhaustive description would be almost without end Our aim here, however, is neither to provide such descriptive detail nor to discuss the functions of the state in general, but to grasp the specific mechanisms which filter the task inputs and thus define which issues are of relevance to the particular type of state. The basis of this structuring mechanism is the *specific relation between state and society*. Clearly this will vary with the mode of production – the capitalist state does not relate to its society in the same way as the feudal or socialist state.

The character of this state-society relation, then, is expressed primarily in those regulative principles which determine *the form of the issues of concern to* the state, but also in the *relative weight of the diverse general functions of a state*. In a third dimension, *the quantitative role of the state* is determined by the extent of social practice encompassed in its tasks.

A useful starting-point for our analysis will be an investigation of the qualitative form of the task inputs under capitalism. The issues with which the bourgeois state is concerned are, in fact, defined by the characteristic *distinction between the private and public spheres*: the state occupies itself only with the latter. In his *What is the Third Estate?*, Abbe Sieyès was already making the point in the following way: 'What does a nation require to survive and prosper? It needs *private* activities and *public* services.'[54] Under the impact of the French Revolution, Hegel was later to develop this distinction into one between state and civil society.[55]

[54] Here quoted from M. Williams (ed.), *1775–1830 Revolutions*, Harmondsworth 1971, p. 93.
[55] I have analysed the emergence of this distinction in *Science, Class and Society*, op. cit., pp. 155–6.

Characteristic Technologies of State Organization

| Most immediately determinant class relations | Directive dynamic | Mode of Activation | | | | |
| | | Command | | Leadership | | |
		Personal	Impersonal	Mediatory	Charismatic	Unifying
Feudal: Hierarchy of rights and privileges	Social superiority and/or personal confidence-loyalty	Seigneurial (independent delegated or bought)				
Capitalist: Competitive market and 'factory despotism'	Stratified monopolization of intellectual knowledge: formal-legal		Bureaucracy			
	Personal qualities of national representativeness and mass appeal			Parliamentary politics		

Social character of productive forces, monopolistic market and 'factory despotism'	Stratified monopolization of intellectual knowledge: substantial-technical	Technocracy
	Personal qualities of national representativeness and mass appeal	Plebiscitary politics
Socialist: Collective appropriation and individual subordination (to managers and bureaucracy)	Uneven degree of political commitment and experience	Cadre
(*Communist*) (Collective appropriation and management)	(Everyday collective experience)	(Collective)

This opposition between what is private and what is public is rooted in the class relations of capitalist society; it is continually reproduced by competition between individuals on the market and by the command of private capital over labour. The formal equality of buyers and sellers appears in the 'public' domain of politics as the common 'interest' of independent and equal individuals. The polity has a necessary but separate role, and it is this separation that is clearly expressed in the private-public distinction.

The struggle of the rising bourgeoisie centered on issues concerning both the state and society. It demanded that the state be separated from the private realm of aristocratic lineage and be firmly based on 'public opinion'; it should be concerned only with matters subsumable under general principles, and not with the material or legal interests of particular individuals or categories of individuals. The distinction was intrinsically related to the concept of bureaucracy – of the *bureau* as a public office separated from the household of the king and the aristocrats. As regards society, the conception of the private was directed against the estates, guilds, village communities, royal charters and all other quasi-public corporations that restricted the action of the individual.

The location and sharpness of the line of demarcation between private and public has varied considerably with the conjuncture of the class struggle. Generally speaking, the private sphere has extended to the choice of occupation and place of work, the choice of marriage-partner, and the ideological convictions, consumption habits and life-style of the individual. In other words, it has comprised the labour market, capital accumulation, the bourgeois nuclear family, and the whole field of bourgeois 'individualism'. Sexual morality, religion and the public expression of political ideology have at times been matters for state repression, although in principle they form part of the private sphere of bourgeois democracy. (Once ideological non-conformism reaches the level of collective organization, however, it invariably becomes the concern of the bourgeois state's forces of intelligence and repression.)

Three major trends of capitalist development have had a considerable influence on the private-public distinction. Two of these have substantially expanded the public sphere of state tasks, whereas on another level the third has separated the private sphere more sharply. Firstly, the increasingly social character of the forces of production has established a new kind of connection between the state and the processes of production and exploitation. State intervention has grown in order to meet the need for large-scale, long-term investment that is too risky for private capital to undertake, and the need for a degree of economic coordination that cannot be realized by the market. The dependence of monopoly capitalism upon a few giant corporations has further encouraged *ad hoc* state action to rescue ailing companies. A second trend – which is largely a consequence of the increasingly social character of the productive forces – is the growth and strengthening of the working class itself. Directly or indirectly, this has focussed public concern on new issues: the content and effects of centralized wage deals, job safety, the length of the working day, the power of command in the workplace, the distribution of income, and social security.

On the other hand, a strong tendency towards the privatization of life has appeared with such phenomena as increasing horizontal mobility, the growth of city suburbs, the intensification of labour through speed-up, and the development of new consumer goods, particularly the motor-car and television. The private sphere has become more isolated from the public, the nuclear family more secluded from society as a whole.

Feudal and socialist states are organized around definitions of tasks that are quite different from the private-public principle, even though they themselves stand at opposite poles to each other. Under feudalism the state is 'privatized', whereas under socialism it is private life that is 'made public'. However, such a characterization remains within the frame of reference of capitalism and does not identify even the general distinctive patterns of the two systems.

The feudal state and feudal society were not the private property of the king. The polity was not based on the *Gefolgschaft* – the armed retainers of the ruler and military commander – which was the form prevalent among Germanic 'barbarian' tribes. It rather expressed a fusion of this institution with the appropriation of the means of production (land) by individual lords, of whom one rose to the position of king.[56] Feudal social relations were characterized by a hierarchy of personal services and obligations that regulated the tasks of the state. This principle can be seen most clearly in the system of noble

---

[56] Joseph Strayer has described these as 'the two levels of feudalism'; see *Medieval Statecraft and the Perspectives of History*, Princeton 1971, ch. 6. Cf. O. Hintze, 'Wesen und Verbreitung des Feudalismus', op. cit.

assemblies, estates and parliaments, and in their relationship to the king.[57]

The feudal monarch and the representative assembly dealt typically with appeals for protection and assistance. The assembly would request that the king remedy specific grievances, settle disputes, answer demands for exemption from burdens, and so on; while he would demand financial aid and armed levies for his household and administration, and for his military exploits. He would also ask his subjects to countersign, or simply register their assent to, new obligations and prescriptions. This system of personal-official bargaining persisted *sub rosa* even in the epoch of feudal absolutism and the eclipse of the representative assemblies. On the very eve of the French Revolution, the king had to summon the Estates-General to ask them to bail out the bankrupt royal administration.

If we look not just at the apex but at the feudal polity as a whole, then it is clear that the system outlined above led to the compartmentalization of issues dealt with by the state. The relevance of a particular matter did not depend on whether it had a general public character, but on whether it fitted into the hierarchical relation in which it was raised. However, the most detailed questions concerning work, property or marriage might come up there for consideration, and the area of discretion was so large that it was often not possible to calculate the acceptability of an issue in advance. The king kept a fairly free hand to decide whether or not it was his task to settle an appeal that came before him.

We should now turn to an examination of the characteristic tasks of the socialist state. These are broadly determined by the fact that the collective workers (or the class bloc led by the proletariat) have replaced the individual market agent and the lord-peasant relation-

---

[57] See for example F. Carsten, *Princes and Parliaments in Germany*, Oxford 1959; R. Holtzmann, *Französische Verfassungsgeschichte*, Munich and Berlin 1910, part II, chs. 2–3, part III, chs. 1–4. An extremely valuable overview of the feudal system of protection and aid may be found in O. Brunner, *Land und Herrschaft*, Brünn/Munich/Vienna 1943. The English Parliament soon showed a marked difference from the assemblies of other feudal states, even though it had a similar origin: 'The original reason for calling Parliaments was . . . that the king wanted assistance in the tasks of government. The purposes of the sitting were produced by him – to consider the nation's affairs . . . to consent to aids and tallages, to see justice done.' G. R. Elton, *Studies in Tudor and Stuart Politics and Government*, Cambridge 1974, vol. II, pp. 30–1.

ship. It is not only in the effective elimination of private enterprise that the bourgeois distinction between 'private' and 'public' is transcended. The collective character of proletarian rule makes necessary a continual struggle against any form of individual sub-ordination of this previously exploited and downtrodden class – in particular against the form that is reproduced in the sphere of per-sonal choice, where formal equality conceals the practical inequality of individuals. The divisions between manual and mental labour, between town and country, and between the labours of the two sexes can also only be overcome by a conscious, collective struggle against their reproduction. Asserting a fundamental principle of Soviet law, Lenin wrote during the NEP period in a letter to the People's Commissar for Justice: 'We do not recognize anything "private", and regard everything in the economic sphere as falling under *public* and not *private* law. Hence the task is to extend the application of state intervention in "private legal" relations, to extend the right of the state to annul "private contracts".'[58]

The class rule of the proletariat supersedes not only the individual market agent but also the anonymous market itself that decides the success or failure of men and women. Moreover, the expression of working-class rule by the state is not equivalent to the absorption of the private sphere by a public bureaucracy. In a socialist society, private life is made public by a number of proletarian and popular mass organizations apart from the state apparatus itself. In this way, the sharp delimitation of the state as an apparatus with special tasks and personnel tends to be eroded – which is essentially what is in-volved in the notion of the withering away of the state.

The existing socialist states would seem to be flourishing rather than withering away; nevertheless, they incorporate mechanisms and institutions, which in widely varying degrees display the characteristic organization and relationship to society of the socialist state.

Administratively, the individual is connected with the state apparatus proper by a whole network of non-professional, elected bodies – at a house, street, neighbourhood or village level; in Europe this structure is probably most developed in the GDR. Besides the repressive forces of the state, voluntary militias and public order bodies operate at the workplace; and in the USSR for

[58] V. I. Lenin, 'Letter to Kursky', *Collected Works*, vol. 36, p. 562.

instance, a system of non-state 'comrades' courts' deals with minor offences.

The field of competence of the state may also be formally shared with other organizations. In Eastern Europe, for example, problems of labour safety and work hygiene are the responsibility of the trade unions, but the enforcement of trade union action is a state task; the Soviet Komsomol plays a direct role in the running of state schools; and in East Germany, the Workers' and Peasants' Inspectorate combines state, party and mass forms of control over the state administration.[59]

In contrast to the atomization and privatization of capitalist society, the pattern of personal relations is the concern of the party and of the mass organizations – trade unions, youth organizations, etc. But how this functions in practice needs to be carefully investigated: to what extent is it primarily an authoritarian preoccupation with external ideological conformity, and to what extent does it serve to foster solidarity, egalitarianism and democratic popular participation?

Another problem concerns the mass organizations' independence of the state organs of administration and repression. The degree to which the former possess a specific dynamic in the post-Stalinist socialist states is of enormous importance to the position of the proletariat as the ruling class. For the state apparatus *per se* is never, strictly speaking, a workers' state – except during its brief and partial fusion with the councils of armed revolutionary workers. It is a workers' state in so far as its specialized apparatuses are controlled and subordinated *from the outside* by the working class collectivity. But for this to take place, the latter must have an independent organized existence.

The leading role of the party is equally dependent on its differentiation from the state apparatus. To a varying extent, all socialist countries do in fact maintain a line of demarcation between party and state – both at the local level, in the separation of the offices of managerial head and party secretary, and at central level, in the different composition of the supreme organs of party and state. Thus, managers of the economic, administrative and repressive apparatuses of the state make up only a minority, albeit the very large one of

---

[59] See for example P. Gélard, *Les organisations de masse en Union Soviétique*, Paris 1965; G. Brunner, *Kontrolle in Deutschland*, Cologne 1972, pp. 413 ff.

45%, of the Central Committee of the CPSU.[60] Since the time of Stalin, the Politbureau and the Council of Ministers have been more clearly delimited from each other: whereas in 1951 ten out of eleven members of the former were also in the latter, in 1971 only three out of fifteen Politbureau members served on the Council of Ministers.[61] However, one consequence of the lingering system of institutionalized authoritarianism is the confusion between the leading role of the party and the coercive powers of the repressive and other state apparatuses.

The tasks of the state are patterned not only by the predominant social relations, but also by the specific dynamics of the mode of production. Under feudalism, where landed property (incorporating a number of tied peasants) was the principal means of production and where consumption was oriented towards noble consumption, the characteristic social dynamic was the urge to acquire and subjugate more land and to extract a greater surplus from what was already possessed.[62] Since land could not normally be bought and sold on the market, armed conquest was the chief means to expand the property and sources of consumption of the nobility. Military proficiency was the only specific skill of the ruling class, and the preparation and waging of war was a major preoccupation of the state, in both its medieval and absolutist forms.

Of course, the raising of production levels on existing land was always an important alternative or supplementary means of increasing consumption. However, the productive forces developed very slowly within the hierarchical system and were not directly propelled by the feudal relations of production, since the landlords were external to the production process proper. Any substantial increase could be obtained only by the redefinition of the services and obligations of the exploited classes. Another important task of the feudal polity was accordingly adjudication of claims concerning the traditional rules governing relations between the nobility and the peasantry.

[60] The figure is calculated from B. Meissner, 'Parteiführung, Parteiorganisation und soziale Struktur der KPdSU', *Osteuropa* No. 8/9 1976, pp. 607–8. It refers to the CC elected by the 25th Congress in 1976. The composition of the CC elected in 1971 is described by P. Gélard in *Les systèmes politiques des états socialistes*, 2 vols., Paris 1975, vol. 1, pp. 124 ff.

[61] T. Rigby, 'The Soviet Politburo: A Comparative Profile 1951–1971', *Soviet Studies* vol. 24 no. 1 (July 1972).

[62] Cf. Anderson, op. cit., pp. 31–2.

In contrast, the accelerated tempo of the capitalist mode of production constantly demanded new and clearly defined legislation, on which individual agents could depend in the fluctuating conditions of the market.

Capital is essentially mobile and is based on a form of exploitation that resembles a non-zero-sum game. Both wages and profits can rise if there is an expansion of the productive forces and a growth of relative surplus value. The defence of capital accumulation by the state is thus not reducible to its tasks of violent repression and ideological indoctrination. It also has the following important functions: economic penetration of other countries and restriction of access to the national territory; stimulation of economic development; and management of cyclical fluctuations. Although their armed might has grown enormously, the capitalist states are today less concerned with military affairs, and, as two world wars have shown, productive capacity is now of great strategic importance in any conflict among them. As regards their internal structure, state intervention in the field of 'social welfare' is not necessarily an obstacle to capital accumulation: as Bismarck already understood, it can even strengthen the capitalist regime against challenge and revolt. In early bourgeois society, the term 'police' covered nearly every kind of internal non-judicial and non-fiscal administration. Today, in spite of the erection of a formidable repressive apparatus, it is the stimulation of economic growth and the provision of social security that constitute the most significant policing tasks of the advanced capitalist state.

The defence of socialism and workers' power invests the state with new politico-ideological tasks, rendering certain functions of organization and ideological orientation much more central than they were in previous types of state. Thus, the state has not merely to manage the production of use-values, but must draw up a *political* plan for the economy, whereby work relations will be developed in the direction of classless society. Defence of the socialist mode of production involves above all maintenance of the collective supremacy of the working class and elimination of the (re-)production of individual subordination.

We can express this best by the following distinction: *the proletarian state is by its very essence 'politicized' and 'ideologized', whereas the bourgeois state is 'economized', and the feudal 'militarized'*. Where collective ownership and planning have replaced private property, the market and the hierarchical feudal contract, the functions of rule-making and rule-application tend to be fused, the latter diminishing in importance. It is true, however, that greater attention has been given to the judiciary since the Twentieth Congress of the CPSU raised the serious problem of 'socialist legality' after the experience of Stalinism.[63]

The character of the state-society relation and the forms of state organization are so dissimilar that it would be of little use to make a quantitative comparison of the tasks of the general types of class state. Within each type, however, an important distinction must be drawn, according to the extent that the state apparatus concentrates class rule; or, to put it another way, according to the extent of diffusion of that rule throughout society as a whole.

In this respect there are important differences between medieval and absolutist feudalism, between parliamentary and dictatorial forms of capitalist rule, and between the earlier soviet and the later state and party socialism. Of course, these are themselves very broad categories, which all contain significant variations. Nor, by the way, should a non-utopian view of socialism assume *a priori* that the possible forms of socialist state are fewer than those of bourgeois rule.

Personnel

Birth and kinship played a critical role in the recruitment of personnel to the feudal state. Nevertheless, it would be rather misleading to employ the conventional sociological jargon of 'ascription versus attainment' to locate the distinction between feudal and bourgeois recruitment criteria. Indeed, from one important viewpoint, it is the *feudal* personnel who are recruited on the basis of achievement, and the *bourgeois* on the grounds of ascription.

If a single formula could express the nature of the feudal hierarchy, it would be *personal service (rendered or promised) to a superior*. This principle pervaded the whole feudal system, and, within the polity, characterized both lord-vassal and lord-retainer relations. It governed also the contractual relationship between the king and his subjects, although in the era of absolutism the 'Christian prince' was considered responsible only to his own conscience and to God. The factor of royal or noble 'blood' operated rather in the manner of an intervening variable: personal services were transmuted into services

[63] The Chinese have retained a more informal political judicial system; see J. A. Cohen, 'The Criminal Process in China', in D. Treadgold (ed.), *Soviet and Chinese Communism*, Seattle 1967.

rendered by prior generations and into the collective service to the realm of the nobility as a whole. Under the absolutist monarchies, this tendency of closure was counteracted by the growth in number and importance of non-noble administrative servants of the crown, who might subsequently be rewarded by ennoblement. It was also possible to enter the state machine by the quite unique service of buying a post. In 17th century France, for instance, this practice was officially encouraged on a large scale in order to bolster the finances of the royal administration.

This recruitment criterion was one of the distinctive political aspects of feudal class rule. It created a common bond between the king and the aristocracy, and between the non-noble state personnel and the monarch – the first among the aristocrats. It was thus thoroughly incompatible with bourgeois rule. For the feudal principle of personal service to a superior, the capitalist state was to substitute two interrelated criteria: *personal intellectual abilities* and *personal qualities of representativeness of the national 'public'*. The latter refers to the personnel of the legislature and of the government, the former to that of other state functions.

The French Declaration of the Rights of Man and of the Citizen (1789) proclaimed that 'all honours, posts and employment should be open to all according to their different abilities, without any distinction other than that created by their virtues and talent'. The language is unambiguous: there is here no mention of achievement – only references to the attributes of individuals. Even if 'virtue' is regarded as an achieved property, it is nonetheless secondary to ability and talent. Competition among gifted individuals thus replaces the pledge of personal service as the mechanism of entry into the state apparatus.

The qualities required of the personnel of the capitalist state have always been of a special kind, as can be seen from the filtering processes of education, selection and training. Two particular aspects stand out clearly. In the first place, experience of manual labour has never played any role in recruitment; only certain intellectual talents of an openly elitist character have entered into the selection procedure. For example, it was in order to deepen this exclusivist basis that the teaching of Latin and Greek was reintroduced or given renewed emphasis in 19th century secondary schools. Such considerations also underlie the German *Juristenmonopol* (the requirement of extensive legal training), the more literary Oxbridge education of 'gentlemen', and the more straightforwardly bourgeois *grandes écoles* in France. The influence of this educational system over the patterning of careers is asserted by the informal criteria of entry into the state machine; by the operation of elaborate 'old boys' networks', including the very special *esprit de corps* of the special corps that groups upper civil servants in France; and by the very important principle that the road to high office is normally opened by these educational channels, rather than by promotion from the lower rungs of the administrative ladder. Another selection mechanism, which has been especially well developed in Germany, is the payment of extremely low salaries during the early stages of a higher administrative career.

Secondly, the training of state personnel has focussed on the systematic inculcation of one particular leadership quality. This is not the capacity to weld together a collective organizational team, but the ability to exercise authority over and ensure the respect of subordinate members of the staff. Boarding-schools and the student fraternities of elite universities are devoted to the development of self-discipline and self-confidence in such leadership cadres.[64]

The formal equality proclaimed by the French Declaration of Rights has thus been combined with a *de facto* bourgeois monopoly and with the power of command of intellectual management over manual labour. This recruitment policy has been remarkably successful for the bourgeoisie: in terms of efficiency, loyalty and class representativeness of the state apparatus. As regards social origin, one or two centuries of 'equality' have resulted in a level of non-working class recruitment to the higher civil bureaucracy of between 80 and 95%:

Proportion of upper civil servants having a manual working class father and proportion of same belonging to female sex, as percentages of total. Circa 1970.

	Working class fathers	Female sex
Britain	18	2
Italy	9	0
Sweden	15	3
USA	18	2
West Germany	8	1

[64] An American scholar, John Armstrong, has written a fascinating comparative historical account of the selection and induction processes of higher state personnel in Russia, Prussia/West Germany, Britain and France; see *The European Administrative Elite*, Princeton 1973.

Source: R. Putnam, 'The Political Attitudes of Senior Civil Servants in Britain, Germany and Italy', in M. Dogan (ed.), *The Mandarins of Western Europe*, New York 1975, pp. 96–7. The figures refer to comparable representative samples of top civil servants.

Italy, West Germany and, probably, France[65] make up one sub-variant of the overall pattern. Another is formed by aristocratic Britain; Sweden, as it was after forty years of Social Democratic government; and the United States – a country with neither a feudal past nor a significant political labour movement, and with a supposedly high labour mobility. What little variation there is in the grim uniformity of sexism points in the same direction as do the figures on class.

Membership of the governmental apparatus of the capitalist state is regulated by the criterion of national representativeness. This was the new principle of legitimacy proclaimed by the bourgeois revolutions in the struggle against the dynastic authority of the 'Christian prince', who protected rather than represented his people. However, the mechanisms of representation have varied considerably – from the mystical bond of 'ein Volk, ein Reich, ein Führer' (one people, one state, one leader) to the parliamentary vote of confidence or the support given to an elected president. Similarly, the 'national public' has been defined in diverse ways, ranging from a tiny minority of large property-holders to the whole adult population.

One interesting and important feature is common to electoral and non-electoral modes. In neither case is bourgeois national representativeness institutionalized by binding politicians to a specific mandate from their constituency. This is made very explicit in classical parliamentary theory and procedure, as well as in that of dictatorships. The representativeness of the politician is invested rather in his personal ability, his individual conscience and presumed commitment to the 'public good'.

Bourgeois democracy – the rule of a tiny minority through institutions of universal suffrage and free elections – is a very significant and intriguing aspect of the advanced capitalist states. However, as I have shown empirically elsewhere[66], it is a late

---

[65] From Ezra Suleiman's fine study, *Politics, Power and Bureaucracy in France* (Princeton 1974, p. 88), it may be calculated that, between 1953 and 1968, persons with manual working class backgrounds composed only six per cent of the total of 1,017 entrants to the *Grands Corps* and *Corps d'Administrateurs Civils* coming from the Ecole Nationale d'Administration.

[66] G. Therborn, 'The Rule of Capital and the Rise of Democracy', op. cit.

phenomenon, accomplished after long and bitter struggles of the working class against the bourgeoisie. The latter's resistance was so strong that the labour movement never succeeded without the help of allies, be they foreign armies (as in Germany, Italy and Japan), the petty bourgeoisie (Australia, Denmark, and other countries), or sections of a divided but powerful bourgeoisie (Britain, France, the United States). Indeed, the most important single factor in the rise of bourgeois democracy has been external war.

Although universal suffrage was initially conceived outside the narrow circles of the bourgeoisie, it would nevertheless be a mistake to regard it as related in a purely external and contingent manner to the dictatorship of that class. As Bismarck quite consciously understood[67], the popular vote advances one of the central aims of the bourgeois revolution – the integration of all social layers into the political and ideological framework of the national (but not necessarily liberal) state. Particularly in the epoch of monopoly capitalism, franchise restrictions have given way to new and more subtle ways of excluding the working class from decisive control over political affairs. If these mechanisms ultimately prove to be inadequate, then the more drastic solutions of fascism, military dictatorship or foreign intervention are always available and invariably employed. But except in situations of acute threat, particularly those of social revolution or internal disintegration due to an incompleted bourgeois revolution, one form or another of elected government arises in correspondence with the inherently competitive character of capitalist relations of production.

Bourgeois control over the formation of national 'public opinion', together with the exclusive ritual of parliamentary activity, has rigidly restricted the qualifications required by an elected deputy. As a result, working class representation in bourgeois-democratic parliaments has been successfully kept at a minimal level: in the

---

[67] From his experiences of the aftermath of 1848, Bismarck soon came to the conclusion that: 'I do not want lawyers to be elected but loyal peasants', and that to drown the liberal intelligentsia it was 'absolutely necessary to widen the circle of voters in order to obtain a legislature which was more national, less dogmatic, and less hostile to the legitimate prerogatives of the monarchy'. He had good reasons at that time: 'If I, for example, could send here in Prussia 100 workers from my estate to the ballot box, then they would outvote every other opinion in the village to the point of destroying it.' Bismarck's aim of a national monarchy involved a two-front war against both the reactionary legitimist wing of the aristocracy and the liberal small and medium bourgeoisie. See T. Hamerow, *The Social Foundations of German Unification 1858–71*, Princeton 1972, pp. 186, 187.

advanced capitalist countries, it has varied between 0 and 10%. Furthermore, after their election, this handful of workers generally become full-time politicians. The sexist tendency is as blatant as the anti-working-class one.

Workers and women elected to the legislature, as a percentage of the total.

	Workers	Women
Belgium 1961	9	—
Canada 1963	—	1
Finland	8	17
France 1968	3	2
Italy 1968	10	3
Norway 1969	9	9
Sweden 1961	3	12
Switzerland 1971	0.5	6
United Kingdom 1970	8	4
USA 1968	1	3
West Germany 1961	6	—

Sources: For Sweden, L. Sköld–A. Halvarsson, 'Riksdagen sociala sammansättning', in *Samhälle och Riksdag*, Stockholm 1966, Vol. 1, pp. 441 and 445 (on class structure); and *Förteckning över Första Kammarens ledamöter 1961* and *Förteckning över Andra Kammarens ledamöter 1961* (on sex structure); for Switzerland, J. Ziegler, *Une suisse au-dessus de tout soupçon*, Paris 1976, pp. 130–1; for the other countries, J. Blondel, *Comparative Legislatures*, Englewood Cliffs 1973, p. 160.

Note: The percentage of women in the Swedish Diet, which was then the highest ever, rose to 21% in 1975; the proportion of workers, however, declined from a 1933 peak of 10%. I have not included Blondel's exceptionally high figure of 22% workers for Austria in 1970, because on closer investigation, it turned out to include labour movement functionaries. See K. Steiner, *Politics in Austria*, Boston 1972, pp. 231–2. As the rigour of national statistics may vary in other respects, the principal conclusion to be drawn from the table is the uniformity with which workers are absent from bourgeois legislatures, rather than any international differentiation.

The changes that have occurred within modern capitalism should be seen within this general framework of sexist and anti-proletarian recruitment. Among officials, the percentage of persons with technical training, both economic and natural-scientific, has risen at the expense of those with legal or literary backgrounds. Among politicians, active entrepreneurs and rentiers have, except in the USA, been displaced by professional hangers-on of the bourgeois class. Plebiscitary politics has also involved the recruitment of 'media personalities', whose main capacity is to make a good showing in the mass media.

The basic social characteristic of proletarian class rule – collective supremacy combined with individual subordination – is expressed in the criteria of recruitment of state personnel. The dominant principle is that of *class representativeness, which is supplemented by the requirement of expertise*. These are not two distinct principles referring to different state apparatuses (as are national representativeness and expertise under capitalism), but a single, combined criterion. For instance, the Eighth Congress of the CPSU in 1919 decided that the Red Army should 'have a definite class character' and that it should include 'military specialists', who, given the nature of the Tsarist army, were generally of non-proletarian origin.[68] The application of this principle and the combination of its two elements have been realized in widely varying ways, according to the country and the period.

Two fundamental types of enforcement mechanism may be distinguished. One was the original soviet system, under which workers' and peasants' councils and their various committees fused governmental functions with administrative ones. The Soviet Constitution of 1918 explicitly denied the bourgeoisie and the commercial petty bourgeoisie access to these bodies, and even deprived them of the right to vote. Prior to the decisions of the Eighth Party Congress, the repressive forces were directed by soldiers' councils under elected commanders. The party operated as a guiding force within a wider structure of class rule.

Later, the party became the decisive authority on matters of personnel recruitment. The *nomenklatura* system gave the relevant party organ the power to plan and supervise recruitment to the state apparatus, and this rapidly replaced the capitalist method of in-

[68] R. Kolkowicz, *The Soviet Military and the Communist Party*, Princeton 1967, p. 41.

dividual competition for posts. Whatever the mechanism and its mode of functioning, the anti-capitalist revolution has effected a drastic change in the class composition of state functionaries. One indication of this is the social origin of the officer corps.

Officers of working class origin, as a percentage of the total.

Soviet Union 1923	14[1]
Soviet Union 1927	22[1]
Czechoslovakia 1952	53
Poland 1963	49
GDR 1960s	over 80
West Germany 1960	0
USA 1959	14[2]
Sweden 1962	13

---

1. The peasantry accounted for 53% in 1923 and 56% in 1927. In 1926–27 the proletariat (excluding employees) made up about 17% of the Soviet population. Calculated from E. H. Carr, *Foundations of a Planned Economy*, Vol. 2, Harmondsworth 1976, pp. 520–1, on the assumption that employees had as many dependents as workers.
2. For the ranks of naval captain and colonel upwards.
Sources: R. Garhoff, 'The Military in Russia 1861–1965', in J. Van Doorn (ed.), *Armed Forces and Society*, The Hague 1968, p. 247 (for the USSR); J. Wiatr, 'Military Professionalism in Poland', in ibid., p. 235 (for Poland); W. L. Warner et al., *The American Federal Executive*, New Haven 1963, p. 30 (for the USA); B. Abrahamsson, *Military Professionalism and Political Power*, Stockholm 1971, pp. 46 ff. (for all the other countries).

Little is known about the operation of the *nomenklatury* by the party, but apart from the requirement of technical competence, the major criteria seem to be ones of a very diffuse political, rather than formal class nature.[69] This immediately raises the highly contro-

---

[69] J. Hough, *The Soviet Prefects: The Local Party Organs in Industrial Decision-Making*, Cambridge, Mass. 1969, ch. VIII.

versial question of the class representativeness of the ruling Communist Parties themselves. We cannot now enter that vast and heavily mined territory, and will merely make a few observations that go beyond current factional polemics to touch on some real issues that need to be discussed.

One aspect that is crucial to the class representativeness of the party is, of course, the ideological-political training of new members. There would clearly be a grave danger if managerially competent individuals were coopted into the party mainly on the basis of their expert merits, and were thus not educated in the history, battles and ideology of the party that led the proletarian revolution. Such a pattern is no doubt discernible in the Soviet Union and Eastern Europe, but, contrary to the hopes of anti-communist researchers, the tendency in this direction that appeared during the Khruschev period seems to have been reversed. Indeed, the proportion of 'coopted specialists' at regional party leadership level was lower in 1967 than it had been prior to the Twentieth Party Congress.[70]

However, in the formation of leaders who are representative of the class, ideological training and organizational work among the masses can hardly serve as substitute for day-to-day experience of working-class life. It is quite natural that capable party members should rise from the ranks of the working class to full-time positions of cadre responsibility in the construction and running of the socialist state and society. However, they may after a time become distanced from the working class, whereas progress towards communism presupposes an increase of direct workers' supremacy.

Official reports on the social compositions of the government Communist parties usually refer to occupation at the time of application for membership, and therefore overstate their proletarian character. Nevertheless, the published figures convey a number of interesting patterns and tendencies: the uniquely high peasant contingent in the Chinese Communist Party (CCP) – although the figures available are rather old; the strong de-proletarianization of the CPSU and the East European parties after the revolution; and the re-proletarianization of the CPSU and the East German SED from the 1960s onwards.

---

[70] R. Blackwell, 'The Soviet Political Elite: Alternative Recruitment Policies at the Obkom Level', *Comparative Politics*, Oct. 1973, pp. 99 ff.

Social Composition of Communist Parties. Percentages.

	Workers			Peasants		
	1947–8	1956–8	1966–9	1947–8	1956–8	1966–9
Bulgaria	—	36.1	—	—	34.2	—
China	—	13.5	—	—	66.5	—
Czecho-slovakia	57.0	—	33.4	31.0	—	2.6
GDR	48.1	33.8	45.6	9.4	5.0	6.4
Hungary	56.0	—	34.6	37.3	—	8.7
Poland	62.2[1]	—	39.7	28.2[1]	—	11.5
USSR	41.0[2]	32.0	38.0	28.0[2]	17.0	16.0
Yugo-slavia	—	—	31.2	49.4	—	7.4

1. 1945.   2. 1921.

Sources: K.v.Beyme, *Okonomie und Politik im Sozialismus*, Munich 1975, p. 143; M. Lesage, *Les régimes politiques de l'URSS et de l'Europe de l'Est*, Paris 1971, p. 289; E. Fortsch, *Die SED*, Stuttgart 1969, p. 104; T. Rigby, *Communist Party Membership in the USSR 1917–1967*, Princeton 1968, p. 414.

A better indicator, however, is the composition of leading party bodies. (The following information has been compiled from available biographical material.) In 1967, among the members and candidates of the Central Committee of the SED, only a third registered a working-class occupational background. Most of the remainder had gone through some kind of intellectual education, and only four out of 181 currently held a working class job.[71] A survey of six republican Central Committees in the Soviet Union, conducted in 1966, reported that only 71 out of 778 members were workers or kolkhoz and sovkhoz peasants. But even this small proportion represents a substantial increase over the 1956 level of 24 out of 644.[72] The present composition of the CPSU may be summarized in the following table:

[71] P. C. Ludz, *Parteielite im Wandel*, Cologne and Opladen 1968, pp. 338 ff. Out of the 189 members and candidates elected to the Central Committee by the Eighth Congress of the SED in 1971, only three were then workers. T. Baylis, *The Technical Intelligentsia and the East German Elite*, Berkeley 1974, p. 282.

[72] Hough, op. cit., p. 322. A similar change is noticeable at lower levels of the CPSU; see ibid., pp. 20–1. In 1966, 4 out of 195 members of the Central Com-

Composition of CPSU in 1975, in percentages.

	Workers and peasants
Party	56
Congress delegates	32
Central Committee members	4

Source: Calculated from B. Meissner, 'Parteiführung, Partei-organisation und soziale Struktur der KPdSU', *Osteuropa* No. 8/9 1976, pp. 607–8, 643, 646.

It should perhaps be added that, as against the ten ordinary workers and peasants on the Central Committee, there were only four heads of state enterprises and two kolkhoz chairmen.

The upheavals of the Chinese Cultural Revolution did not lead to a significant proletarianization of the party leadership, although a few top positions were filled by local cadres from working-class or peasant milieux – people like Wang Hung-wen (now expelled as one of the 'gang of four') and Chen Yung-kwei (the leader of the Tachai Commune). The proletarian contingent of the Central Committee of the CCP, elected by the Tenth Congress in 1973, is about the same as that of the CPSU. Of its 195 members, only 7 (that is, 3.5%) are known to be peasants or workers. After making unspecified assumptions about those whose occupations are unknown, the compiler of their biographies, Wolfgang Bartke, has raised the figure to 12 (or 6%), six workers and six peasants.[73] As for a country which has experienced a long period of Social Democratic government, not a single worker has sat on the Swedish Social Democratic party executive of 35 members for many decades.

---

mittee of the CPSU were categorized as workers or collective farmers; see M. Lesage, *Les régimes politiques de l'URSS et de l'Europe de l'Est*, Paris 1971, p. 196.

[73] Calculation from W. Bartke, 'The 195 members of the Tenth Central Committee of the CCP', *Chinese Studies in History*, vol. IX No. 1 (1975). I have counted as workers all those mentioned by Bartke as being definitely or probably workers, excluding those cited as union, party or state officials, but including members of revolutionary committees and brigade chairmen. Another 32 (or 16%) would have to be added, if we were to include as workers those who rose to union office or sub-national party office after the Ninth Congress of 1969. Sexism has not been overcome in any of the socialist states. Thus, women constituted 10% (or 20 members) of the CC elected by the Tenth Congress of the CCP. The Soviet CC of 1971 had only 6 women among 241 members (i.e., 2.5%). See Gélard, op. cit., 1975, p. 131.

The growing need for technically qualified personnel has made the *school system* a more important factor in the functioning of the principle of class representativeness than it used to be. Crucial here are both the criteria of selection and the link between schools and working class experience. Education in the socialist countries is free of charge, and entry into higher education usually depends on a recommendation from the party, youth organization or enterprise. Explicit class criteria were abolished in the Soviet Union in 1935, but they continue to operate at varying levels of formality. In the GDR, Article 126 of the Constitution stipulates that the class composition of secondary-school and university entrants should correspond to the proportion of workers in the area.[74]

From about 1930 onwards, the organization and content of Soviet education had a strongly elitist and intellectually exclusive character. In 1958, however, important changes were introduced, bringing the school into a much closer relationship with production: it became a general principle that secondary education should include an element of manual labour; that the school should be attached to a productive unit; and that admission to university should normally require two years experience of productive work.[75]

The impact of the Khruschev reforms can be gauged from the following study by M. N. Rutkevich.

Full-time Students at Sverdlovsk Mining Institute.

	Social Origin %			Social Position at Entrance %			
	Wor- kers	Em- ployees	Pea- sants	Wor- kers	Em- ployees	Pea- sants	Stu- dents
1940	33.4	30.2	36.4	4.6	5.9	—	85.5
1955	27.7	57.3	15.0	5.1	9.6	—	84.3
1961	59.8	25.0	15.2	62.8	20.2	3.0	14.0

Source: D. Lane, *Politics and Society in the USSR*, London, 1970, p. 413.

[74] R. Enerstvedt, *To samfunn – to skoler*, Oslo 1973, pp. 210 ff. In 1967, 38% of university students in the GDR came from the working class, and another 8% from the collectivized peasantry.

[75] O. Anweiler–K. Meyer, *Die sowjetische Bildungspolitik seit 1917*, Heidelberg 1961; M. Mathews, *Class and Society in Soviet Russia*, London 1972, pp. 288 ff.

The new educational system created a number of problems both in the school and in production, and after the fall of Khruschev fresh changes were made. These led to an immediate and powerful reassertion of elitist tendencies.

Entrants to the Urals Polytechnic

	Social Origin %			Position at Entrance %			
	Wor-kers	Em-ployees	Pea-sants	Wor-kers	Em-ployees	Pea-sants	Stu-dents
1962/3	46.8	38.4	14.8	40.0	32.6	0.3	19.1
1967/8	42.1[1]	56.3	1.6[1]	19.1	12.9	0.2	67.8

---

1. In the intervening period, the majority of collective farms had been transformed into state farms, and their peasants reclassified as agricultural workers. *Source:* D. Lane, op. cit., p. 508.

In response to these developments an anti-elitist trend has re-appeared, but its significance and effectiveness are still unclear.[76]

Recruitment based on free competition of intellectual talents has a strongly anti-working-class character. To the extent that it is reproduced in the socialist countries, it has to be tirelessly combatted in order to ensure adequate working class representation. In this respect, the Chinese Cultural Revolution was by far the most radical experience that has yet occurred. The other socialist states try to tackle the problem by means of specific institutional structures of varying efficiency. For instance, according to a Norwegian study conducted in the early seventies, nearly every school class in the GDR is connected with a workers' brigade from a nearby enterprise, and several months of productive labour form a normal part of a university student's education.[77]

Energy

The primary energy source of capitalist states is taxes and customs and excise duties; funds needed for public purposes are provided by regular and compulsory levies on private individuals and business

---

[76] Mathews, op. cit., pp. 300 ff.
[77] Enerstvedt, op. cit., pp. 222, 237 ff.

enterprises.[78] Feudal and socialist states do not usually derive their material resources in this way, and thus face specific energy problems and crises.

In all socialist countries, taxes on individuals are low and of minor significance to the state. Revenue is drawn principally from public enterprise and is directly bound up with the global planning process and the pricing of goods.

The two main items of budget income are: deductions from enterprise surpluses – a factor of growing importance; and something usually, but misleadingly, called 'turnover tax', which is equivalent to the difference between the wholesale and retail prices of consumer goods, minus a trade margin. The chief problem is not that of balancing budget revenue and individual incentive, but organization of the prices system in such a way that it reflects real costs and corresponds to plan priorities. Also involved is the opposition between central planning and enterprise autonomy.

Special problems arose in the existing socialist countries, since a large industrial sector first had to be created. In the USSR socialist industrialization was initially financed to a large extent out of excise duties, above all those levied on vodka.[79] After collectivization, vodka was replaced by a prices system geared to the extraction of agricultural surpluses, whereby, to take one example, the kolkhoz sold grain to the state at 14% of the wholesale price charged to milling enterprises by the state.[80]

Under feudalism, the state budget depended above all on the size of the royal domain and on the degree of exploitation to which its attached peasants were subjected. A further source of revenue was the fees exacted within contractual relationships such as the dispensation of royal justice or the minting of money. The solvency of the feudal polity was not corporately guaranteed, but was the problem of the king alone. Confronted by the fiscal crisis of the state, he could only appeal to his subjects for aid and engage in protracted struggle and bargaining with other magnates over his more or less permanent demand for extraordinary levies.[81]

[78] R. Braun, 'Taxation, Socio-political Structure and State-Building: Great Britain and Brandenburg Prussia', in C. Tilly, op. cit., p. 244.

[79] E. H. Carr–R. K. Davies, *Foundations of a Planned Economy*, vol. 1, Harmondsworth 1974, pp. 818, 1031, 1032.

[80] A. Nove, *The Soviet Economy*, New York 1961, p. 99.

[81] On early feudal fiscality, see *inter alia* O. Brunner, *Land und Herrschaft*, Brünn/Munich/Vienna 1943, pp. 312 ff.; for its later development see Braun, op. cit.

Classical writers on political economy like Smith and Ricardo, as well as later theorists and politicians of the capitalist state, have all been concerned with the *effects* of taxation upon exploitation and capital accumulation. The feudal fiscal system, on the other hand, was directly part of a mode of exploitation based on the extraction of rent from the peasantry and on the exercise of seigneurial authority over cities and commerce. In feudal Sweden, for instance, the peasantry was divided into three groups: the first paid rent to the royal landlord, the second to the nobility, whilst the third section of 'tax peasants', who owned their own land, had to pay taxes to the monarchy.

Processes of transformation

The Handling of Tasks

The way in which incoming tasks are handled within the state is in general shaped by the dynamics of the given mode of production, and more specifically, by the character of the organizational technology.

Under feudalism, it was above all *interpretation* of existing laws and customs that determined the tasks of the state. The estates were not legislative bodies, nor did they seriously attempt to assert themselves as such; only the English Parliament began to develop in that direction from quite an early date. Their principal functions were to make grants of money and to provide a channel through which specific grievances could be raised. The French *parlements* had the authority to keep a public register of royal edicts, and to ensure that they were compatible with traditional law.[82] Since it was accompanied by the strengthening of the aristocracy vis-à-vis the rest of the population, the development of royal absolutism in Europe did not significantly alter the way in which state tasks were handled; they continued to be bound by the customs of the feudal mode of production, whose slow movement only occasionally made new rules necessary.

However, royal and seigneurial 'interpretation' obviously gave considerable leeway for discretionary judgements, which might gradually evolve and crystallize into new 'customs'.

[82] R. Holzmann, *Französische Verfassungsgeschichte von der Mitte der 9. Jahr-hundert bis zur Revolution*, Munich and Berlin, pp. 218 ff.; Carsten, op. cit.; Elton, op. cit.

A further characteristic norm of the feudal polity was the *differential handling* of tasks *according to* the *social position* of the person or persons involved. Nobles could only be judged by nobles, for instance, and the settlement of juridical and fiscal matters typically depended on the class that was affected by them. State procedures were pervaded by the logic of war, rule-adjudication, and royal and seigneurial consumption.

The handling of tasks within the capitalist state has been described with deep insight by Max Weber. Apart from the peculiar case of Britain, the basic operational criterion is a formal constitution, according to which new rules are laid down in prescribed form by *legislation*. Subsequent interpretation of these laws plays a role that is quite subordinate to their *impersonal* and calculable *application*. The material substance of this formal legal and administrative rationality is provided by the economic requirements of the market and of capital accumulation.

In dictatorial bourgeois regimes, the forms of rule-making are usually much more variegated and improvised, although as the example of the Salazar dictatorship shows, this is not necessarily the case. On the other hand, the bureaucratic form of rule-application is normally retained in all its essentials.

Strictly fascist regimes, like Mussolini's Italy and Hitler's Germany, present a rather more complex picture. Since one of their distinctive features was the existence of a mass movement consciously modelled on the labour movement, there always existed tensions between the fascist apparatus and the civilian and military state bureaucracy. The bourgeois state machine and monopoly capital were able to frustrate the petty-bourgeois hopes of a sweeping reorganization of society and of a 'revolution from the right'. Although fascism retained its own dynamic and was never simply reducible to the violent dictatorship of monopoly capital, nevertheless it was allowed to develop its destructive tendencies only in the bureaucratic organization of war and mass murder. The orderly annihilation of the Jews by specialized apparatuses of the state represented the ultimate union of the fascist movement and the bourgeois state machine.[83]

However, many tasks of the modern interventionist bourgeois

[83] See the remarkable study by M. Broszat, *Der Staat Hitlers*, Munich 1969, pp. 433 ff. and *passim*.

state, whether democratic or dictatorial, cannot be handled by means of general regulative legislation and prompt, mechanical application. Intervention in business cycles, promotion of growth, and other such policies require the use of managerial-technocratic, rather than legal-bureaucratic, methods. Formal legislation has lost ground to wide discretionary powers, whereby the government and top administration dispose of public funds in accordance with their economic strategies and statistical information. The administrators of the state's economic policies are not restricted to application of legal rules. Above all, they direct state money to favoured recipients on the basis of bargains with private corporations and other powerful groups, and technically organize state units for the efficient execution of policy objectives. In the state of monopoly capitalism, general regulative legislation and impersonal rule-application are increasingly supplemented by *selective budgeting, administrative decree, top-level bargaining.* and *the furthering of productive and destructive technology.* The abstract generality which characterized the state of the competitive market has been supplemented and surpassed by discriminatory management of monopolistic competition.

Socialist states also exhibit formal law-making and law-applying practices. Indeed, the terrible experience of Stalinist arbitrary rule has reinforced their contemporary importance in the Soviet Union and Eastern Europe. On the other hand, it is impossible to reduce a process of global social transformation to purely formal terms. The inherent tension between collective proletarian dominance and individual subordination will not be abolished by legislation; it can be overcome only by a constant struggle that is always changing in form. A socialist state must above all be permeated by the logic of the defence and development of working class power.

In order to deal with this fundamental problem, the socialist states have elaborated new methods of handling tasks. These are concentrated in *the party principle (partinost')* or in the formula *politics in command.* In practice, these involve essentially the implementation of laws and rules according to *campaign directives* that provide the criteria for interpretation, emphasis and priority. Thus, non-state decisions taken by party bodies become criteria of decision-making within the state, and tasks are handled through mass involvement under the direction of cadres.

The point here is not that the cadre system is an ideal of efficiency, or even of democracy, but that it constitutes an original kind of organization. This may be illustrated by the way in which it is differentiated from management at enterprise level. A Swedish journalist, Rolf Berner, has published a well-informed eye-witness account, based on a month's stay in 1973 at the Cherepovets steel-works in the Vologda *oblast* of northern Russia.[84]

Of the 35,000 employees, 4,980 are CPSU members. They are organized in 116 plant branches and, at a lower level, 345 party groups. There are twenty full-time party cadres. Workers make up two-thirds of the full members and four-fifths of those passing through the one-year period of candidate membership. A good quarter of the total are women, but none of them are on the 13-man party plant committee. Although the party is outside the adminis-trative chain of command, all managerial appointments have to be approved by the party – in the case of foremen by the party bureau of the relevant base organization. The cadre presence ensures that enterprise administration and fulfilment of plan targets are under the constant supervision of a mass organization endowed with a political programme and highly unspecified powers. (These powers do not, at plant level, include the right of command or the right to dismiss workers, but they are very real ones.) Furthermore, at col-lective meetings of party members – of whom the large majority are not managers – all aspects of the factory organization are at the centre of discussion, forming the subject of resolutions and recom-mendations, as well as of ongoing ideological training and propa-ganda. The tasks of the plant – in this case, production of steel – are handled in a continuous process of collective political involvement, but are led from above.

The Patterning of Personnel

The patterning of personnel is dependent both on the form of state apparatuses and offices and on the system of social relations among office-holders. It should be remembered, however, that the feudal state was not primarily a structure of apparatuses and offices, but a pattern of persons invested with diffuse seigneurial rights, namely, the king, the aristocrats and their various servants and retainers. Although the relationship between them was essentially hierarchical, it was neither one of unconditional personal obedience nor one of rank as defined by the statutes of a common organization. It was

---

[84] R. Berner, *Rysk arbetare*, Stockholm 1976.

rather a *contractual hierarchy*, which linked partly independent persons and groups on the basis of assurances of 'protection' and 'aid'. Relationships between king and aristocracy, and between king and councils or estates were all governed by this kind of contract. It assumed a new form in the late feudal era, when the growth of commodity production and mercantile capitalism promoted the buying and selling of offices and services.

Traditional law and custom were such weighty criteria of decision-making that a specialized legislative body for rule-applying administration developed only very rarely. For a long time, the only central state apparatuses of importance were the ones that arose out of fiscal, judicial and military functions.[85]

The contractual hierarchy and the role of customary law account also for the distinctively *heteroclite* character of the feudal state apparatus. As existing laws were interpreted and reinterpreted over the centuries, there grew up a vast array of new bodies that were only very loosely integrated with the old ones and with each other. In the end, the absolutist state presented a veritable mosaic of over-lapping, conflicting and disproportionate institutions and jurisdictions, that were to be swept away by the bourgeoisie in the process of revolutionary national unification.

The feudal state expressed class relations *in a direct and unmediated manner*. This is the most important social aspect of the lack of a clear, 'bureaucratic' demarcation between on the one hand the household, land and attached peasants of the king or local seigneur, and on the other hand the sphere of state administration. The two were rather fused in the royal court or the noble estate.

This unmediated expression of class relations in the state is one element of a more general coalescence of polity and economy, which is a characteristic feature of feudalism and which is mirrored in the fusion of economy and ideology in the landowning church. Closely related to this is the fact that whilst the aristocracy individually appropriates the means of production and determines their orientation towards noble consumption, nevertheless the process of production is not under the direct management and supervision of the landowners. In this mode of exploitation, the economic unit is at the same time a military-judicial one, and conversely the political unit

---

[85] O. Hintze, 'Die Entstehung der modernen Staatsministerien', in op. cit., pp. 265 ff.

is also an economic one. The polity is the manor writ large, or to put it more precisely, it is a chain of interlinked manors.

By contrast, the bourgeois state is not patterned after the capitalist enterprise, nor can it be described as in any sense an agglomeration of enterprises. Economic units are interrelated through the market, and the function of the state is not to establish connections among them, but to manage and defend the market, to represent the capitalist class as a whole. The patterning of state personnel, therefore, only expresses the class relations of society in a mediated way. The unity of the personnel is defined not by their possession of monetary wealth, but by the structure of the apparatuses and of relations among office-holders – a structure that reproduces the distinction between private enterprise itself and the public servicing of it. This pattern, then, has two aspects: one is *public* and essentially consists in the representation of the bourgeoisie as a whole (or of an entire fraction of the class), whilst the other involves the public *service* of private enterprise, that is to say, assistance to and management of the dynamics of private capital.

One of the most important consequences of the bourgeois revolutions was the emergence of a unified, centralized and deprivatized bureaucratic machine – an *office hierarchy*. At the centre of this new state apparatus was placed a legislative body that represented the public and expressed its demands in original general rules.

Public control over the state was ensured by a system of 'checks and balances', and by the 'separation of powers' into those of the legislative, the judiciary and the executive. The various executive bodies were further separated from one another, and each central apparatus was given a precise field of competence and jurisdiction. In effect, the bourgeoisie was applying the old maxim of divide and rule to its own servant, although in times of crisis the overriding priority has been to marshal all the powers of the state into a unified striking force to be used against the class or national enemy.

The considerable expansion of the state apparatus under monopoly capitalism, particularly in the health, social security and education sectors, has involved the influx of a large number of employees who are not patterned in the same way as the traditional administrative officials. They are regarded in practice as a subordinate collective, rather than as individuals on different rungs of a hierarchical career ladder. The position of a growing number of state employees is thus similar to that of workers in a capitalist enterprise: mental and manual labour are kept separate in, for example, the rigid hierarchy of doctors, nurses and ancillary workers; intellectual labour is under the sway of managerial power, and every member of staff is subordinated to the authority of school, hospital and social service administrators; techniques of supervision and speed-up are imported from the private sector; and finally, trade unions and labour-management conflicts have begun to appear within the state apparatus itself. Public enterprises, which are here treated as lying outside the capitalist state apparatus proper, are run on lines more or less identical to those of their private competitors.

Fascism revealed with particular clarity, and in its own stark and cruel colours, another general feature of modern bourgeois state organization. The Fascist regimes exercised the rule of monopoly capital, even though, as a political movement, they cannot be reduced to that rule. We pointed above to the difference between bureaucratic organization and that of both the private entrepreneur and corporate management. After the defeat of the petty-bourgeois tendencies in the Fascist movement, the anti-bureaucratic conception of organization common to Fascist politics and monopoly capital found expression in rearmament and the war economy. The West German historian Martin Broszat has formulated this very well: 'In the organization of the war economy of the Third Reich, the prevalent war-time demand for the highest possible efficacy was so to speak surcharged by the fundamentally anti-bureaucratic motif of the National-Socialist Führer-principle. Since the Party had no contribution to make in the field of the economy . . . the private entrepreneurial form of large industry corresponded most closely to the Nazi principles of leadership. Unconditional priority to accomplishment of ongoing projects, greatest possible organizational flexibility, wide personal freedom of action for leading agents entrusted with the confidence of directors (or managers), conduct regulated by powers of proxy rather than strictly defined official duties – all these principles were shared in common by private business and by the Party.'[86]

In the monopoly capitalist state, the bureaucratic hierarchy has been undermined both from above and from below: from above, through the development of an array of *ad hoc* commissions and

[86] Broszat op. cit. p. 377.

plenipotentiaries – though not to the extreme degree obtaining under conditions of total war; and from below, through the growth of a vast army of state workers. The separation of apparatuses is overshadowed by the predominance of the government executive.

Whereas the feudal state integrated individual seigneuries at a political level, and whereas the capitalist state represents the totality of private entrepreneurs, the socialist state must first *constitute* the intrinsically collective power of the proletariat as the *Zusammenfassung* or condensation of the social collectivity. It is only after the seizure of state power and of the state apparatus that the appropriation of the means of production by society can begin.

On the other hand, the existence of a centralized state machine reproduces the individual subordination of workers and thus stands in the way of the development of classless communist society. Although the conquest of the state constitutes the proletariat as the ruling class, its power does not derive from the state, nor by the way from the appropriation of the means of production, but from the *working-class movement*.

The socialist state, then, is at the same time centrally important and fundamentally antagonistic to the rule of the proletariat, and in both these respects it differs from feudal and capitalist regimes. Under feudalism, the polity is fused with the economy and directly reproduces the specific class relations. Although it remains a necessary instrument of power, the bourgeois state is in one sense external to the rule of capital; it does not directly reproduce class relations, but defends the conditions of their reproduction.

On the other hand, the state is the primary mechanism by which the bourgeoisie and the feudal aristocracy are politically organized as a ruling class. Their other collective institutions, such as the noble assembly or the bourgeois party and employers' federation, are of only secondary importance. The absence of a feudal or capitalist 'movement' comparable to that of the working class, is evident in the enormous organizational complexity and variety of bourgeois as opposed to proletarian revolutions.

Under socialism, where the basic problem is the supremacy of the working class movement over the state apparatus, the bourgeois principle of the separation of powers is useless as a guarantee of popular sovereignty. Two attempts have been made so far to provide a solution to this difficulty. Marx and Lenin envisaged, and the early Soviet republic realized the fusion of the state apparatus with the labour movement, under the hegemony of the latter. Workers'.

peasants' and soldiers' councils took charge of the state apparatus, elected officials and commanders who were subject to instant recall, and organized the administration of society.

In the existing circumstances, however, the soviet system was unable to ensure either the unity of the working class or an adequate level of administrative and technical competence, and it has since been superseded by a dual hierarchy of party and state institutions, under the supreme control of the party. This solution also involves a very different structure of competences and relations among the state personnel than exists in capitalist society. Its most obvious feature is the primacy of non-state office over state functions: from the local unit up to central government, the administrative director is subordinated to the party secretary and party committee. This relation is not a legal-administrative one and seems to work in very complex and subtle ways. Nevertheless, the primacy of the cadre over the bureaucrat and technocrat can be clearly perceived throughout the system.[87]

Secondly, the state hierarchy is not only controlled from outside, but is also internally dissected. In the repressive forces, for example, the chain of command is supplemented by a network of political commissars, departments and officers, whose primary responsibility is to organs of the party.[88] Party cells exist in all units of the state apparatus, and higher officials are usually members of them. However, they do not occupy leading posts within their party unit and are exposed to censure and criticism by comrades who are their administrative subordinates.[89] In addition, these party cadres have the right of appeal to higher bodies against their boss.

---

[87] For a revealing analysis of party-state relations at regional and local levels in the USSR, see Hough, op. cit., chs. IV, V and *passim.*

[88] There were military commissars in the French Revolution too. But they were commissars of the civilian parliamentary *state* apparatus – the Convention and, later, the Directory. See the immense monograph by Jacques Godechot, *Les commissaires aux armées sous le Directoire,* 2 vols., Paris 1937.

[89] We cannot adequately answer here the decisive question of the practical frequency and importance of party criticism and self-criticism within socialist societies. However, the available information shows that they do play a real role. Kolkowicz (op. cit., pp. 379 ff.), for example, mentions an instructive incident that occurred in the Soviet Army. In December 1960, the central organ of the army political administration related how a general had been criticized by a subordinate officer for his unduly privileged and immoral private conduct. The general tried to retaliate by invoking his superior rank, but he was summoned before a party commission, which obliged him to make a far-reaching self-criticism. In this way he managed to avoid expulsion from the party, although he was reduced to the status of a candidate member on probation.

Thirdly, the principal mechanism of distribution of state personnel is not the capitalist one of competitive application and promotion according to ability or seniority, but the cadre policy of the party.

The Transformation of Energy

We shall only mention briefly the specific problems faced by different types of state in the process of transformation of material inputs. The feudal state had to struggle with poor means of communication and with difficulties of conversion into useful energy of qualitatively diverse inputs. A typical solution to these problems was the devolution of the transformation process on to individual office-holders, whether in the form of fiefs or by way of tax-farming and the appointment of commander-entrepreneurs. In the medieval and Renaissance periods, both the monarchy and the lord of the manor also had to engage in commercial activities in order to monetize the product extracted from the peasantry.

In contrast to the problems facing the feudal polity, both capitalist and socialist states dispose of characteristic mechanisms to re-allocate incoming material resources. Under capitalism, this is essentially a question of budgetary allocation among the administrative and repressive apparatuses of the state. 'Fiscal crises' here refer mainly to the problem of securing adequate funds for payment of the state personnel and for transfers of income. In modern monopoly capitalism, the incoming resources are transformed so as to be geared to the management of the market (by adapting the state budget to trade cycles) and to the current problems of private capital accumulation.

As regards the socialist states, the reallocation process involves primarily determination of plan priorities. This is clearly illustrated in the composition of the government of the USSR, where in the late sixties 51 out of a total of 59 ministries were charged with economic and technical planning.[90] What corresponds to the fiscal problems of the bourgeois state is distribution of social resources between investment and consumption and between the producer and consumer goods sectors, in such a way as to balance long-term goals with immediate needs. Disruption of this delicate equilibrium has given rise to a number of economico-political crises in the

[90] Calculated from Lane, op. cit., p. 556.

USSR and Eastern Europe, of which perhaps the most dramatic is that which has arisen recently in Poland.

Outputs

Tasks I: Foreign Policy

Foreign policy may be defined as the external pursuit of the policies of a given ruling class. In one sense, it may be regarded as the continuation of domestic policy, but it is differentiated from the latter by its concern above all with relations between ruling classes of separate states. As we would expect, feudal, capitalist and socialist states all reveal characteristic forms of foreign policy and of inter-state relations, which are in turn rooted in the relations prevalent within the ruling class.

Now, the matter is further complicated by the regular coexistence of different types of state within a particular international system. At the present time, for example, socialist states are related not only to each other, but also to capitalist ones. As a result, there emerges a special kind of international class struggle and class solidarity.

In the feudal polity, the main task inputs were demands for military and juridical protection, whilst relations within the dominant class were determined by the extent of ownership of productive land and by a complex network of rights and obligations, which were increasingly transmitted along lines of family descent. The history of foreign policy and inter-state relations is filled with conflicts over questions of seigneurial jurisdiction and sovereignty and of legitimate descent; the material content underlying these was of course the struggle for control of land and of the surplus extracted from the peasantry. Especially noteworthy were the disputes that arose between the pope and various kings and emperors, and between the emperor and the princes. In the Nordic countries, analogous conflicts broke out over the union monarchy, and the problem of dynastic legitimacy was at the heart of the Anglo-French Hundred Years' War in the 14th century and of the struggle for the Spanish and Austrian succession in the 18th.

Ideological issues – above all religion – entered the international arena cast in the typical feudal mould. Control over the church became a central issue in the jurisdictional conflicts between the pope and a number of kings and princes. In certain acute cases, from the Crusades to the Spanish Armada and the Thirty Years' War, religious dissensions took on a directly military form.

The forces of competition and monopoly structure relations among capitalist states, as they do relations within each bourgeois class. The international expansion of capital is impelled neither by jurisdictional claims nor by the search for new land to provide increased means of consumption. It involves instead the capture and monopolization of sources of raw materials and of markets for exported commodities and capital. This is the fixed centre of inter-imperialist relations: from the explosive conflicts of World Wars I and II to the peaceful cycles of free trade and protectionism; in the struggle for economic influence in weaker countries, from the Marshall Plan to OECD and EEC cooperation; from the successful displacement of the Spanish and Portuguese feudal empires by the English and Dutch, to contemporary relations between the United States and Latin America, or between Japan and capitalist South-East Asia.

However, capitalist foreign policy is not only modelled on the internal relations of the bourgeoisie. As we have already seen, the capitalist state is a representative of the national public, and strictly nationalist factors play a role in the formation of foreign policy alongside the dominant contradiction between different national capitals. This has been of particular importance for foreign relations when rival territorial claims have brought states into conflict with one another: for example, the disputes between France and Germany over Alsace-Lorraine, and those among many of the new European nation-states in the inter-war period.

This is an appropriate point at which to mention the question of *national liberation*. In the struggle against feudal and other pre-capitalist polities, one of the major achievements of the bourgeoisie was the unification and liberation of the nation. Of particular importance were the breaking of the domination of feudal Spain and Portugal over Latin America; the collapse of the Habsburg and Romanov empires in Eastern and Central Europe; and the independence of the Balkans and the Arab countries from the Ottoman Empire. The specific bourgeois form of imperialism is not based essentially on national subjugation, but on the combination of exploitation and oppression by capital with precapitalist modes of production. It has not been irreconcilable with, nor even implacably hostile to the acquisition of state independence by its colonies.

There are three principal reasons why national liberation struggles have played such an important role in recent decades: First, there are a number of exceptions to the general colonial pattern – a pattern illustrated in India and most African countries according to which the new Asian and African bourgeoisies gained independence in a relatively easy and peaceful manner, after they had attained a certain degree of development and internal unification. The exceptions have occurred when an imperialist state, driven by economic weakness to maintain traditional forms of colonialism, has been challenged by national forces of liberation. This was the case of France in Indo-China and Madagascar; Holland in Indonesia after World War II; and, most clearly of all, Portugal in her African colonies.

Secondly, these new bourgeoisies have in some areas encountered the rival bourgeois nationalism of settler groups (Palestine, Algeria, Rhodesia, South Africa). Thirdly, the existence of powerful socialist countries has created the possibility that national unification and liberation may take a non-capitalist road (Vietnam, Korea, Angola). In the last two instances, imperialism has put up a ferocious resistance to the process.

Today, the foreign policy of capitalist states concerns not only *inter-capital* and *inter-nation* relations, but also the organization of international class solidarity, that is, the defence of other bourgeoisies against the threat of socialism. There is nothing original in this: it was already practised in the coalition of feudal states against the French Revolution, and in the role of Tsarist Russia as the gendarme of last resort in 19th century Eastern and Central Europe; it also informs the policies of 'proletarian internationalism' conducted by socialist states. Common to all types of state is the use of armed intervention, but there are additional forms of solidarity that are specific to each class. The capitalist state, for example, disposes of potent economic mechanisms: boycott, blockade, political restrictions on credit: the use of economic sanctions against the young Soviet republic, the blockade of Cuba, the blackmail of Portugal since 1975, the current economic threats to Italy, to mention just a few cases.

We have already given considerable stress to the fact that working class power, and thus the socialist state, is based primarily on the class organization of the labour movement. The equivalent of relations between national capitals is *inter-party policy*. So far, however, socialist states have had to operate in a world dominated by capitalism, and their foreign relations have typically been of an inter-state character. In the earlier history of the Soviet Union, this policy took the most devious routes in order temporarily to divide and ward off the hostile capitalist powers. The most extreme examples were the Stalin-Hitler Pact and the secret clauses of the Rapallo Treaty of 1922, whereby the Soviet Union committed itself to provide facilities for German military training that were forbidden under the Treaty of Versailles.

Nevertheless, socialist policy vis-à-vis capitalist states always contains an important and distinctive element of relations between political parties and movements. The offensive struggle against capital is waged by fraternal Communist parties, who have often been charged with heavy responsibilities for the protection of the socialist states. In addition to the traditional weapons of diplomacy and military preparation, the fostering of mass movements in other countries has been an integral part of defence policy. The 'Hands Off Russia' campaign after the October Revolution, the Peace Movement in the fifties, and the Vietnam movement in the sixties all testify to that.

Relations between socialist states have by no means been a model of equality, fraternity, and freely consented unity. However, the pattern of contention among them is very different from that which exists among capitalist states. Conflicts between the Soviet Union and Yugoslavia, Hungary, Albania, China and Czechoslovakia have all been of a politico-ideological nature, rather than concerned with Russian economic advantages or rival territorial claims (although the latter did play a role in the course of the Sino-Soviet dispute). Khruschev's drastic withdrawal of Soviet technicians and aid from China was certainly a measure of economic constraint, but the quarrel has mainly consisted of mutual ideological abuse.

In fact, until the Chinese began to court every conceivable anti-Soviet state and political tendency, the Sino-Soviet split was strikingly similar to divisions among left-wing parties and groups within the same country. It centered on political and ideological questions, such as anti-capitalist strategy and models of socialism. The only antidote that capitalism can offer to such acrimonious controversy is the absence of ideological struggle, exemplified by the bourgeois-democratic policies of appeasement of the fascist states, which only ended in war because of economic and territorial rivalry.

In light of the fact that differences over the character of socialism have not infrequently brought non-ruling groups and factions to the point of physical confrontation, it is easy to see that this may assume a military form in relations between states. The invasion of Czecho-slovakia was not launched in order to defend Russian economic positions, and it did not lead to an intensification of Russian economic 'exploitation'. Nor did the Prague Spring pose a threat to Soviet 'national security': there was no imminent danger of an anti-Communist or anti-Soviet take-over. The occupation sprang rather out of an authoritarian and sectarian political practice that is alien to the rationality of capitalist imperialism.

If it were true that the Soviet Union operates as a profit-seeking, 'state capitalist' corporation, then there should be clear evidence of this in its economic relations with Eastern Europe. However, the fact that no serious analysis has been made of these links says a great deal about the 'scientific' character of such arguments. In fact, the available data strongly suggest that Soviet policy towards Eastern Europe is not of the kind practised between national capitals. It may perhaps be argued that this is refuted by the joint companies set up in Romania, Hungary and Bulgaria after the war as part of Soviet reparations policy. However, these were dismantled between 1954 and 1956, and the shares of the USSR were sold off to the respective governments.[91] Moreover, the deviation of Comecon prices from those of the capitalist world market has not generally favoured the USSR at the expense of the smaller member states, but has worked to the advantage of all countries. When Comecon price bases were revised in 1966, the result seems rather to have been detrimental to the Soviet Union.[92]

The one serious economic dispute that has arisen within Comecon also reveals a definite specificity. I am referring, of course, to the resistance of other Eastern European states, and in the early stages particularly of Czechoslovakia, to the prioritization of heavy indus-trial development in Romania. The opposition to the policy of Bucharest came mainly from economists, economic geographers and

[91] G. Amundsen, *Le conseil d'entraide économique*, Strasbourg 1971, pp. 34 ff. These joint companies were most significant in Romania; see J. Montias, *Economic Development in Communist Rumania*, Cambridge, Mass. 1967, pp. 19 ff., 50 ff.

[92] Amundsen, op. cit., pp. 450 ff.

foreign trade officials, in Czechoslovakia, East Germany and the Soviet Union. However, when the Romanians launched their counter-attack, the most outspoken of these were criticized and disowned by more authoritative Soviet and East German spokesmen. The logic of commercial interest was able to develop in the economic and ideological apparatuses of these socialist states, but it was not allowed to become paramount. On the other hand, although the peaceful character of the conflict contrasts starkly with the brutal reaction to the 1968 events in Czechoslovakia, it does not provide a model of proletarian internationalism untarnished by considerations of economic advantage and cost. The Soviet Union never went back on its refusal to furnish cheap credits for the Romanian Galati steel mill.[93]

Tasks II: Domestic Policy

It will be remembered that we are concerned here only with the characteristic forms of the policy output of the state. The problem of its class content is part of the question of state power, which I have tried to analyse elsewhere. The form of domestic policy does however vary with the form of class rule, and it has to fit both with the internal relations of the ruling class and with its relations with other classes. We can thus identify a distinctive *mode of state intervention*, in spite of the fact that we are dealing with the policies of states that have many elementary administrative and repressive functions in common.

The feudal state seems to operate principally by means of *juridical regulation and judicial protection* of particular individuals and collectives, according to the interpretation of traditional law and custom. More specifically, the state machine is used for the following purposes: endowment of the chain of vassals or of the estates with certain unequal rights and privileges; conferment of membership of the ruling class by the act of ennoblement; juridical recognition and regulation of the various exploitation rights of noble landowners; the grant of town charters to burghers of particular localities and of trade privileges to individuals and groups; and legal recognition and protection of artisan labour and organization.

---

[93] Montias (op. cit., ch. 4) devotes a long section to the dispute within Comecon in a solid and well-documented study of the Romanian economy.

Under capitalism, many of the feudal juridical regulations are replaced by the economic mechanisms of the market. The public tasks of the classical capitalist state concerned above all the provision of *a unified and universalistic legal framework* for free enterprise, and *the furthering of the development of the productive forces*, particularly the means of transport and communication, and institutions of research and training. In addition to these modes of intervention, the modern bourgeois state has developed *administrative regulation* and *market operations* by means of public spending and differential rates of taxation. It sets out no longer to free but to regulate competition; while the market is boosted or restrained by the direct and indirect effects of public spending; through countercyclical and investment policies; and through the social security expenditure of what the West Germans call the 'social state'.

The socialist state also has a distinctive mode of intervention. Although its domestic policy output evidently retains legal, administrative and juridical forms, it assigns a key role to ideological *mobilization* of the masses. Thus, state economic policy goes beyond the establishment of plan targets by legislative and administrative means, to embrace campaigns of economic mobilization and the organization of 'socialist emulation'. Similarly, the state discharges its tasks of political and ideological transformation both by enactment of laws and decrees and by stimulation of movements among the masses.

The extent to which it operates through non-military mass mobilization is a sensitive, although by no means sufficient, indicator of the proletarian and popular class character of a state. The basis of working class power is class organization, and if this is not or cannot be activated, then something must be seriously wrong. This difference between socialist and capitalist states is most clearly revealed by comparative analysis of the development strategies of relatively backward countries: China and India, North and South Korea, North and South Vietnam (before 1975), Cuba and Venezuela or Peru, or Bulgaria and Greece.

Laws and decrees of socialist states are not always universal in form. They sometimes contain class references that explicitly differentiate between fractions of the peasantry or even of the bourgeoisie (national and comprador), as well as between the intelligentsia and the working class.

Personnel I: State Personnel in Inter-State Relations

The external policy of the feudal state personnel was structured not by the nation, which is essentially a post-feudal phenomenon, but by relations among various royal and seigneurial families and their retainers. Dynastic marriages constituted inter-state affairs of the highest significance, as they usually involved political dowries, transfers of land, the forging of military alliances, the grant of subsidies, etc. – *felix Austria*. The ruling classes of European states often spoke the same language, which differed from that of their subjects: Latin in the Middle Ages, French in the age of Absolutism. Moreover, aristocratic families moved easily from one country to another. An extreme example of this was the new aristocracy that settled in Bohemia after the Habsburg victory over the rebellious Bohemian nobility in the 1620s; it came from all over Europe – Italy, Germany, Austria, Slovenia, Wallonia, Lorraine and Ireland.[94]

The bourgeois state is organized around the very different entity of the nation of free individuals integrated by the market and by common public interests. To be sure, capital itself is international, and bourgeois external relations have oscillated between nationalist rivalry and mercantile cosmopolitanism. However, capitalist officials are representatives primarily of the nation, rather than of a particular lord or capital. This is true even when the ruling class of a given country is in fact the bourgeoisie of another, and the national form is thus quite hollow; such is the case of many Latin American states, whose personnel was thoroughly Anglicized in the 19th century, and Americanized in the 20th.

In periods of intense imperialist rivalry, such as those of the two world wars, state nationalism and capitalist transnational expansionism may merge in a single movement. The extent of mass mobilization and the scope of the war itself are then incomparable to the limited commercial wars that were fought among the Dutch, French and English states in the 17th and 18th centuries.

The period since World War II has witnessed the emergence of a number of international agencies such as the World Bank, the International Monetary Fund, the European Economic Community, NATO, the United Nations organizations, and so on. Although these are organizations of sovereign states, their personnel have also to represent the agency itself. The World Bank and the IMF are

[94] Anderson, op. cit., pp. 307–8.

both important instruments of capitalist blackmail which may be directed against socialist or excessively reformist governments.

The very formulation 'proletarian internationalism' expresses clearly the composite nature of the external relations of socialist states: they are at the same time nation states and integral parts of an international class organization. Thus, the personnel relate not only to officials of other nation states, but also to representatives of fraternal parties and movements. This may be elucidated by a study of the patterns of foreign aid and official invitations, and of the accessibility of the domestic state apparatus to different categories of foreigners.

Although military alliances are a common feature of European politics from the 17th and 18th century broad coalitions to NATO and the Warsaw Pact, there are other kinds of inter-state bond and organization that are specific to the particular type of class state. Among feudal states – for example among participants in the Vienna Conference – the typical links are marriage and kinship, and other 'blood' relations central to dynasties of 'legitimate descent'. Capitalist states have developed their own characteristic forms in the League of Nations and United Nations, the OECD and various international trade communities. Whilst they participate in certain inter-state bodies, socialist regimes also pursue an independent policy of alliances through class organizations like the Cominform and international communist conferences.

Personnel II: State versus Non-State Personnel

As we have noted above, the feudal polity threaded together the economic units of exploitation. Neither in theory nor in practice did it rest upon a distinction between state and civil society. Since leading state officials were almost invariably large landowners, it was indeed difficult to make a clear conceptual division between the two functions. In some cases, this coincidence of political and social hierarchy was strictly formalized: in Tsarist Russia from 1831 to 1917, the state office of a noble was juridically defined in terms of his hereditary rank.[95]

Under capitalism, it is the public authority of the state that structures the relations of its personnel with ordinary citizens. To be an administrative official, a judge or an army or police officer is to

[95] Ibid., p. 346.

occupy a specialized, full-time position. Although members of parliament are normally allowed to follow a private occupation, government ministers are either required or clearly expected to relinquish professional posts and activity whilst they are in office.

The system of patronage that is so marked in Italy and many non-European countries is a symptom of the underdevelopment of the bourgeois state, and of the strength of pre-capitalist forces. In its more advanced forms, the state fits its personnel into the prevailing class structure in more characteristic ways. Officials are not linked to sections of the popular masses by chains of patronage, but rather *cut off* from them by a variety of mechanisms.

This insulation from society is most apparent in the case of the repressive forces, who tend to be housed in barracks and exposed to special regimentation. Often, the state personnel is demarcated by its possession of exceptional rights – for example, security of tenure, respect of ordinary citizens – and by the restriction of certain others, such as the freedom to engage in trade-union and non-administrative political activity.

Representative politicians must establish some rapport with the population at large, but once elected, they are not answerable to their constituents. Party leaders and prime ministers are usually made and unmade by parliamentary groups, rather than by extra-parliamentary bodies of their party. In no bourgeois democracy is it considered a serious anomaly that parliamentary majorities may be based on the support of a minority of the electorate.

Classical bourgeois parties operated primarily as caucuses of parliamentary deputies and local notables. Only the rise of mass workers' parties significantly changed the character of the political arena, and their implicit challenge to its seclusion from the life of the masses has been a constant preoccupation of the bourgeoisie ever since. All the same, attempts to integrate the Social Democratic parties into the political order have generally met with great success: the centre of power has been firmly located within their parliamentary bodies, and social-democratic governments and prime ministers have accepted that they are responsible first of all to parliament and only secondarily to their own party membership.[96] With the

[96] When the first social-democratic government was about to be formed in Sweden in 1920, one of the demands of the king was that it should act quite independently of the influence of 'external bodies'. E. Palmstierna, *Dagjämning*, Stockholm 1954, p. 58.

exception of the Nordic countries, where bourgeois political culture is relatively weak, the highly stylized parliamentary form of activity has led to a 'natural selection' of lawyers and academics even as deputies of reformist workers' parties. The influx of labour members has thus done little to alter the distinctive style and decorum of these assemblies, which are closer in spirit to a bourgeois club than to a trade-union meeting.

In a parallel process to the severance of links with the working class, the income and social standing of top figures within the state personnel have placed them on a par with the bourgeoisie. The salaries of senior civil servants are correlated with those of middle and upper layers of management. Thus, one ironic effect of popular pressure has been that the bourgeois politician, who was once expected to have 'independent means' (i.e., a private fortune), is now rewarded for his 'services' in the same way as a relatively well-paid manager. On the other hand, the supremacy of the non-state sphere and of private enterprise is still expressed in the much broader opportunities that are open to a skilled profiteer.

We have already seen that, contrary to the suggestion of Max Weber, the capitalist state bureaucracy handles its tasks according to decision-making criteria that are different from those of the entrepreneur or top business executive. It is therefore not surprising that private enterprise and the state bureaucracy have not developed side by side in a fully even and harmonious manner. In France and Prussia, for example, the rapid and energetic rise of officialdom was not related to an equally vigorous capitalist industry, even though it was the clear result of a bourgeois, anti-feudal revolution. In Britain and the United States, the inverse was true: the development of bureaucracy lagged behind the economic thrust of capital.

In the monopoly stage of capitalism, when the public-private distinction becomes less sharp, the upper reaches of state administration tend to merge with private corporate management. The mechanism that fuses monopoly capital with the state attained its highest degree of perfection during the two world wars. It involves a close collaboration between top military or civilian officials and representatives of private capital in such tasks as the following: organization of military supplies, investment coordination (or 'indicative planning'), administrative regulation of prices and incomes, maintenance of the supply of labour to industry, promotion of exports, and sponsorship of research projects. This connection between the state personnel and capitalist management often becomes institutionalized in joint bodies, on which a trade-union representative may also sit. Of course, the state does not thereby embrace the working class and specifically working-class policies: the workers themselves are excluded from such committees, which contain only senior union officials (or quite frequently, expert intellectuals hired by the union), and which have as their goal the administration of monopoly capitalism. The sole purpose of the incorporation of workers' and farmers' organizations is to cut their ties with their popular base and to convert them into instruments of state control over their members. At the bottom of the state, however, ordinary, non-managerial, non-bureaucratic employees are now frequently drawn into the orbit of the working class.

Under socialism, the state has to strive in the opposite direction to that of the capitalist state: to break down barriers that separate and insulate its personnel from the working class; to subordinate itself, as far as possible, to the organizations of the class. It is only in this manner that the 'withering away' of the state can become a reality. These themes informed the writings of Marx and Lenin on the new type of state – the dictatorship of the proletariat – and were translated into practice by the October Revolution and the short-lived Soviet republics in Hungary and parts of Germany. During the Chinese and Vietnamese revolutions, a similar tremendous change took place in the liberated villages.[97]

In Russia, the act of insurrection was presented by the Bolsheviks not to a ritualized parliament, packed with dignitaries and intellectuals who had progressed in the school of bourgeois law and journalism, but to a tumultuous meeting of workers', peasants' and soldiers' deputies in Petrograd. Local risings throughout the vast territory of Russia involved not party putsches but the seizure of power by broad masses, who proceeded to replace the lofty old city dumas and village councils with new, popular soviet organs. Administration of society was assumed by these bodies; courts and commanders were elected by largely illiterate peasants and workers; the old repressive forces were dissolved and detachments of armed workers created in their place.[98] At the level of central government,

---

[97] See the fascinating account of the Chinese revolution by a participant observer – W. Hinton, *Fanshen*, New York 1966.

[98] See Oskar Anweiler's seminal study of the Russian soviets, of which there is a recent French edition: *Les Soviets en Russie*, Paris 1974.

however, the Council of People's Commissars was from the beginning responsible more to the Central Committee of the Bolshevik
Party than to the all-Russian Supreme Soviet.

For a number of reasons, the original revolutionary soviet system
had rather a short life, and it is still these dramatic historical
experiences that demonstrate most clearly the fundamental tendencies and potentialities of socialist revolution. Nevertheless,
existing socialist states exhibit a relationship between state personnel
and citizens that differs radically from that of bourgeois states. It is
most clearly expressed in the range of the cadre concept, which in
both the Asian and East European socialist states covers state and
non-state personnel, whether professional or non-professional. An
East German work on cadre policy defines the concept thus:
'[Cadres are] above all leadership forces or functionaries in the
different areas of social life – in the party, in the state (including the
police and the army) in the economy, in mass organizations, in
scientific and cultural institutions, and so on – in other words, cadres
are a category of people who by reason of their knowledge and competence are entrusted with the responsibility of leading other people
in the performance of their appointed tasks, or who work in a
leadership collective. They can include either major or honorary
office-holders.'[99] This definition lumps together bureaucrats, managers, senior intellectuals, and political organizers – from whom the
concept has been extended, and to whom it is restricted in this essay.
The result serves to obscure the contradictory modes of organization under socialism. But it is significant that it subsumes the state
official under the conception of the political organizer, since: 'the
highest rule of socialist cadre policy is to promote the leading role of
the working class and its party.'[100]

The publicization of private life and the massive political mobilization of the people also lessen the distinction between state and
non-state personnel, brought together in common tasks. This
characteristic form can be seen in a number of mechanisms and
institutions that vary greatly in importance and practical correspondence with theoretical norms.

Although strict one-party rule has deprived the soviets of much

[99] R. Herber–H. Jung, *Wissenschaftliche Leitung und Entwicklung der Kader*,
Berlin 1964, p. 10. Quoted here from E. Förtsch, op. cit., p. 76.

[100] Heinrich Rau (another SED writer on cadre policy) in *Neuer Weg* No. 18
1959, cited from Förtsch, op. cit., p. 79.

of their power, deputies are not full-time politicians and their function as representatives of the rank-and-file and as conveyors of grievances cannot be dismissed out of hand.[101] They are obliged to report back regularly to their electorate, and can be mandated and recalled from below: nominating organizations can at all times request that a by-election be held. Forty-two per cent of deputies to the Supreme Soviet of the USSR in 1972–3 were manual workers or kolkhoz peasants.[102] In 1968, the working-class contingent to the East German *Volkskammer* comprised 44% of the total number of delegates.[103]

The positions of judge and procurator are not administrative careers but elected offices or appointments determined by political criteria. Furthermore, the cardinal principle of party control asserts the effective primacy of a non-state organization over the whole of the state personnel, from the Prime Minister to the lowest-ranking bureaucrat. However, the fact that the party is run by full-time functionaries reduces the significance of this principle for the closeness of relations between the working class and members of the state apparatus.

A radical means to ensure popular supremacy is the submission of state officials to public criticism in mass meetings. This 'mass line' has been developed above all in China, where it was already being applied on a large scale in the mid-forties to land reform cadres in the liberated areas.[104] During the Cultural Revolution it was extended to state personnel at virtually every level.

The relation of state to society is affected by a distinctive official organ of general control and supervision. In the GDR this bears the name that was first used in Lenin's Russia – the Workers' and Peasants' Inspectorate; in the Soviet Union it is currently called the

---

[101] Lane, op. cit., pp. 157, 167 ff.; Lesage, op. cit., p. 316.

[102] J. Hough, 'Political Participation in the Soviet Union', *Soviet Studies*, Jan. 1976, p. 11. The corresponding figures for 1954–55 and 1963–64 are 14 and 32, respectively. Among deputies to city soviets, the working class component rose from 28 to 47 (i.e., to 59.5%) in 1972–73. The more powerful Presidium of the Supreme Soviet contains individual manual workers, foremen and kolkhoz chairmen. See *The Soviet Form of Popular Government*, Moscow 1972, p. 125. This work uses a broader definition of workers and peasants than that of Hough, giving (p. 97) a total of 50% for deputies elected in 1970 to the Supreme Soviet. (We noted above similar problems of definition in Blondel's table on parliamentary social composition). 30.5% of the total are women (op. cit., p. 97).

[103] Blondel, op. cit., p. 160.

[104] Hinton, op. cit., part IV.

Committee of Popular Control. Usually these are joint party-state bodies with supervisory powers roughly similar to those of the parliamentary Ombudsman in Sweden. There are, however, two important differences: in the USSR and Eastern Europe, they are concerned primarily with the fulfilment of central plans and directives (which is only a minor aspect of the role of the Ombudsman); secondly, they are mass institutions, involving more than 100,000 people in the GDR, and over 3 million in the USSR.[105]

As we have already pointed out, the repressive forces of the socialist state have been deeply politicized and thoroughly transformed in social composition; only the guerrilla armies of China, Vietnam and Cuba seem to have been more closely connected with the life and work of ordinary citizens. Another measure that has somewhat narrowed the distance separating the repressive apparatus from the masses is the introduction of non-state organs, such as the comrades' courts and volunteer public order squads in the USSR, in order to deal with petty offences.

The administrative personnel also occupy an original position within society. In revolutionary Russia, the pre-capitalist Tsarist machine was largely, though not entirely, broken up; whilst in Eastern Europe the special privileges and obligations that had been legislated by the bourgeois regimes were abolished after 1945.[106] In all cases, the administrative apparatus was restructured according to the principles of cadre administration. It is thus hardly accidental that the concept of cadre may be applied to both state and non-state personnel, to both full-time functionaries and worker-militants.

The level of remuneration of the state personnel is another aspect of its relationship with the rest of the population. Lenin demanded in his April Theses that 'the salaries of all officials . . . should not exceed the average wage of a competent worker'.[107] However, the urgent need to recruit military and civilian specialists rapidly forced the new Soviet state to deviate from this egalitarian programme, and since that time, little attention has been paid to the problem except in China and Vietnam.

In the USSR itself, criteria applicable to the remuneration of professional revolutionaries were taken up and developed in a greatly

---

[105] Ludz, op. cit., pp. 128 ff.

[106] Balla, op. cit., pp. 164 ff.

[107] V. I. Lenin, 'The Tasks of the Proletariat in the Present Revolution', *Collected Works*, vol. 24, p. 23.

expanded, state form. In principle, the cadre hands over all his personal income to the party, which then takes on responsibility for his material support. What in fact occurred was that a special system of consumer supply was established for the party and state cadres. As long as mechanisms function to ensure permanent political commitment, this need not lead to the creation of a privileged elite. However, it cannot fail to set top officials apart from the masses. The extent to which this distance can grow is well brought out by an episode in the novel *The New Appointment* by the Soviet writer, Alexander Bek. Towards the end of the Stalin era, a minister finds himself abandoned by his chauffeur in the streets of Moscow; he goes into a Metro station, but he has to ask what is the fixed fare, and in any case he soon realizes that he has no cash.

In order to resist the differentiation from the working class inherent in the work of state officials, some socialist regimes have institutionalized a system of periodical involvement of functionaries in manual labour. For example, this has been introduced in the GDR[108], in Cuba (in the organization of the sugar harvest or *Zafra*), in Vietnam, and above all in China, where Article 11 of the new Constitution of 1975 states explicitly: 'Cadres at all levels must participate in collective productive labour'.

Relations between the state personnel and the population as a whole are also influenced by relics of the capitalist or pre-capitalist apparatuses that existed prior to the proletarian revolution. The principal effect of this residue, which is *reproduced* within the new structures, is of course the intensification of the alien and distant features of the state. One aspect of this problem is the carefully guarded wall of *secrecy* built around the discussions and operation of the central apparatus. The lack of a tradition of bourgeois public opinion has led to and been compounded by the obstacles placed in the way of the development of proletarian public opinion on critical matters. In China, the holding of the last National People's Congress was not announced until after the event, and at the height of the Cultural Revolution, a strange code of behaviour still prevailed, according to which prominent personalities could be criticized by name only upon a signal from above. Even peaceful leadership changes, such as the removal of Khruschev in 1964, are still realized

---

[108] Balla, op. cit., p. 233 n. This was in the fifties and early sixties, and its practical import does not seem to be known. (Cf. Förtsch, op. cit., p. 81.)

in a secretive and conspiratorial fashion. In some cases, the methods of repression have themselves been taken over from the previous regime. Thus in the Soviet Union, the extensive use of deportation is modelled on Tsarist practices; in the Stalin period, and more recently in Poland, the secrecy and isolation of the repressive forces even led to a resurgence of anti-semitism within them.

A peculiar feature of the bloody Stalinist repression was the fact that it ravaged the top state and party personnel as well as the ordinary population. Before the machinery of the purge, citizens of all ranks and positions were equal – equally defenceless. But the system of suspicion institutionalized under Stalin and still largely in existence today has in many important ways cut off the top leaders of both state and party from the life of ordinary citizens. Leading politicians of socialist states cannot be expected to be seen shopping in a department store, walking their children to a day-care centre, or commuting on a suburban train to their office; they are supplied by special outlets and driven in guarded, chauffeured cars. This breeds, at best, overpoliticized insensitivity to the concerns of everyday life; at worst, cynicism born of privilege and profound political and ideological hollowness. (It should not be forgotten that there are also real reasons for vigilance and suspicion, as the revelations of the CIA's many plans and attempts to assassinate Fidel Castro make clear. But nor should it be overlooked that Fidel survived these plots while moving about among the people to a much greater extent than many other socialist leaders.)

We can now summarize the various types of link between state and non-state personnel. Under feudalism, *lord* and *subject* form the two poles of a relation that pervades the whole social hierarchy. In the bourgeois state, this is replaced by the distinction between *public government* and *individual citizen*, and there appears the characteristic problem of maintaining simultaneously governmental responsibility to bourgeois public opinion and the inaccessibility of the processes of state to the 'dangerous' working classes. In the monopoly stage, relations between government and public opinion expressed through parliament, journals, clubs and salons, have increasingly given way to joint state-capital ventures, networks of bodies which fuse the summits of various organizations, and to the mass communication politics of '*stars*' and '*fans*'.

Thirdly, to the extent that they are organized according to principles of cadre administration, the socialist countries exhibit a distinctive politico–ideological relationship between the organizer and the organized, between the *vanguard* and the formerly downtrodden and exploited *masses*. In the difficult and complex course of this relationship, the crucial variables seem to be: the vanguard's relative size and prior experience of bourgeois democracy; the breadth of the popular layers that it represents; and the extent of the tradition of self-organization already accumulated by the masses.

Energy Outflow

Although its expenditure evidently had a certain effect upon the economy, the feudal state directly consumed the greater part of its material resources. This practice was justified by the household conception of political economy that pervaded the cameralist and mercantilist doctrines of the period. The expenditure of the Swedish state in 1573 may be cited as an illustration of this structure:

Items of Swedish state expenditure in 1573. In percentages.

'Reductions' of payable rent, i.e., various enfiefments	15
The Court	12
Wages, drink, food and fodder of local civilian administration	13
Military wages, food and fodder, and other military expenditure	about 50
Construction, mining and diverse civilian expenditure	6
Ransom for the fortress Älvsborg	4

Source: B. Oden, *Rikets uppbörd och utgift*, Lund 1955, ch. IX. pp. 375 ff., 409. The figures are approximate calculations. 1573 was a year of peace in Sweden.

By contrast, the expenditure of the capitalist state is directed mainly towards the servicing of the private sphere, and towards the production of certain effects upon the market and the population. The following comparative tabulation of the Swedish budgets of 1873 and 1973 clearly indicates the trend:

Items of Swedish state expenditure, as percentages of the total budgets presented in 1873 and 1973.

	1873	1973
Court	2	0.002
Administration, incl. judiciary and police	14	12
Defence	31	11
Infrastructural services: communications, promotion of the economy, labour market policies	21	12
Social services and welfare	9	51
Of which: Health, education, social services	9	21
Transfers	—	30
Capital expenditure	10	11
Debt service	11	1

Sources: Calculated from government budgets presented to the Diet in 1873 and 1973. The figures are only approximations, since the boundaries of the various rubrics are often difficult to determine in the official report.

Note: The relatively high figures for capital expenditure and debt service in 1873 are explained by the fact that the 1870s were a period of intensive railway construction in Sweden.

The characteristic patterns of energy outflow may be concisely defined as follows: whereas the feudal state is essentially *consumptive* (i.e., its outflow is mainly indirect), and the capitalist *redistributive*, the socialist state is *productive*. What is expressed here is the fusion of the feudal state with the process of exploitation; the regulative separation of the capitalist polity from the market; and the collective appropriation of the means of production under socialism. The capitalist apparatus does not redistribute wealth primarily among the classes, but among different sectors of the economy (by means of customs and excise duties and taxes), in its management of the capitalist economy as a whole. It further reallocates resources among the various areas of personal life, among generations (by its pensions policy), between periods of sickness and health, between the ages of childbearing and childrearing, and other periods.

The productive character of the socialist state involves the apportionment of the major part of productive investment through the central budget. This mechanism constitutes an important aspect of the appropriation of the means of production by society as a whole. Part of what are the social services of a capitalist state are furnished by the price structure (for example, low-rent housing).

The distinctive patterns of outflow of socialist and other states are clearly revealed in the following table:

Patterns of state expenditure, in rounded percentage figures.

	Feudal Sweden	Capitalist Sweden		USSR
	1573	*1873*	*1973*	*1966*
Total administration, incl. court, judiciary and police	40	16	12	6[1]
Defence	50	30	11	13
Non-productive consumption	90	46	23	19
Social services and welfare	—	9	51	39
Infrastructural services	6	25	12	about 15
Productive redistribution	6	34	63	54
Productive Investment	—	10	11	about 28
Debt service	5	11	1	—

1. Includes 'Other expenditure' (i.e., police, allocations at the disposal of the Council of Ministers, etc.).
Sources: For Sweden see the two previous tables. For the Soviet Union see A. Nove, *Det ekonomiska systemet i Sovietunionen*, Stockholm, 1969, pp. 112 ff.

The Effects of Technology

The output of the state technology may be defined as the effect it produces upon those who are organized by it, or in other words, as the allegiances it manages to construct. For instance, feudal structures typically inspire a relation of *deference*, which is based on recognition of the personal eminence and distinctiveness of the hereditary rulers. This attitude is normally expressed in highly ritualized forms of submission, from those of courtly ceremony to the bow of peasants standing bareheaded in a ditch as the landowner passes by.

By contrast, capitalist bureaucratic and managerial authority rests on the cultivation of *discipline*. If the organizational technology is functioning correctly, then legitimate orders will receive prompt and unquestioning execution. All the administrative and repressive apparatuses of the state, as well as the capitalist enterprise itself, generate a spirit of discipline and a structure of command that are functional to the formal rationality of market accumulation and to the tempo of the productive forces; while managerial technocracy assures the modern capitalist state of a certain *technical flexibility* in its interventions on the market.

Of course, discipline has for a long time had a positive connotation within the labour movement, where it denotes the renunciation of personal interest and inclination in favour of collective ones. However, unlike feudal or capitalist rulers, the proletariat does not organize a different class, but rather itself. The working class cadre is already part of the collective within which he works, and in principle he cannot enforce claims to deference or discipline with any special means of compulsion. Successful working class organization, then, relies heavily on *commitment and solidarity* – individual devotion to a common cause – rather than on formal orders and hierarchies. In socialist states, this discipline of commitment is characteristically produced and sustained by the mechanism of politico-ideological education – within the state administration, the armed forces and the police, as well as at the point of production and in all areas of social life.

However, if the cadre does not share the material existence and frame of reference of the collective that he organizes, and adopts an aloof and domineering attitude towards it, then his politico-ideological message will be hollow and unconvincing; he will be able to arouse only fear and an outward show of loyalty. To the extent that he loses his politico-ideological role, he comes to resemble the boss of the US political machines and business unions, standing

Summary of Structural Characteristics of State Apparatuses

Structural Element	Characteristic Organizational Form in:			
	Feudalism	Capitalism	Monopoly Capitalism (additional forms)	Socialism
Input: Tasks	Hierarchical privatization Militarization	Separation of public and private sphere Economization	Public expansion and private atomization	Politicization of all spheres, incl. 'private life'
Input: Personnel recruitment	Personal service to a superior	Intellectual talent and personal qualities of national representativeness	Technical and plebiscitary accentuation	Class representativeness and expertise
Input: Energy (material resources)	Revenues from royal lands and prerogatives, plus bargaining with estates	Statutory taxation	Massive increase	Revenues from public enterprise structured by price system
Transformation: Handling of tasks	Interpretation of given laws and customs; differentiation according to social position	Legislation, impersonal rule-application	Selective budgeting; administrative decree; top-level bargaining	Mass involvement according to political line

Transformation: Patterning of personnel	Contractual personal hierarchy; overlapping and conflicting areas of competence	Office hierarchy, separation of apparatuses	Ad hoc agencies at the top, collectivity of workers at the bottom; executive preponderance	Unified apparatus subordinated to working class organizations or party cadres
Transformation: Energy	Devolution to individual office-holders	Budgetary allocation	Budget adaptation to market management	Plan prioritization
Output: Tasks I Foreign policy	Jurisdiction and control of land	Inter-capital and inter-nation policies of competition, monopoly and rivalry	Imperialist expansion in search of markets and raw materials	Inter-party policies based on political line and ideology
Output: Tasks II Domestic policy	Juridical regulation and protection	Unifying legal framework; furthering of productive forces	Administrative regulation, market operations	Mass mobilization
Output: Personnel I Inter-state	Family relations, direct or delegated	National representation	Incorporation in international agencies	National and party representation
Output: Personnel II Domestic	Fusion of private-public;	Separation of public officials from the people	Merger of top officials with private executives; inclusion of many below into working class	Breakdown of barriers between state officials and non-state organizers
Output: Energy	State consumption (only indirect output)	Redistribution	Massive increase	Productive investment
Effects of technology	Deference	Discipline	Technical flexibility, fan spirit	Commitment, solidarity, mobilization

in charge of a fragmented and uncommitted mass of workers, and becoming subordinated himself to bureaucrats and managers.

Only in such exceptional circumstances as war is the bourgeois state significantly concerned with ideological mobilization – and then it takes a sharply nationalist form. We should however mention one effect of the bourgeois technique of leadership by mass communication. The relationship between the pop-fan and the 'star' is probably the closest analogy with the spreading cult of political personalities, who are drained of all concrete political content. In the bourgeois world, it is this *fan spirit* and discipline that correspond to commitment, solidarity and collective mobilization.[109]

A Note on Petty-Bourgeois Effects on the State

Although the petty bourgeoisie has never been able to create a sovereign state of its own, it has often constituted an important social force, and has at times even succeeded in making a definite imprint upon the state apparatus. The peculiar social position of these strata has given rise to two distinct types of effect. On the one hand, where they have attained a high degree of strength and independence, direct expression has been given to the relations of petty commodity production. On the other hand, the state has developed special modes of protection of the interests of the petty bourgeoisie, when its position within capitalist society has been seriously threatened. We may place both these effects under the heading of 'populist' aspects of the state.

Petty-bourgeois social relations are essentially ones of exchange and competition among self-employed, independent and equal individuals, or more precisely nuclear families. In reality, the petty bourgeoisie proper cannot always be sharply differentiated from

---

[109] The Stalinist regime obviously cannot be scientifically and politically comprehended by the official terminology of the 20th Congress: 'the cult of the personality'. Nevertheless, the Stalin phenomenon certainly included a personality cult, even if it was radically different from the idolization of US political 'stars' like Kennedy, Nixon and Carter. The class character and political functioning of the cults of Stalin, Mao Tse-tung and Kim Il-Sung, remain to be analysed. But in contrast to bourgeois forms, they were devised as mechanisms of a kind of politico-ideological mobilization, rather than as means to create a disparate following for a politician virtually devoid of a programme.

traditional patriarchal families, who are predominantly self-sustaining and linked to one another only by spatial cohabitation of varying density. Usually, however, the so-called patriarchal mode of production involves a village collective as an important element of its relations of production. It is the urge to individual and family consumption that inspires the relatively slow-paced dynamic of petty commodity production. If a society were wholly composed of independent producers, it would contain no classes and thus, according to Marxist theory, would require no special state apparatus. Historically, the weight of the petty bourgeoisie has been used precisely to limit the separateness of the state apparatus. This may be clearly seen in a number of US and Swiss institutions and practices: for example, in the power of recall of officials under the spoils system and also of elected politicians at state or lower level; the elective character of numerous minor posts and the correspondingly low number of bureaucratic career offices in the United States; in the militia army of Switzerland and the National Guards and earlier posses of deputy marshals in the United States; in the right of citizens to bear arms in both countries; in the determination of important legislation by means of referenda; and in the central role of the jury within the judicial system. Of course, all these petty-bourgeois institutions have increasingly operated within a global bourgeois framework, and can function very well as instruments of repression of the working class: US marshals and National Guards, for instance, have frequently been used against labour organizers and workers' struggles. Nevertheless, they have served to soften the distinctions between state and society and between the public and private spheres, and have set limits to the growing autonomy of the specialized legislative, administrative, judicial and repressive apparatuses of the state.

Another aspect of these restraints is the investment of the state with the moral and ideological concerns of the petty bourgeoisie. This is illustrated by the creation of new state cults of Reason and of the Supreme Being by left-wing Jacobins during the French Revolution, and by official concern with adult heterosexual practices in a number of American states.

As capital accumulation develops in scope and intensity, both monopoly capital and the working class confront the petty bourgeoisie with a serious threat. The acuteness of this depends on the global weight of middle strata within society, the availability of economic reserves, and on the character of the politico-economic conjuncture. The petty bourgeoisie will turn in the direction of popular fronts and people's democracy only if it sees before it a strong labour movement, sensitive to its need for protection, and if its own experience of politics and alliances leads it to identify the monopolies and the landowners as its principal enemies. When these conditions are absent, it will focus on such characteristic demands as those for cheap credit, antimonopoly legislation or agricultural and other subsidies, and in situations of acute crisis, it will gravitate towards more or less authoritarian forms of populism that are based on the cult of the leader.

In this second variant, the petty-bourgeois effect also involves curtailment of the separateness and specificity of the state. However, the need for protection then becomes the craving for an individual *protector* who will constitute and control an anti-bureaucratic part of the state machine; the petty bourgeoisie hopes to entrust its interests to such a populist leader, to whom it will have direct access and be able to appeal over the heads of capitalist officials. Both European fascism and Latin American presidential populism contain elements of this kind, and demonstrate that, depending on the strength of the working class, such movements may be directed primarily either against the old semi-feudal or palaeo-capitalist oligarchy or against the menacing organization of the working class. The fatal contradiction of the populist state is that its social base cannot sustain a non-capitalist mode of production, whilst its petty-bourgeois aspects disrupt the public servicing of capital accumulation. In the fascist states, the problem was solved by the rapid subordination of the aspirations of the petty bourgeoisie to the needs of monopoly capital, and in Latin America by the overthrow of populist regimes by the forces of imperialism and the domestic bourgeoisie.

Was Lenin Right? A First Conclusion

What has been presented above is only a basic framework for analysis of the class character of state apparatuses: substantive results will be obtained only through verification and application of the model. However, if we assume that it contains a degree of truth, then the experience of sixty years allows us to answer in a slightly more concrete way Lenin's old question: What is the nature of the relationship of the socialist proletarian state to the bourgeois state, of proletarian democracy to bourgeois democracy?

There appear to be sufficiently strong grounds for affirming that the state expresses, in its irreducible specificity, a particular set of societal relations – those which Marxists see as class relations. That it does so is clear not only from the content of its policies and of the social order its repressive apparatuses are prepared to defend, but also from the form of its administrative organization and governmental representation. The very organizational form of the state apparatus manifests social class relations and contributes to their reproduction. It is thus part of the rule of the ruling class.

Marx and Lenin asserted that the existing state apparatus must be 'smashed' in any socialist transformation of society. What are to be smashed are neither the various agencies of the state (though some will no doubt be abolished) nor the personnel who work in them (though some will have to be removed). *To smash the state apparatus means to smash the class character of its technology or organization*, as well as the manifestations of the latter in the mode of regulating tasks, personnel and material resources. In a socialist revolution, this involves dismantling bureaucracy, technocracy, and the exclusive and ritualistic forms of parliamentary and plebiscitary politics.

It now seems possible to disentangle the strengths and weaknesses of Lenin's *State and Revolution*. If the above analysis is not completely misguided, then Lenin was right to raise the problem of the class character of the state apparatus; he was right to assert that the existing state has to be smashed in any socialist revolution; he was right in his indication of the direction that this change would have to take.

In relation to the Marxism of the Second International and to the summit of bourgeois thought on the state (Max Weber), Lenin's achievement was of the utmost scientific as well as political significance. He was nevertheless wrong when he confounded a socialist society and its state with a classless communist society. This defect lends his work a utopian ring and has made it possible for a number of substantial problems of socialist construction to go untheorized. In essence, Lenin limits the problem of the transitional and contradictory character of socialism to the aspect of its *external* defence by force against the bourgeois enemy at home and abroad – hence his emphasis on the *armed* proletariat. But *within* the armed fortress of the proletariat, he tends to assume a state endowed with a degree of equality, efficacy and transparency possible only in a future communist society – hence the assertion that the armed workers can control and supervise everything.

This essay has argued instead that socialist society is erected upon a fundamental contradiction between, on the one hand, the collective supremacy of a previously downtrodden and exploited class – a supremacy invested in its overall direction of the state and the orientation of socially appropriated means of production towards collective use – and, on the other hand, the subordination of the individuals who compose that class to a bureaucratic and technocratic expertise that still remains necessary. The main instrument of this collective superordination is the political organization of the working class. But, like all other classes, the proletariat is not a homogeneous collectivity made up of equally committed and capable individuals – as Lenin was, on other occasions, very well aware. It too needs special forms of organization and leadership. In its history of struggle, the labour movement has developed a distinctive technique of organization, with the collective organizer and leader, the cadre, as its central figure. Cadre organization of the state and economy is, then, the instrument of working class collective supremacy.

Each type of state apparatus exhibits a specific dialectic – specific contradictions of class domination and the execution of class domination. In the feudal state, these affected the relation between, on the one hand, direct seigneurial rule involving the possibility of disintegration, and, on the other, royal centralization carried forward with the help of non-aristocratic retainers. Later, under the impact of the rise of mercantile capital, feudal relations of confidence, loyalty and enfiefment were recast in the mould of venality and commodity relations, thus undercutting the power of the landowning aristocracy and barring the full emancipation of the bourgeoisie as a whole. The legalistic bureaucracy and parliamentary politicians of the classical bourgeois state were poorly equipped to handle the monopolized market, the social character of the productive forces, and the rise of the working class. Today, the collusion of state managerial technocrats with sectors of big capital endangers the unity of the bourgeoisie; the vast expansion of the state drives masses of state employees close to, and into the arms of, the class enemy – the proletariat; while the technocrat and plebiscitary demagogue, although equally necessary, govern in conflicting ways.

The socialist state has no immunity to dialectics. In the struggle to defend itself and develop a productive base for the abolition of divisions between mental and manual labour, and town and country, the state has to utilize bureaucratic and managerial techniques which simultaneously reproduce these same divisions. In order to direct and control bureaucracy and technocracy, it has to assert political cadre leadership. But that in turn involves reproduction of the cadre-worker or vanguard-masses distinction, which blocks the road to the collective self-organization of communism.

However, dialectics also teaches that contradictions do not remain enclosed in an unsurpassable stalemate; their dynamic is one of change and development. Thus the position of the cadre is also contradictory. He owes his relationship to managers and bureaucrats to his links of representation with the masses. Thus, as the latter grow and develop, the cadre will have either to integrate himself with the collectivity or to be thrown onto the 'dustheap of history', once his epochal task is fulfilled.

State Power – on the
Dialectics of Class Rule

Class, State and Power

A Line of Demarcation

What is the character of the relationship between, on the one hand, social classes – basically defined by their position within the economy – and, on the other, the exercise of political power through the state? Is there a ruling class in this or that country? If there is, which is that class? How does it exercise its rule? How may it lose its power? Although the last of these questions raises complex problems of prediction and strategy, the others seem quite simple and straightforward. The real difficulty arises when we attempt to answer them. If we disregard prejudices of an ideological nature, the issue involved here appears to be the famous one of scientific method. This essay, indeed, is intended as a methodological contribution to analysis of certain crucial scientific and political problems of class, state and power.

Discussion of these questions has given rise to an intensive as well as extensive polemic. But can we be sure that genuinely different replies are being proposed? From what we know of 'paradigms' and 'problematics', would it not rather be naive to assume that the writers concerned, whose scientific and political formations are extremely diverse, are referring to the same problem – even if they use the same, or similar, words?

Upon closer consideration, this does prove to be an unwarranted assumption. However, our aim here is not to present a critical survey of the overabundant literature, but to outline a set of questions and propose methods with which to answer them. We shall not adopt a new, idiosyncratic approach, but rather follow an old-established one – hopefully with greater rigour than has been done in the past. But before we can begin, it is first of all necessary to draw a sharp line of demarcation between this and other types of question.

Leaving aside subtler points and distinctions, we may identify three basic approaches to the study of political power. By far the most common of these centres on the question: *Who has power?* It asks, for example: Who governs this country? Who rules America? Does anyone at all run this community?[1] We may call this the *subjectivist* approach, in the sense that it seeks to locate the subject of power. It evidently includes the further question: How many hold power? A few or a large number? A unified group of families, an institutional elite of top decision-makers, or competing groups? Everyone or no-one really? Within this shared problematic, many different analyses and solutions may then be proposed; particularly in the United States, a lively debate has emerged in relation to both methods and conclusions of research. Truly there seems no end to the polemics among theorists of 'pluralism', 'the power elite' and 'the ruling class'.[2]

Remaining essentially within the framework of liberal political

[1] See, for example, Robert Dahl, *Who Governs? Democracy and Power in an American City*, New Haven 1961; W. Domhoff, *Who Rules America?* Englewood Cliffs 1967; N. Polsby, 'How to Study Community Power: The Pluralist Alternative', in *Journal of Politics*, Vol. 22 1960.

[2] The methodological debate has been fought out above all in the pages of the *American Political Science Review* (APSR). An overview may be gained from the Reader edited by R. Bell, D. Edwards and H. Wagner: *Political Power*, New York 1969. An earlier, European survey, conducted from a liberal-pluralist point of view, is: R. Aron, 'Classe sociale, classe politique, classe dirigeante', in *Archives Européennes de Sociologie* 1960 No. 2, pp. 260–82. In 1971, the APSR published another round, between F. Frey and R. Wolfinger (Vol. 65, pp. 1081–1104). As for the radical, 'elitist' theorists (so called not because they are elitists, but because they find elitism to be the prevailing doctrine) the most important writings include: P. Bachrach–M. Baratz, *Power and Poverty*, New York 1970; S. Lukes, *Power: A Radical View*, London 1974. The methodology of the Domhoff school was expounded in a special issue of the US journal *The Insurgent Sociologist*, 'New Directions in Power Structure Research' (ed. W. Domhoff) 1976. Among the principal contributions to the substantial polemics are the following: a) from the elitist side: F. Hunter, *Community Power Structure*, Chapel Hill 1953; C. W. Mills, *The Power Elite*, New York 1956; W. Domhoff, op. cit. 1967 and several later, more specialized works; M. Creson, *The Un-Politics of Air Pollution*, Baltimore 1971; and R. Miliband, *The State in Capitalist Society*, London 1969 – a book which, although coming from a tradition of Marxist research, falls essentially within this category; and b) from the pluralist side: D. Riesman et. al., *The Lonely Crowd*, New York 1953; R. Dahl, op. cit. and *Pluralist Democracy in the United States: Conflict and Consent*, Chicago 1967; and a work which leans in this direction: A. Giddens, *The Class Structure of the Advanced Societies*, London 1973.

ideology, or at least political theory[3], the debate has accepted liberal conceptions of democracy as its starting-point and proceeded to investigate whether or not contemporary manifestations of democracy in the United States correspond to ideal norms.

The second approach enjoys much more limited currency outside a few highly specialized departments of academia. Its focus is the businessman's question: How much – how much power, that is to say? It lays stress on 'power to do' rather than on 'power over', and on the exchange and accumulation of power rather than its distribution. Since analysis of political power is, in this case, modelled on one or another form of liberal economic theory – textbook marginalist micro-economics (Buchanan-Tullock, Downs), economic development theory (Huntington), or more sophisticated contemporary liberal economic analysis (Coleman, Hernes) – we may term this the *economic* approach.[4] In its micro-economic variants, it occupies a framework which is much the same as that of the more rigorous subjectivists: power is studied in terms of preferences, alternatives, choices, and so on. In fact, some of the 'economic' theorists are also interested in questions of 'power over'.

The Marxist, *historical-materialist* approach is profoundly different. In contrast to the two others, it starts not from 'the point of view of the actor' but from that of the ongoing social process of reproduction and transformation. If it were to be condensed into a single question comparable to the others, it would be formulated thus: What is the character of power and how is it exercised? The historical-materialist mode of investigation, then, seeks above all to define the nature of power, not its subject or quantity. This feature is expressed in the scandalous interrogation of Marxism-Leninism: Democracy of which class? Dictatorship of which class? *Capital* itself was not written primarily in order to reveal 'who are the rich and who are the poor', or to assess the magnitude of existing wealth. Marx's central objective was rather to lay bare 'the economic law of

---

[3] While C. Wright Mills, for instance, was unquestionably a radical liberal, writers like Lukes or Miliband start out from premises of liberal political theory without politically adhering to liberalism.

[4] T. Parsons, 'On the Concept of Political Power', in idem., *Sociological Theory and Modern Society*, New York 1967; S. Huntington, *Political Order in Changing Societies*, New Haven 1968; A. Downs, *An Economic Theory of Democracy*, New York 1957; J. Buchanan–G. Tullock, *The Calculus of Consent*, Michigan 1962; J. Coleman, *The Mathematics of Collective Action*, London 1973; and G. Hernes, *Makt og avmakt*, Oslo 1975.

motion of modern society', to show how wealth and poverty, domination and subjugation are (re-) produced and changed. Thus, the basic focus of analysis was neither property nor property-owners, but *capital* – that is to say, specific historical relations of production connected in a determinate manner to the productive forces, the state, and the social ensemble of ideas.

This approach has important implications which should be spelled out clearly from the outset. Marxists are interested in the relationship of classes to state power for a very particular reason. They view the state as a separate material institution, functioning as the nodal point of the relations of power within society. The state as such has no power; it is an institution where social power is concentrated and exercised.[5] According to the axioms of historical materialism, class and state condition each other: where there are no classes, there is no state. In class societies, moreover, social relations are first and foremost class relations. Thus, by definition, every state has a class character, and every class society has a ruling class (or bloc of ruling classes). In other words, Marxist discourse does not pertain at all to the subjectivist debate on whether there exists a ruling class. If it seeks to identify the ruling class and the class character of state power, it does so in order to discover the characteristic social structures and relations which are promoted and protected above all others by the material force of the state; and in order to determine the conditions under which they may be changed or abolished. The class character of a given state power does not necessarily refer to back-stage string-pulling; it denotes the societal content of the actions of the state, and indicates thereby the ruling class of that society. There then arises the question of how this class rule is grounded and maintained, and how it can be overthrown.[6]

. . . and its rationale

In a scientific mode of discourse, lines of demarcation should be motivated by reference to procedural canons. Now, although the historical-materialist approach to political power constitutes a

---

[5] This point has been emphasized and elaborated in the very important works of Nicos Poulantzas: *Political Power and Social Classes* (NLB 1973) and *Classes in Contemporary Capitalism* (NLB 1975).

[6] Cf. the authors' introduction to J. Fabre–F. Hincker–L. Sève, *Les communistes et l'état*, Paris 1977 – a book of great theoretical and political import; and François Hincker's interventions in the debate on 'Crise du capitalisme, crise de la société, crise de l'Etat', in *La Nouvelle Critique*, February 1977.

specific problematic, it may in fact be compared with the other two in respect of analytical value. For this purpose we may discuss all three in the loose and general terms of 'power to do' and 'power over'. Individual contributions to analysis may, of course, rest upon blatant ideological distortions of their own. But the basic inadequacy of the two non-Marxist approaches may be said to lie in their failure to grasp their own limitations. Furthermore, their own achievements deal with specifications and special cases of the more general overall problematic of historical materialism and are thus susceptible to incorporation by the latter.

The problem of 'power to do' raises the question: Power to do what? It is naturally not without importance to identify and quantify the range of politically influential subjects, or to assess the power resources of a given state. (To take but one extreme example, which has at times been tragically neglected by not a few Marxists, a competitive democracy must evidently be distinguished from a Fascist dictatorship or a murky oligarchy, even though all three may be manifestations of bourgeois class power.) But once we have located the most influential power subject or subjects, we are faced with another problem: What does this power subject do with its power? What do the rulers do when they rule? Where do the leaders lead the led? In non-Marxist discourses, this whole area is either ignored or treated in a manifestly inadequate fashion. It would involve only a slight caricature to say that the pluralist-elitist debate comes down to the following opposition: Look, many have power, that is good! No, look, few have power, that is bad!

The typical reply given to the question 'power to do what?' is 'power to realize one's interests'; or, as Talcott Parsons's Panglossian conception of world would have it, 'the interest of the effectiveness of the collective operation as a whole'.[7] In view of the enormous variety of historical forms and systems of power, this can hardly be considered a satisfactory answer. Only within a given social form and time-perspective does it seem possible to attach a precise empirical meaning to the utilitarian notion of 'interest'. What, for example, is the interest of a Fascist or military dictator, or that of a democratic prime minister? In the short run, it may be suggested, to stay in power. But does that really illuminate the matter? Similarly, while the marginalist models of micro-economics may provide a

[7] Parsons, op. cit., p. 308.

picture of market transactions, they contribute little to our understanding of the rise and dynamics of capitalism, or of the mechanisms and crises of capital accumulation.[8]

By ignoring or evading the problem of 'power to do', the non-Marxist approaches tend to be unable to account for historical social change. Characteristically, the classical elite theorists, who really thought through the consequences of their analyses, held that society does not basically change at all. This is true of all of them: Gumplowicz, Mosca, Pareto, Michels. Instead, they depicted an eternal cycle of the rise, rule, degeneration, and fall of elites, tending ultimately to reduce people and society to biology.[9] Now, although men certainly are biological organisms, it is an obvious fact that human society has changed over the ages and assumed a number of different forms. The task of social science must be to analyse these historical modes and their processes of transformation – a task which cannot be accomplished if the psyche, will and interests of the subjects of power are taken as the starting-point. These subjects must be brought into systematic relationship with the historical social context in which they rule. It is with this, and not the detection of dark conspiracies, that Marxism is concerned.

From the historical-materialist standpoint, classes are the bearers of definite relations of production. Thus, to identify the bourgeoisie as the ruling class involves the location of state power within the matrix of the dynamics and contradictions of capitalism, as it presents itself, with its particular tendencies, possibilities and problems, at a given stage and conjuncture. Similarly, every government is related to a particular ruling class within a specific historical social matrix which circumscribes what is done by the state and determines the possibilities of change.

From one point of view, the non-Marxist analyses may thus be said to deal implicitly with a number of significant specifications of class rule, while from another they appear as *de facto* concerned with a special case of it. This distinction will become clear upon examination of an aspect of 'power over'. Are the various moments of the rule of power-subjects related to one another? Should we

[8] Cf. my 'Ekonomiska system: Vetenskap och ideologi', in my *Klasse och ekonomiska system*, Staffanstorp 1971. A provisional English translation has been made for Frank Roosevelt at Vassar College, Poughkeepsie, New York.

[9] For a demonstration and references see G. Therborn, *Science, Class and Society*, NLB 1976, Ch. 4 part III.

conclude that social power is random and unpatterned wherever it does not emanate from a unified power-subject, such as an autocratic group or individual, or a consensual social collective? If not, how should the relationship be studied, and how may it be grasped?

The contemporary Western debate between theorists of pluralism and elitism has concentrated on the secondary problem of whether there is an *interpersonal* relation between the different moments of the exercise of power in society. Are they united by a cohesive elite which takes all the major decisions in important areas? Or is decision-making power fragmented among groups which have little or no connection with one another? Such a formulation of the issue effectively ignores the fact that interpersonal fragmentation of decision-making does not necessarily imply a random and unpatterned structure of events. Indeed, it is a basic, and seemingly legitimate, assumption of social science that all occurrences in human society are in some way patterned and therefore susceptible to comprehension by scientific analysis. Pluralist and elitist contributions have thus focussed on only a single possible form of the patterning of power – one, moreover, which is hardly the most important form in complex modern societies.

Little is to be gained by the observation that, apart from interlocking membership in cohesive power groups, another kind of interpersonal identity exists: the sharing of ideas, a consensus of values.[10] For in contemporary societies, such a consensus is extremely general and abstract, and the precise modes of its emergence, functioning and maintenance still have to be explained.[11] It

[10] Robert Dahl has written: 'democratic politics is merely the chaff, it is the surface manifestation, representing superficial conflicts. Prior to politics, beneath it, enveloping it, restricting it, conditioning it, is the underlying consensus among a predominant portion of the politically active members.' *A Preface to Democratic Theory*, Chicago 1956, p. 132. But what if 'consensus' is the surface manifestation of something else, which 'envelops', 'restricts' and 'conditions' both the consensus and electoral politics?

[11] This is a weak spot in Ralph Miliband's otherwise well-substantiated critique of the pluralist thesis (*The State in Capitalist Society*). Miliband shrinks in the end from analysis of those forms in which neither the governmental personnel nor the upper echelons of the administrative apparatus are essentially recruited from the economic elite. In such cases, he merely refers us to the ideology of the political leaders as a part of the bourgeois consensus. (See Ch. 4 part IV.) Although he provides some empirical material and suggestions for a study of the problem, the latter remains fundamentally outside his mode of analytical control. For analysis of advanced bourgeois democracies, as well as of reformism, fascism and military regimes, it would seem indispensable to elaborate a more complex model than that

must further be shown how different forms of 'consensual power' pattern people's lives and give rise to certain objective social structures and relationships.

Bachrach and Baratz[12] and more recently Lukes[13] have developed important methodological critiques of pluralism, introducing the notions of institutional 'mobilization of bias', 'non-decision-making'[14] and, in the case of Lukes, latent conflicts and effects of inaction.[15] But they do not deal with the present problem of 'power over'. In fact, the subjectivist orientation of these writers seems to preclude a solution on the basis of the theory of elitism. While their refined methods are able to sound deep-lying manifestations of elite rule, they can hardly be expected to find social patternings of the exercise of power other than those of a unified power-subject. In the case of Bachrach-Baratz, this limitation is strongly implied in their view of power as an inter-personal relation between A and B, as well as in associated concepts.[16] Lukes, for his part, is led by his moralistic preoccupation with responsibility to disregard impersonal forms of domination and concentrate on cases where it may safely be assumed that the power-subject could have acted in a different manner from the one he chose. In this context he actually throws in a distinction between power and fate![17] For Lukes too, then, power should be

---

of Miliband. Similarly, the valuable work of William Domhoff on the upper-bourgeois backgrounds and connections of American politicians and administrators, and on the cohesiveness of the top stratum of the US bourgeoisie, would greatly benefit if it were located within a much more elaborate conceptualization and analysis of the power structure and contradictory development of US society.

[12] Bachrach-Baratz, op. cit. See also their articles: 'The Two Faces of Power' and 'Decisions and Non-decisions: An Analytical Framework', in *APSR*, vols. 56 and 57 (1962 and 1963) respectively.

[13] Lukes, op. cit.

[14] A non-decision denotes 'a decision that results in suppression or thwarting of a latent or manifest challenge to the values or interests of the decision-maker.' Bachrach-Baratz, op. cit. 1970, p. 44.

[15] Lukes, op. cit., Chs. 4 and 7. The author draws upon the work of Creson (op. cit.).

[16] Bachrach-Baratz, op. cit. 1970, Ch. 2.

[17] Lukes, op. cit., pp. 55–6. Cf. Marx: 'I do not by any means depict the capitalist and the landowner in rosy colours. But individuals are dealt with here only in so far as they are the personifications of economic categories, the bearers of particular class-relations and interests. My standpoint, from which the development of the economic formation of society is viewed as a process of natural history, can less than any other make the individual responsible for relations whose creature he remains, socially speaking, however much he may subjectively raise himself above them.' *Capital*, Volume 1, Penguin/NLR 1976, p. 92. Of course,

analysed primarily with a view to finding its subjects – identifiable, free and responsible originators of acts (and non-acts). He seems to remain stuck within the pluralist-elitist alternative: either a unified elite or various elites and leadership groups. (It remains obscure, moreover, how the inter-relationship of these groups functions as a relation of power over others – unless they themselves are aware of the connection between them.)

Marx opened up a path out of the pluralist-elitist impasse. But it has gone almost completely unnoticed among sociologists and political scientists, including those who have in a more or less critical fashion explicitly referred to Marx. The radical novelty of the Marxian approach seems to have been all but drowned in subjectivist treatments and re-interpretations. Marx argued that study of a given society should not just focus on its subjects or structure, but also and at the same time inquire into its process of *reproduction*. Significantly, it is in examining the latter process that Marx analyses the class relationships of exploitation and domination.

Capitalist production, therefore, under its aspect of a continuous connected process, does not create only commodities and surplus-value. It also produces and reproduces the capital relation itself: 'on the one hand the capitalist, on the other the wage-labourer.'[18] In a refutation of subjectivist conceptions of market exchange prevalent in 18th and 19th-century economics, Marx also provided a critique *ante diem* of 20th-century sociologists: 'To be sure, the matter looks quite different if we consider capitalist production in the uninterrupted flow of its renewal, and if, in place of the individual capitalist and the individual worker, we view them in their totality, as the capitalist class and the working class confronting each other. But in so doing we should be applying standards entirely foreign to commodity production.'[19]

From the perspective of reproduction, the dominant question of all subjectivist approaches to the study of power – Who rules: a unified elite or competing leadership groups? Is the economic elite identical with or in control of the political one? – is displaced by the

Marx's view implies not that the power of the capitalist is a fate to be accepted, but that it can be combated and abolished. His argument does suggest, however, that it is rather pointless to accuse the capitalists of not behaving as something other than capitalists. From Marx's standpoint, the arm of criticism is ultimately replaced by the criticism of arms, that is, by the class struggle in all its forms.

[18] Marx, op. cit., p. 724.
[19] Ibid., p. 732.

interrogation: What kind of society and what basic relations of production are being reproduced? By what mechanisms? What role do the structure and the actions or non-actions of the state (or local government) play in this process of reproduction? Do they further it, merely allow it to take place, or actively oppose it?

The analysis of reproduction enables us to explain how the different moments of the exercise of power in society may be inter-related, even in the absence of a conscious inter-personal connection. They are, in reality, linked to one another by their reproductive effects. Thus, the given relations of production may be reproduced – and furthered or permitted by state intervention – even where the exploiting (dominant) class, as defined by those relations, is not in 'control' of government in any conventional sense of the word. The fact that a specific form of exploitation and domination is reproduced constitutes this too as an example of class rule. The importance of this reproduction in the exercise of power within society is clear from this instance.

Excursus for Sociologists

In order to elucidate the distinctive character of Marx's *démarche* and make comparison possible within a sociological context, it may be useful at this point to take a fresh look at the classical, and still very important, source of sociological anti-Marxism in the fields of class, power and stratification – namely, Max Weber's treatment of these themes in *Economy and Society*. We intend here not to undertake a comprehensive analysis, but only to spell out the relationship between the Marxist problematic and the object of Weber's pre-occupation in these texts.[20] We say 'texts' in the plural because *Economy and Society* deals twice with class, status and power – both in the first part, which presents Weber's conceptual system, and in the second part, which, although written earlier, contains an elaboration of this system.[21] Weber's concepts are introduced separately: parties in the third chapter on *Herrschaft*; estates or 'status groups' (*Stände*) and classes in a fourth chapter of their own. Later, however, they are treated together, in a single section of the chapter on political communities.

[20] In my *Science, Class and Society* (op. cit), I have attempted to locate the theoretical core and historical context of Weber's sociology.

[21] Max Weber, *Economy and Society: An Outline of Interpretive Sociology*, New York 1968, pp. 481–88, 500–17, 926–38.

In one of the best introductions to Weber, Gerth and Mills write about his concept of class: 'In locating the class problem in the market and in the streams of income and property, Weber points towards production and its modern unit, the capitalist enterprise.' The authors imply that Weber here concurred with Marx, and they go on to indicate what they see as the additional contribution made by Weber: 'By making this sharp distinction between *class* and *status*, and by differentiating between types of classes and types of status groups, Weber is able to refine the problems of stratification to an extent which thus far has not been surpassed.'[22] Essentially the same view of Marx and Weber is presented by Giddens, although he has his own criticisms of Weber and of his theories of class. Giddens also thinks that the two theorists had the same conception of the market: 'In clarifying some of these matters we may start from the premise, which is fundamental for both Marx and Weber: that, in capitalism, the market is intrinsically a structure of power, in which the possession of certain attributes advantages some groups of individuals relative to others.'[23] According to Giddens: 'There are two principal respects in which the [Weber's] analysis differs from Marx's "abstract model" of classes. One is . . . differentiation of "class" from "status" and "party". The second . . . equally important . . . is that, although Weber employs for some purposes a dichotomous model which in certain general respects resembles that of Marx, his viewpoint strongly emphasizes a pluralistic conception of classes.'[24]

However, in order to understand Weber's view of stratification and power and to compare it with that of Marx, it is essential to realize that Weber's notion of capitalism issued from highly diverse sources: Austrian marginalist economics, German historicism, and some elements of the Marxist analysis – above all the attention paid by it to a historical economic system called capitalism.[25] One of the effects of this interesting combination of influences is the tendency of modern-day readers to take Weber's Marxist-sounding words, like class or capitalism, as denoting Marxian concepts.

As Gerth-Mills and Giddens quite rightly point out, Weber defines class in terms of position in the market. Weber emphasized:

[22] H. Gerth–C. W. Mills (eds.), *From Max Weber*, New York 1958, p. 69.
[23] Giddens, op. cit., pp. 101–2. Cf. the similar view of Frank Parkin in his *Class, Inequality and the Political Order*, London 1971, p. 31.
[24] Giddens, op. cit., p. 42. Emphasis added.
[25] Therborn, op. cit. 1976, pp. 270 ff.

'But always this is the generic connotation of the concept of class: that the kind of chance in the *market* is the decisive moment which presents a common condition for the individual's fate. Class situation is, in this sense, ultimately market situation.'[26] Now, provided that one's powers of vision have been sharpened through a difficult social process, it is sufficient to read the first six chapters of *Capital* to see that Marx's analysis followed quite another course. Towards the end of Chapter 6 Marx writes: 'The consumption of labour-power is completed, as in the case of every other commodity, outside the market of the sphere of circulation. Let us therefore, in company with the owner of money and the owner of labour-power, leave this noisy sphere, where everything takes place on the surface and in full view of everyone, and follow them into the hidden abode of production, on whose threshold there hangs the notice "No admittance except on business". Here we shall see, not only how capital produces, but how capital is itself produced.'[27]

The focus of Marx's analysis is not the market and the relations of circulation, but the relations of production. He conceptualizes classes in terms not of their market bargaining power, but of their function as agents or 'supports' of the relations of production within the process of social reproduction and change. In order to understand the two principal classes of capitalist society, it is, in Marx's view, necessary to grasp the 'law of motion' of capital and wage-labour.[28] Only after fifty-one chapters did Marx embark upon an exposition of the concept of class; and, as is well known, this remains only in the form of an unfinished draft.

For Weber, by contrast, classes are not agents of specific socioeconomic mechanisms, but market subjects (albeit only partially aware of their common identity) whose bargaining opportunities are determined by their differential endowment with certain properties or acquisitions. Accordingly, the class to which A belongs is decided by the question: *How much does he have?* (i.e., how great are his market resources?); whereas for Marx the crucial factor is: *What does he do?* What is his position in the process of production? Weber's interrogation is in turn the answer to his primary problem

[26] Weber, *Economy and Society*, II, p. 928.

[27] Marx, op. cit., pp. 279–80.

[28] 'These classes are . . . an empty phrase if I am not familiar with the elements on which they rest. E.g. wage labour, capital, etc.' Karl Marx, *Grundrisse*, Penguin/NLR 1973, p. 100.

of class: *How much is he likely to obtain?* (i.e., how great is his likeli-
hood of 'procuring goods', 'gaining a position in life', and 'finding
inner satisfactions'?[29]) But Marx poses the issue in a different manner: *What is he likely to do?* Will he essentially maintain or change
the existing society?[30]

It is in the light of his strict market definition of class that Weber's
concept of status groups has to be understood. Weber does not really
think of class and status as two distinct dimensions of stratification,
relating respectively to economic position and social status; he sees
them rather as opposites. Status groups derive from non-capitalist
societies, are contrary to market rationality, and, by their survival in
the modern world interfere with the free development of capitalism.
'Those men whose fate is not determined by the chance of using
goods or services for themselves on the market, e.g., slaves, are not,
however, a class in the technical sense of the term. They are, rather,
a status group.'[31] 'Acquisition classes are favoured by an economic
system oriented to market situation, whereas status groups develop
and subsist more readily where economic organization is of a
monopolistic and liturgical character and where the economic needs
of corporate groups are met on a feudal or patrimonial basis.' A
certain group may be both a class and a status group and Weber
remarks that 'Property classes often constitute the nucleus of a
status group.' But he then comes to his main argument: 'Every
status society lives by conventions, which regulate the style of life,
and hence creates economically irrational consumption patterns and
fetters the free market through monopolistic appropriations and by
curbing the individual's earning power.'[32] In the section on class,
status and party in the second part of *Economy and Society*, Weber
tells us: 'Now status groups hinder the strict carrying through of
the sheer market principle. In the present context they are of interest
to us only from this one point of view.'[33]

[29] Weber, op. cit., I, p. 302.

[30] From *The German Ideology* and *The Communist Manifesto* onwards, Marx's
conception of class and class struggle developed out of a confrontation with German idealism and utopian socialism. Central to this new viewpoint was the
discovery of agents and mechanisms of social change over and above well-meaning
intellectuals, secret conspirers, education or *coups d'état*: namely, the oppressed
classes themselves and their struggles against their exploiters.

[31] Weber, op. cit., II, p. 928.

[32] Weber, op. cit., I, p. 307.

[33] Weber, op. cit., II, p. 930.

In Marxist terms the distribution of status honour is an aspect of the functioning of ideology in society. It has been shown – for instance, by Frank Parkin – that this distribution does not rest on 'the moral evaluations of the population at large . . . but mainly [on] the evaluations of dominant class members.'[34] This is a correct observation. But the essential point in this context is the following one: the Weberian dichotomy between market class and status honour, deriving from the dichotomy between feudalism and capitalism as neo-classical ideal economic types, hinders an analysis of the functioning of ideology in capitalist class societies. On the one hand, ideology plays an inherent and central role in the reproduction and class struggles of capitalist society, rather than the external and dysfunctional one suggested by Weber's marginalist-inspired conception of capitalist rationality. On the other hand, there seems little basis for assuming *a priori* that the effective role of ideology is reducible to prestige stratification; or even that the latter is of greater significance than, for example, structuring of the visibility of performance and reward, formation of individual and collective self-confidence and aspiration, or canalization of discontent. It may be argued from a Marxist point of view, then, that *Weber's distinction between class and status* attributes not too much, but too little importance to the role of social values in the analysis of class.

'Now: "classes", "status groups", and "parties" are phenomena of the distribution of power within a community.'[35] Weber's famous section on class, status and party revolves around a typology of subjects of power. It is thus not surprising that he illustrates the fatal flaw of the subjectivist approach which we identified above. At first sight Weber may seem to be presenting an attractive, circumspect, common-sense view of the place of parties in the 'sphere of power': 'In any individual case, parties may represent interests determined through class situation or status situation, and they may recruit their following respectively from one or the other. But they need be neither purely class nor purely status parties; in fact, they are more likely to be mixed types, and sometimes they are neither.'[36] While conceiving of politics as a 'play of interests', Weber notes that 'in this context "interests" is by no means necessarily an economic category. In the first instance, it is a matter of political interests

[34] Parkin, op. cit., p. 42.
[35] Weber, op. cit., II, p. 927.
[36] Ibid., p. 938.

which rest either on an ideological basis or on an interest in power as such.'[37]

The outcome of this view of parties and power is best illustrated by Weber's examination of various kinds of party (seen as a power-seeking and power-holding subject). 'The classic example of parties in the *modern* state organized primarily around patronage are the two great American parties of the last generation. Parties primarily oriented to issues and ideology have been the older types of Conservatism and Liberalism, bourgeois Democracy, later the Social Democrats and the [Catholic] Centre Party. In all, except the last, there has been a very prominent element of class interest. After the Centre attained the principal points of its original programme, it became very largely a pure patronage party.'[38]

This approach to political parties follows more or less directly from Weber's conception of sociology as the attempt to grasp the subjective meaning which individuals attach to their actions.[39] It certainly does not take us very far towards an understanding of power in society. To know that the American parties are organizations of pure patronage, or that politicians are brought into government through parties 'solely concerned with the attainment of power for their leaders and with securing positions in the administrative staff for their own members. (Then they are "patronage parties".)'[40] – this tells us nothing of the kind of society which they help to maintain and develop. The Weberian method completely avoids analysis of what parties actually do with their patronage, and thus throws little light on problems of the distribution of power: either in the post-Civil War period in the United States (the age of 'robber barons', the rise of populism, and the origins of US imperialism), or in Weimar Germany (where the Centre Party was to play a specific role within the coalition of parties).

[37] Weber, op. cit., I, p. 285.
[38] Ibid., p. 287.
[39] Ibid., pp. 4, 7.
[40] Ibid., p. 285.

2.

Finding the Ruling Class: Defining the Class Character of State Power

So far we have set forth two basic guidelines for a historical-materialist analysis of the problems of class, state and power. First, the central question must concern the class character of state power, since the ruling class is defined as such by its exercise of that power. Secondly, state and political power must be analysed in relation to the ongoing processes of social reproduction and transformation. The primary focus is thus neither the inter-personal relations of various 'elites' (ranging from family background to current social intercourse), nor the decision-making process *per se* (decisions and non-decisions, as well as the issues affected by them). The crucial object is rather the *effects* of the state upon the production and repro-duction of given modes of production, whether actual or hypo-thetical.

How then does the state affect and enter into the processes of social reproduction and change? This is determined by *what* is done (and in certain key cases, *not* done) through the state, and by *how* this is done through the state. The second aspect, which is addressed in the other essay of this volume, refers to the structure of the state apparatus – to the class character of the organizational form of the state. The first aspect refers to state power. When we say that a class holds state power, we mean that what is done through the state positively acts upon the (re-) production of the mode of production, of which the class in question is the dominant bearer. The classical expressions 'taking' and 'holding' state power should not be inter-preted in the sense that state power is a thing which can be grasped in the hands. It is rather a process of interventions in a given society effected by a separate institution which concentrates the supreme rule-making, rule-applying, rule-adjudicating, rule-enforcing and rule-defending functions of that society. To take and to hold state power signifies to bring about a particular mode of intervention of the special body invested with these functions.

An Analytical Schema

In order to study the place of the state within the processes of social reproduction, we have first of all to ask: What is to be reproduced? In answer, we may identify three basic objects: the relations and forces of production, the character of the state apparatus, and the particular ideological superstructure with its specialized apparatuses of qualification and subjection. In all three spheres – economic, administrative-repressive and ideological – positions and processes are reproduced at the same time as suitable individuals are reproduced (or freshly recruited) in sufficient number to fill the positions. That the state has to reproduce itself is probably obvious. But it may be asked why we refer here only to the state apparatus, and not also to state power. It is principally a matter of the order of analytical exposition. In this section we are concerned with the definition of state power in terms of the reproductive effects of state interventions; it would not be very meaningful to locate the character of something in its effects upon the reproduction of itself. Below we shall reverse the sequence: having defined the class character of state power and the ruling class, we shall go on to look at its determinants and the way in which it is maintained.

Since the class character of state power denotes the class character of what is (re-) produced through the interventions of the state, a number of further definitions need to be made. The character of the relations of production raises no difficulty, since it was in terms of these that we originally defined classes. The problem of the class character of the superstructure, however, has hardly ever been systematically tackled by Marxists. In the other essay of this book, we attempt to elaborate the character of the state apparatus. Concurrently, I am working on a class analysis of ideology. But, for the moment, we shall have to leave this as a blank box in the schema of analysis, humbly asking the reader to assume, provisionally, that the class character of ideologies and ideological apparatuses may be determined in a rigorous fashion. Some rough indications that this is so are already rather commonplace.

Finally, we have to order the effects of the state interventions in some way. At least as a first approximation, we may distinguish four types of effect. Three of these are fairly evident logical possibilities. An intervention may further (increase), allow (maintain) or break existing relations of production. However, state power is exercised not according to a pre-established functionalist harmony, but in and through the struggle of antagonistic classes. In this process it may be necessary to have recourse to concessions and compromises, whereby, for instance, the state goes against the logic of capital accumulation without breaking it.

It should be noted that the analysis presented here does not make use of the notion of class interest. Class character is defined by reference to observable relations and structures, the class nature of which is derived from the basic definitions, axioms and propositions of historical materialism. Marxists who have employed the notion of class interest have encountered great difficulty in giving it a precise empirical meaning[41]; and, whether or not it is agreed that application of the concept outside an extremely limited range is inherently dubious, it seems clear that it is dispensable for most scientific purposes. In a theory of rational action, 'interest' may be assigned an exact meaning as part of a definite game, applying to a number of clearly demarcated social situations, on the market and elsewhere. But when used in more complex contexts to denote 'long-term', 'objective' or 'true' interests – that is to say, something other than factual preferences – the notion seems to provide a spurious objectivity to essentially ideological evaluations. Be that as it may, my use of the concepts of class and relations of production should be perfectly acceptable to Marxists, and, at least for the sake of the argument, to non-Marxists as well.

On the basis of the above remarks, we may now propose the following analytical schema for location of the ruling class and assessment of the class character of a given state power.

[41] At least this is my impression even of Poulantzas's treatment of the subject in *Political Power and Social Classes* (op. cit) and *Fascism and Dictatorship* (NLB 1974). The same point is cogently argued in Claus Offe's penetrating essay: 'Klassenherrschaft und politisches System. Zur Selektivität politischer Institutionen', in his book *Structurprobleme des Spätkapitalistischen Staates*, Frankfurt/Main 1972.

Class character of state power (=effects of state interventions).

Effect on class character of state apparatus	Effect on relations of production			
			Go	
	Further	Maintain	against	Break
Further	1	2	3	(4)
Maintain	25	6	7	8
Go against	9	10	11	12
Break	(13)	14	15	16

The logical possibilities 4 and 13 appear to be empirically out of the question. Strictly speaking, we should also have charted the effects upon the class character of the ideological superstructure. But that would have yielded 4^3 (i.e., 64) cells, and there are typographical limitations, if none other, on even my taxonomic zeal. In fact, the schema is intended not as a collection of pigeon-holes, but as a guide to, and reminder during the course of, concrete analysis. It is proposed as an instrument with which to answer questions such as that which was posed by Maurice Dobb in his debate with Paul Sweezy over the transition from feudalism to capitalism: Which class ruled in England prior to the 17th-century Civil War?[42] It is also relevant to the current debate in France on whether contemporary state power in that country is monopoly-capitalist or bourgeois in character[43], as well as to the seemingly interminable dispute on the Left about the nature of the Soviet Union.

However, a number of further points have to be clarified and specified in order to render the schema capable of application. The only effects we can consider in the present context are direct and immediate ones; if we were to go beyond these, we would incorporate the dialectics of social contradictions into the definition of state power, with, at times, the most absurd results. For example, on the eve of the Great French Revolution, in the throes of a deep fiscal crisis, the *ancien régime* continued to uphold a fiscal structure based upon noble privilege. This quite rapidly proved to be a major cause of the outbreak of the Revolution. In the medium term, then, this manifestation of state power had the effect of breaking up the nobility's feudal privileges and establishing a bourgeois state. But

[42] M. Dobb, 'A Reply', in R. Hilton (ed.) *The Transition from Feudalism to Capitalism*, NLB 1976, p. 62.

[43] See, for instance, the debate in *La Nouvelle Critique*, February 1977, op. cit.

it would be ridiculous to call the fiscal policies of the *ancien régime* an expression of bourgeois state power. In view of this extreme possibility, a rigorous analysis cannot allow tampering with the time-scale, even though the consequences may not always be so fatal.

At the same time, it is clear that, in a particular situation, there are a number of different ways in which the existing relations of production or class state may be maintained or furthered. Thus, a certain intervention may very well go against prevailing ruling–class opinion, while objectively furthering or maintaining its mode of exploitation and domination. A well-known case in point is Roosevelt's New Deal: 'The rich may have thought that Roosevelt was betraying his class; but Roosevelt certainly supposed [reflecting in spring 1935 on the mounting opposition from business circles] . . . that his class was betraying him.'[44]

This frequent phenomenon, which is of major importance in understanding social dynamics, is obscured by the concentration on 'issues' and 'decisions' characteristic of the methodology of the pluralist subjectivists.

State Power and State Apparatus

In the practice of both science and politics, the problems of state power and the ruling class assume great complexity. Normally, within a single society there coexist several different modes of production, as well as three or more classes each capable of different forms of alignment. Moreover, these classes are often divided into fractions, whose precise comparative power it may be crucial to assess. To take another example, the schema itself provides for a number of ambiguous combinations, such as maintenance of given relations of production together with breaking of the corresponding state apparatus, or vice versa. All these problems are the subject of intense debate within the labour movement and have to be tackled head on.

State power and state apparatus are analytically distinct concepts – that much is quite clear. But what is their range of variation in relation to each other? Is it adequate to name class A the ruling class, even where the state apparatus is still maintained and impregnated

[44] A. Schlesinger, Jr., *The Age of Roosevelt*, Vol. III, London 1960, p. 273.

by class B, on the grounds that the mode of exploitation represented by class A is furthered above others by the state? This is not an exercise in abstract thinking. The transition from feudalism to capitalism raises just this question in a number of instances.[45] On the eve of the English Civil War, little remained of feudal relations of production, but the absolutist Stuart state apparatus was still fundamentally feudal in the sense elaborated in the other essay of this book. Nor did the abolition of serfdom in Russia involve any change in the Tsarist state. In fact, in most countries other than France, such disjunctures seem to have been the rule rather than the exception. Similar ones may also be found in the transition from capitalism to socialism, with the important qualification that here a decisive change in the state apparatus precedes transformation of the relations of production. The NEP period in the USSR, when maintenance of a new socialist state apparatus was combined with the fostering of both capitalist and petty-commodity production, is probably the clearest example of such a phenomenon.

These well-known cases of disjuncture between state and economy provide glimpses of a number of areas of complexity. Not only do several different classes and modes of production co-exist; they also inter-penetrate one another in many ways, giving rise to hybrid forms and special transmutations. Neither relations of production nor forms of state and ideology are single entities which either do or do not exist. For instance, neither in Prussia nor in Russia did the abolition of serfdom and the development of grain-growing for the export market entail the disappearance of labour rent and a dependent labour force on the noble estates.[46] The English aristocracy continues to dominate the countryside to this day; and among the feudal forms retained by the English state apparatus is a House of

---

[45] For an overview see Hilton, op. cit.; the international historians' colloquium published as *L'abolition de la 'féodalité' dans le monde occidental*, 2 vols., Paris 1971; and the vast panorama brilliantly drawn by Perry Anderson in his *Lineages of the Absolutist State*, NLB, London 1975.

[46] Anderson, op. cit., pp. 273 f., 348 ff. The classical works are: Lenin, *The Development of Capitalism in Russia*, in *Collected Works* Vol. 3, Moscow 1964; and the summaries of Max Weber's research into the subject contained in his essays 'Entwicklungstendenzen in der Lage der ostelbischen Landarbeiter', and 'Agrarstatische und sozialpolitische Betrachtungen über zum Fideikommissum in Preussen', in his *Gesammelte Aufsätze zur Sozial- und Wirtschaftsgeschichte*, Tübingen 1924, and *Gesammelte Aufsätze zur Soziologie und Sozialpolitik*, Tübingen 1924, respectively.

Lords, which had more than a purely symbolic and ceremonial significance as late as the time of the 1945–1951 Labour Government.[47]

The above schema is intended as an instrument with which to unravel these complexities and particularities, not as an *a priori* grid serving to conceal or ignore them. It will be of little use if it is applied in mechanistic manner. The attempt to determine the class character of state power and the ruling class necessarily involves risky judgments and qualitative analysis. But if it is grounded on conceptual clarification and elaboration of criteria, the undertaking need be neither arbitrary nor unrealizable. The problems we have just mentioned call for further specification in at least three important respects: the weight to be attached to the character of the state apparatus; the meaning of class alliance; and the content of hegemony within an alliance composed of entire classes or fractions thereof.

On the whole, Marxists have tended to allot a crucial importance to the character of the state apparatus – from the government to the repressive apparatus. Thus, they have not suggested that the bourgeoisie was the ruling class in Tsarist Russia between 1861 and 1917, or that it constituted, together with the petty bourgeoisie, the ruling class of the USSR from the launching of NEP to the campaigns of collectivization and industrialization. Similarly, analysis of the bourgeois revolution in England has centred on the period between 1640 and 1689, rather than on the earlier dismantling of seigneurial rents and rights. But if these approaches have been correct, and if the distinction between state power and state apparatus is valid, then attachment of such weight to the character of the latter must still be grounded in a theoretical elucidation! At first sight it may even appear to contradict a fundamental proposition of historical materialism: that which concerns the determinant role of the economic base.

The key role accorded to the character of the state apparatus derives from the definition of the latter as a material crystallization of the relationships and division of labour dominant in society. Its tenacious materiality thus provides an objective point of insertion of a time dimension into the analysis of state power. In order to pre-

---

[47] The Lords delayed implementation of the government's steel nationalization bill until after the new elections of 1950. See D. Howell, *British Social Democracy*, London 1976, p. 155.

clude *ad hoc* juggling with the time scale and with long and contradictory chains of indirect causation, we have had to confine the
analysis of state power to the direct and immediate effects of state
interventions. However, there is evidently a strategic time dimension to the consolidation and preservation of state power and the
position of the ruling class, situated as these processes are within the
confrontation of opposing classes. The character of the state
apparatus is crucial to the indirect and delayed effects of state interventions in the economy and ideological superstructure. But these
may be taken into account without recourse to an elastic time scale,
so long as the direct and immediate effects of state policies are
assigned primary importance in study of the character of the state
apparatus.

The state apparatus occupies this special place in relation to the
positions of the ruling class for two main reasons. First, everything
that is done by the state is done through the state apparatus; it thus
provides a filter determining the modality of state economic and
ideological interventions. Moreover, the manner in which state
economic and ideological policies of a given aim and content are
actually implemented is a crucial determinant of their effects, particularly those of an indirect and intermediate kind.

Secondly, the state apparatus, as a material condensation of class
relations, affords a strategic base for an overall change in state policy.
Once it is entrenched in the state apparatus, the ruling class or
hegemonic class of an alliance enjoys a privileged position of
strength, from which it may proceed to withdraw concessions and
end or shift alliances.

Perhaps the most obvious illustration of the way in which the
character of the state apparatus influences the outcome of various
policies is provided by the effects of ostensibly anti-feudal land
reforms upon landowner-peasant relations. The impact of these
varies greatly indeed from the French Revolution through 19th-
century Prussia and Russia to the contemporary Third World. In
France, the revolutionary bourgeois state carried through such a
radical abolition of feudalism that even the post-1815 Restoration
was unable to reverse the process; whereas the control exercised over
the state by the Prussian Junkers and Russian *dvoryanstvo* for a long
time made it possible for them to maintain their rule over the countryside with only slight modifications here and there. Nationalizations
of capitalist enterprise offer another example. Although the post-

war nationalizations in Western Europe – from Finland to France, from Britain to Austria – indicated a real temporary weakness of the bourgeoisie, they posed no threat to its power. For the capitalist character of the state apparatus ensured that the nationalized enterprises were from the very beginning administered on capitalist lines, and thus easily reintegrated into the bourgeois order.

The second reason for the particular importance of the state apparatus is best illustrated by the early history of the socialist revolutions – from the Russian October to the Cuban experience. If we disregard the shortlived and unsuccessful period of Russian War Communism, all of these revolutions initially fostered peasant petty-commodity production and even capitalist enterprise, at the same time as they brought about a more or less complete smashing and transformation of the bourgeois state apparatus. There thus arose a class alliance comprising the proletariat, the petty-bourgeoisie and the 'national bourgeoisie'. Within this alliance, if has often been said, the working class played the leading, hegemonic role, because the proletarian character of the state apparatus secured for it a decisive position of strength from which to end the alliance and embark upon socialist construction.

In the Russian case, the previous revolutionary transformation of the state apparatus enabled this historical turn to be accomplished within a basic political continuity – even if it did not rule out violence and purges at the top. By contrast, where a particular class complements its economic advance by gaining the upper hand in the state apparatus, the rupture of the former class alliance has tended to take the form of a more or less violent revolutionary break. Although the subject cannot be explored here, the intriguing complexity of most bourgeois revolutions is probably attributable to the fact that the feudal aristocracy did not rule alone before the revolution. In most states, it seems rather to have formed and led an alliance with the bourgeoisie (or a fraction of it). Revolution was then precipitated by a challenge to that hegemony by the bourgeoisie (or by fractions of it, perhaps not previously allied to one another, or newly linked up with subordinate fractions of the aristocracy). In some such way it may be possible to gain a theoretical understanding of the character of Stuart Britain and of the conflicting forces within the Civil War – a war which has been empirically designated by its foremost historian as one of 'country *versus* court'.[48] Fresh light may also be cast

---

[48] C. Hill, *The Century of Revolution, 1603–1714*, Edinburgh 1961, p. 102.

on the large role of non-bourgeois popular forces in bourgeois revolutions, and many other phenomena.

Now, the state apparatus itself bears the imprint of definite class relations: if the economic base of a class undergoes erosion and collapse, or is not set again on solid foundations, then its impact on the state apparatus must evolve accordingly, although perhaps with some time-lag. This process too is well known from the history of the transition from feudalism to capitalism. However, there is more to disjuncture between the state apparatus and the dominant relations of production than just a time-lag. Co-existence of the two involves various forms of inter-penetration and permutation of classes and modes of production. Nevertheless, in any given society there is only a single state. It is true that it is composed of a number of different apparatuses, whose mode of inter-relation tends to correspond to the intricacy of the social formation. But except in times of acute political crisis, these apparatuses form a more unified system than the one produced by the circulation processes which articulate the different modes of production. Thus, while basically determined by the class relations of society, the state apparatuses – as a materialized condensation of those same relations – tend to manifest them with a particular rigidity.

The discontinuity between the specific unified materiality of the state apparatus and the complex pattern of interpenetrating classes and modes of production constitutes another basic reason why state power is not a redundant concept. Much important knowledge would never be produced were we simply to say that the class whose mode of dominance is manifested in the organization of the state apparatus is the one which holds state power and makes up the ruling class. The situation where a state furthers one mode of production while retaining a state apparatus impregnated by the dominant class of another provides us with a valuable insight into the relations between class, state and power, as well as an important key to the future development of society and its class relations.

Definitions and Procedures

Bearing in mind these considerations, we may now propose the following definitions and basic analytical procedures. In order to account for the complexity of social formations, the schema presented above normally has to be applied at least *twice*, in the course of investigating the effects of state interventions upon two distinct relevant types of relations of production, state apparatus and ideological structure. A single class may be the ruling class in cases 1 to 11 (in the schema on page 147), but it does not necessarily rule alone, even in case 1. One exemplification of case 11 is perhaps the first Perón regime in Argentina. In its organization and mobilization of the working class and in its drastic re-distribution policies, it may be said to have largely acted against both the capitalist state and capitalist relations of production; at the same time, however, it broke with neither of these and did not offer a socialist alternative.[49] Quite soon, of course, this proved to be an untenable position, and when the ruling capitalist class re-asserted itself, Perón fled into exile. To take another example, it is clear that Meiji Japan furthered both a capitalist state and capitalist relations of production. But it also maintained important features of the feudal imperial state and the aristocratic estates, as well as of feudal clientelism in both industrial and agricultural relations of production. This combination indicates that an alliance of classes was in power.[50]

Our intention here is not to determine the class character of this or that regime, but rather to indicate the crucial questions involved. Thus, in order to assess the character of state power and find the ruling class, it is necessary to look for the effects on the economic, political and ideological position of *several* classes, not just a single one. This raises the intricate problem of the comparative weight to be attached to the effects on different classes, and to the various policies of a given regime. For instance, Perón not only went against the positions of the bourgeoisie; he also promoted them – particularly, it seems, those of medium-size domestic capital producing for the internal market. No general procedures can serve here as substitute for the tools and skills of the historian, or the perceptive practice of the political cadre. Below, we shall touch on certain strategic aspects to which particular attention must be paid.

[49] The real wages of unskilled workers increased by forty per cent between 1946 and 1948 – a figure which does not take into account the multitude of welfare benefits. See P. Waldmann, *Der Peronismus 1943–1955*, Hamburg 1974, p. 202. With the economic crisis of 1950 Perón turned to the right.

[50] Under external imperialist threat, a fraction of the feudal class came to develop an indigenous industrial bourgeoisie and a new state. For a political history of this fascinating revolution, see *inter alia* W. Beasley, *The Meiji Restoration*, Stanford 1972. The misleading term 'restoration' derives from the fact that the initial goal was to restore to the current emperor (Meiji) an imperial power which had been undermined by the *Shogun-ate* leaders of the upper aristocracy.

It should also be noted that the question of state power and the ruling class has to focus on the content and effects of state policies. It would not be correct simply to compare the positions of various classes before and after a fixed point in time – the fall of a certain political regime, for example. For those positions may have changed as a result of mutations in the parameters of state power, the composition of the productive forces, the character of the international context, and so on.

On the other hand, the analysis must take into account the previous relative positions of two or more classes or different modes of production, investigating the effects of state interventions upon their relations of subordination and superordination. The furtherance of a given mode of production – for instance, petty-commodity production in a capitalist society – may not in fact alter its subordinate position within the social formation. Conversely, policies which go against the upper aristocracy or monopoly capital may not directly undermine their superordinate position in the short or even medium term.

In the interests of analytical order, we shall now attempt to bring the multitude of possible combinations of state interventions into certain delimiting sets or defining thresholds. For purposes of definition only, effects on ideology will be treated as subsumable under those on the economy and state apparatus, although this practice should certainly not be carried over into analysis of the actual dynamics of a particular class rule. Since in this section we are concerned only to define the class character of state power and locate the ruling class, rather than to determine how the latter rules, we shall use the term classes to refer only to the ruling classes of different modes of production – the exploiting classes in the case of exploitative modes.

Rule by a single class (or fraction thereof) will cover systems of state interventions ranging from that in which the state furthers or maintains the positions of one class alone, through that where a specific class has a *predominant* position in at least the state apparatus, to that where the state goes against the positions of a dominant class without furthering the positions of another, and without maintaining those of another economically dominant class (where one exists). The range stretches from the peak of power of a ruling class to the stage when, while still holding a monopoly of power, it is forced to retreat and yield concessions.

The span of *a class alliance in power* touches at one end the simple instance where the positions of two or more classes are furthered by the state; and at the other end the case where the state goes against, in no more than one sphere, the positions of a class which is predominant in at least one sphere – at the same time as it *both* maintains at least one of the dominant positions of that class or furthers its non-dominant positions *and* furthers the positions of one or more other classes. Bare maintenance of the non-dominant positions of a class – such as the petty bourgeoisie in capitalist societies – should thus not be interpreted as evidence of its participation in a ruling alliance.

A class alliance should be distinguished, then, both from relations of political and ideological *support* between two or more classes (that is to say, the situation where one or more classes merely support or acquiesce in the dominance of another) and from *the granting of concessions within* a given economic and political structure (for example, reduction of the working-day and introduction of social security benefits within capitalism). A class alliance is indicated only where the effects touch upon the *type* of relations of production, state apparatus and ideological system. 'Alliance' is here employed as an analytical concept, which should not be personalized by equation with explicit deals. Still, it does denote a real bond between classes, and not merely a relation of co-existence. This link is manifested by the fact that at one and the same time the positions of two or more classes are actively promoted and protected by the state.

Poulantzas's concept of 'power bloc' – referring to an entity distinct from a ruling class alliance – seems to serve little purpose. Poulantzas derived this concept from Marx's analysis in *The Eighteenth Brumaire* of the power constellation which issued from the French February Revolution. But Marx was there discussing the joint rule of different fractions of a single class: the bourgeoisie.[51] Particularly when the 'power bloc' involves only two or more fractions of the same class, the concept appears to be an unnecessary, and at worst positively bewildering, circumlocution. It does, however, point up an important feature of ruling classes, which they

[51] Because of the development of capitalist relations of agricultural production, Marx explicitly regarded the landowners as a fraction of the bourgeoisie. See *The Eighteenth Brumaire of Louis Bonaparte*, in Karl Marx, *Surveys from Exile*, Penguin/NLR 1973, p. 174.

have in common with ruled ones: the fact that they are not homogeneous monoliths.

By the term *class fractions*, we will refer only to those divisions within a class which are rooted in the differential position occupied by certain of its sections within the relations of production. Examples of such layers are: the upper aristocracy and the gentry within the feudal hierarchy; sections of capital differentiated with respect to their level of concentration (big, or monopoly, small or competitive); strata exhibiting various degrees of dependence upon imperialist monopoly capital (comprador and national bourgeoisie); different kinds of capital (mercantile, industrial, financial). The rule of a given class fraction can be assessed by specifying its position vis-à-vis the relations of production and the state apparatus. The state apparatus of monopoly capital, for instance, tends to have a managerial-technocratic character which is in marked contrast to the parliamentary-bureaucratic one of competitive capital.

Class alliances and the cleavage of the ruling class raise the question of *hegemony* or direction. Hegemony developed as a Marxist concept in the Russian labour movement of the late nineteenth century, where it referred to the strategic role of working class leadership of allied classes in the bourgeois revolution against the feudal Tsarist state. In the West, the concept has since then spread through the important and penetrating work of Antonio Gramsci. Gramsci both elaborated and radically extended the concept, using it to designate not only leadership of an alliance but also the 'leadership' of one class over another in an antagonistic relationship – for example, bourgeois hegemony over the proletariat after the end of feudalism.[52]

Since these two types of non-coercive direction are vastly different, they should not be denoted by the same concept. In an alliance the object of reference is leadership of a team for a common task, whereas in the antagonistic relation it is the rule of an exploiter class over another class. We shall employ the term hegemony, then, exclusively to denote direction of a class alliance.[53] Gramsci expounded at length, albeit in fragments, the highly complex modali-

[52] See P. Anderson, 'The Antinomies of Antonio Gramsci', in *New Left Review* No. 100, Nov. 1976–Jan. 1977, pp. 15 ff.

[53] Poulantzas also makes this restriction in his application of the concept of hegemony to internal relationships within the 'power bloc'. See *Political Power and Social Classes*, op. cit.

ties of hegemonic direction. One thing only needs to be emphasized here. Both in the Russian tradition and in Gramsci's writings hegemony does not mainly involve ideological supremacy. It is above all a *political* concept, referring in the former case to the political form of the anti-Tsarist revolution and the post-Tsarist state, and in the latter to the state of the capitalist West – to the mode of leadership exercised by the bourgeoisie in the establishment and maintenance of its rule, as well as to that utilized by the proletariat in its strategy for the overthrow of the capitalist class.[54] Alliance naturally implies a relation of ideological direction and consent rather than one of coercion. Moreover, ideological direction of a heterogeneous alliance involves as a global perspective attention to the needs and demands of all its components. The needs of other sections must be not reduced but related to those of the leading fraction, albeit as a subordinate part. Plekhanov, Axelrod and Lenin, as well as Gramsci, all stressed this task of a hegemonic proletariat. But while hegemony should not be used to designate a structural aspect of the state – which involves relations distinct from that of class leadership – the exercise of hegemony has to be manifested in the form of the state. For the hegemony of a given class or fraction signifies that it will be or is now accorded predominance in the state apparatus as part of a class alliance, either in power or struggling for power.

At this point we should mention a specific problem which has been raised by current conceptions of state monopoly capitalism and by the debates they have stimulated. Does monopoly capital rule alone in the advanced capitalist countries, or is it rather the dominant fraction in the power of the entire bourgeois class? Again, we shall seek here only to elaborate the precise questions that must be answered in any scientific solution of the problem. In the present stage of the capitalist mode of production, big monopoly capital enjoys a naturally dominant position owing to the degree of concentration of capital. Thus, a state which today furthers or maintains capitalist relations of production *ipso facto* essentially furthers or maintains the dominance of monopoly capital.

However, fractions of a single class are naturally more closely intertwined than the classes of different modes of production. It seems reasonable to argue, then, that one of these fractions can be

[54] Cf. C. Buci-Glucksmann, *Gramsci et l'Etat*, Paris 1976.

held to exercise exclusive power only if two further conditions are satisfied – if, that is, the class fractions stand in a conflictual relationship, and if the state systematically intervenes in favour of one of them. To what extent the current relationship between monopoly and competitive capital is marked by conflict is an empirical question which cannot be answered here. Nevertheless, two possibilities should be carefully distinguished: first, the existence of a serious conflict between them, in the sense that advantages to the one are disadvantages to the other; and second, a relationship within which their positions, while not directly colliding, are so independent of each other that a strategy directed against monopoly capital may include maintenance of the positions of the competitive bourgeoisie. The latter variant appears to me more likely than the former one, although it is in any event obvious that there is also an antagonistic relationship between the competitive bourgeoisie and the working class.

Now, conflicts within the bourgeoisie may have either economic or political roots – may be grounded either in the pattern of the circulation of capital or in the interventions of the state. (In the latter case, the state converts non-conflictual economic differences into conflicts over discriminatory treatment.) Whatever the basis of the antagonism, exclusive exercise of state power by monopoly capital would imply that the state systematically goes against the positions of non-monopoly capital. This would involve discrimination against the latter with regard to credit facilities, taxation, subsidies, state purchases, and so on; restriction of its access to and influence over the state apparatus; establishment of a technocratic administration tied overwhelmingly to big monopoly capital; and closure or severe constriction of the channels used by small business in lobbying parliament or the civil service.

However, bearing in mind the distinction we drew earlier between alliance and support, we should note that exclusive rule of monopoly capital precludes neither an appeal to nor assurance of the support of the rest of the bourgeoisie.

Before we can leave the arid path of definitions and specifications for the more exciting open fields of substantial problems, we must say a word about the meaning of 'further', 'maintain' and other terms as applied to different modes of production. Regarding the concept of modes of production, the reader is referred to the exegetic clarification contained in my *Science, Class and Society*; while for the development of the concepts of the feudal, capitalist and socialist state apparatuses, the other essay of this volume should be consulted. On that basis we can make some initial observations.

Generally speaking, to *further* given relations of production means to *extend* them – for example, to subject a free peasantry to feudal obligations, to open up new areas and labour resources for capitalist exploitation, or to increase the socialist sector of the economy. In relation to the state and ideological system, this involves expanding the relevant class-specific apparatuses. But it should also include *intensifying*, within a fixed range, the exploitation or domination of the ruling class of a given mode of production – for example, increasing peasant bondage, seigneurial rent and dynastic-aristocratic grip on the state apparatus; actively promoting capital accumulation and capitalist 'factory despotism', and augmenting the surplus-value extracted from the workers; strengthening the national-bureaucratic or national-technocratic character of the state, as well as its pro-capitalist repressive functions; heightening the collective superordination and diminishing the individual subordination of workers in relation to managers, bureaucrats and intellectuals. (These two aspects – extension and intensification – may not be harmonious with each other, but may express conflicting tendencies which have to be weighed together with careful consideration. Stalinist industrialization provides an obvious example of such discord.)

To *maintain* means more than just passively to accept what exists and to defend it against challenge from the exploited classes. Normally, it involves above all running the system, providing resources and overcoming crises – whether famines, business cycles or planning bottlenecks, dynastic successions, parliamentary crises, or working-class alienation and demobilization – resolving conflicts among different sectors of the population and apparatuses of society, and handling external relations.

To *go against* is essentially the opposite of to further. It involves restriction of a given mode of production and alleviation of the exploitation or domination of its dominant class. As a consistent policy, this is an expression of the power of an adversary class. But a ruling class may also go against the positions of certain of its own members in order to promote the current or long-term position of the class as a whole. To this end, it may, for example, open up an exclusive aristocracy to new entrants, restrict the exploitation of natural resources, employ non-proletarian experts, or keep wages down for the sake of accumulating collective production goods.

The use of state power against the position of the ruling class, even where it may benefit from these interventions in the long run, indicates that that class suffers from a weakness of one kind or another. It is necessary, therefore, to distinguish such measures not only from revolutionary breaks but also from policies which directly promote or maintain ruling class positions.

To *break* the positions of a class is defined not in terms of suddenness and violence, but by qualitative content. In respect of feudalism, this content lies in elimination of seigneurial rents and dues, creation of a free market in land and labour, and dismantling of the dynastic-seigneurial state. The suppression of capitalism puts an end to the situation where production is determined by the profitability of competing individual capitals, by the commodity character of labour, and by the intervention of the bureaucratic-technocratic state. In the case of socialism, a qualitative change would signify privatization of the means of production, and abolition of planned production for social use and of the collective superordination of the working class. Breaking the positions of one class entails, directly or indirectly, creating space for the rise of other classes.

These definitions may be further specified in such a way that they also apply to fractions of classes.

What then does the ruling class do when it rules? Essentially, it reproduces the economic, political and ideological relations of its domination. This rule is exercised through state power, that is to say, through the interventions or policies of the state and their effects upon the positions of the ruling class within the relations of production, the state apparatus and the ideological system. The class character of state power is thus defined by the effects of state measures on class positions in these three spheres. The possibilities and viability of the rule of a class are determined by the tendencies and contradictions of the modes of production within which and in relation to which it is exercised. The next section will deal with this determination. The rule of a class is moreover deployed in struggle with other classes, according to a number of modalities which we shall examine further below.

3.

Determinants of State Power: The State in the Reproduction of Society

In very general terms, the character of state power is defined by the two fundamental processes of determination of the superstructure by the base – processes which in reality are two aspects of the same determination.[55] One of these is the systemic logic of social modes of production, that is to say, the tendencies and contradictions of the specific dynamic of each mode. The other is the struggle of classes, defined by their position in the mode of production. These two forms of determination by the base are logically interrelated in the basic theory of historical materialism, and serious distortions of an 'economist' or 'politicist' nature result from their dissociation. The former determination constitutes the structural fit of state and society; the second the manner in which it is actively experienced and fought out by the ruling and ruled classes. This section and the following one will treat the two modes in turn.

From a structural point of view, there are *four axes of determination of* the character of state power: 1. The stage of development of the relevant mode of production; 2. The place of the mode of production within the international stage of the same mode; 3. The conjunctural articulation of all modes existing within the social formation; 4. The insertion of the social formation in the international system of related social formations at a given point in time. In the Second International these axes tended to be reduced to the first one; the reductionist impasse which resulted was unblocked primarily by the theory and practice of Lenin. Lenin's achievement was to develop the revolutionary strategic thought of the founder of

[55] See my *Science, Class and Society* (op. cit) pp. 398 ff.

historical materialism, after it had been discarded by economistic and parliamentarist evolutionism.[56]

The ability of a particular bourgeoisie (or fraction thereof) to hold state power is thus structurally determined by: 1. the stage reached by capitalism in the society in which it functions; 2. the central or peripheral position, and the advanced or retarded stage, of the capital which it represents, as well as the expansion, crisis or contraction of international capitalism as a whole; 3. the manner in which its relations to feudalism and petty commodity production, as well as its own internal cleavages, have historically evolved and currently manifest themselves in the given constellation of forces; and 4. the international conjuncture facing the social formation – the peculiar strengths and weaknesses of the latter within the international configuration of harmonious or conflicting forces.

The reproduction and transformation of society develops within the space delimited by these four axes of determination. Reproduction of a social formation usually follows the course of what Marx, in his economic analyses, termed expanded (as opposed to simple) reproduction. In other words, society is not as a rule maintained exactly as it was at a previous period: rather its fundamental structure and dynamic are preserved, even though the number, size and concrete forms of the various positions and roles may change, together with the individuals who have to fill them. The stable foundation of the structure is theoretically defined by the concepts of the relations of production, and the class character of the state and ideological system.

In a basic sense, *the reproduction of a society denotes its mode of functioning as an ongoing social process*, throughout which goods are produced, distributed and consumed, laws and commands are issued and applied, violence is displayed and exercised, and ideas are inculcated and lived. Reproduction (as well as transformation) has two objects: the positions of a given social structure and the persons required to fill them.[57] Within the continuous process of

[56] However, Lenin could start from the point reached by Marx. The best example of Marx's complex strategical thought is probably his letter, as a leader of the First International, to Meyer and Vogt on the inter-relationship of the Irish and English revolutions. See 'Marx to Meyer and Vogt, 9 April 1870', in *The First International and After*, Penguin/NLR 1974.

[57] Cf. D. Bertaux, *Destins personnels et structures de classe*, Paris 1977.

society, these aspects are internally related in the mode of mutual reproductive conditioning. Human beings who have been shaped into social individuals by (among other ideological apparatuses) a particular kind of family tend to form the same or a similar kind of family themselves and to submit their own children to it. A given set of relations of production forms part of the universe in which the new generation – entering through class-specific gates and along class-specific paths – has to find its material means of support and, thereby, reproduce those initial relations. In this way the exploited have to deliver surplus labour to their exploiters, who thus acquire the resources to maintain and continue their exploitation. Every state structure provides specific institutionalized channels, which, backed by instruments of repression, delimit the field of possible politics by determining the issues, demands and forms of expression which are politically relevant. Even radical protest tends to be forced to employ these channels, thus contributing to their reproduction.

It is important to emphasize that social reproduction denotes not a special process of cultural transmission or physical coercion, but the very functioning of society as a whole in a constantly ongoing process. But it should also be stressed that the reproduction of a given mode of production always takes place within a concrete social formation – that is to say, in articulation with other modes of production in an international system. Normally, the reproduction of a particular economic mode of production involves exchange – whether forced or free, equal or unequal – with *other* modes. (Sometimes outright plunder may serve as substitute for commerce.) Integral to the reproduction process of feudalism, for instance, was the links of the seigneuries with market trade. The maintenance of the feudal hierarchy of class relations depended to a considerable extent on the ostentatious consumption of the aristocracy – a phenomenon made possible by exchange.

The State and the Economy

A nodal point in the reproduction of society is the interrelation of state and economy. The intense and controversial debate on state monopoly capitalism has centered on this problem as it presents itself in advanced capitalist society[58]; while recently another im-

[58] See, for example, the collective works *Der Imperialismus der BRD*, Berlin 1967, and *Le capitalisme monopoliste d'état*, 2 vols., Paris 1977; R. Gundel et al., *Zur Theorie des staatsmonopolistischen Kapitalismus*, Berlin 1967; Ph. Herzog,

portant Marxist discussion has revolved around the relation of the national state to international capitalism and the so-called multinational corporations.[59] Once again, our purpose is not to enter directly into the complex substantial issues involved, but to contribute, in however summary a manner, to clarification of the basic questions at stake.

First of all, it is necessary to understand that, even prior to socialism and state monopoly capitalism, the state was always an essential part, and not merely an external guardian, of the reproduction of the economy.

Invariably the state enters into the reproduction of the relations of production by providing the latter with a stabilizing legal framework backed by force. The distribution of the means of production is regulated through inheritance laws, enfiefments and *fideicommissa*, legal definitions of what constitutes a valid market contract, and enactment of nationalization and public ownership. Social relations of production are framed by legal rules which define relations between lord and peasant, master and servant, employer and employee, and manager and worker. The goals of production are patterned not only by plan directives under socialism, but also by feudal regulations concerning rent and the legitimacy of trade outlets, and in capitalism by (for example) the provisions of corporation and commercial law which lay down the obligations of management to owners, customers and creditors, and to the workforce. Expanded reproduction of the mode of production has also everywhere been crucially dependent upon different kinds of state practice: acquisition of new lands and subjugation of free peasants; capture of fresh markets and sources of raw materials; and extension of the socialist orbit.

However, the range and modality of state intervention in the economy vary greatly according to the nature and stage of development of the mode of production. Under feudalism, the crown was usually the largest landowner, and thus took an active part in

---

Politique économique et planification, Paris 1971; S. L. Wygodski, *Der gegenwärte Kapitalismus*, Cologne 1972; M. Wirth, *Kapitalismustheorie in der DDR*, Frankfurt/Main 1972; R. Ebbinghausen (ed.) *Monopol und Staat*, Frankfurt/Main 1974; Projekt Klassenanalyse, *Stamokap in der Krise*, West Berlin 1975; and N. Poulantzas, *Classes in Contemporary Capitalism*, op. cit.

[59] R. Murray, 'Internationalization of Capital and the Nation-State', in *New Left Review* No. 67 (1971); and B. Warren, 'The Internationalization of Capital and the Nation-State: A Comment', in *New Left Review* No. 68; and many other works.

reproduction of the system as *primus inter pares* of feudal lords. The state further had the important obligation to supply the urban population with food.[60] (The breakdown of this system in Petersburg during the war-time winter of 1916–1917 was the proximate cause of the February Revolution.)

The capitalist state left this last problem to market forces, subject in varying degree to legal regulation; it acquired instead an important responsibility for development of the productive forces, especially an infrastructure of means of transport and communication, and technical training and scientific research. As the old climatic harvest cycle was superseded by the business cycle, the state became involved in a new type of crisis management: intervention by means of monetary, tariff and fiscal policies.

Recent decades have witnessed an enormous expansion of the state's role in the reproduction of advanced capitalism, to the point where in the United States about 40%, and in several West European countries more than half of the domestic product passes through the state. This marks a highly significant change from the beginning of the century, when in the USA less than a tenth of the nation's newly-created wealth fell within the sphere of the state. But the fact that capitalism continues to be reproduced shows that *there are no fixed 'commanding heights' of the economy.* Despite bourgeois fears that government taxation of capital accumulation would make reproduction impossible, and despite labourist hopes of strategic nationalization of heavy industry and the banks, the expanded reproduction of capital has not in fact been brought to a halt. Reproduction is a constantly ongoing process, which, like a mighty river, will take new courses when obstacles are erected in its way. The experience of extensive post-war nationalizations in Austria, Britain, Finland, France and Italy demonstrates this very clearly. Given this character of reproduction, a social transformation must, if it is to succeed, also be a continuous process.

The vast expansion of state income has not threatened the reproduction of capitalism because it has mostly been channelled back into the circulation of capital – not only, or even mainly, through state purchases and subsidies, but also and above all through transfers to households. Enmeshed in capitalist relations of production,

[60] See, for instance, S. Kaplan, *Bread, Politics and Political Economy in the Reign of Louis XV*, The Hague 1976.

these latter have had to spend their increased income on consumer goods produced by capitalist enterprise.

Behind the current role of the state in the reproduction of advanced capitalism lies a broad complex of economic and socio-political tendencies. These must be dissected with great care, but let us here simply mention three of the most obvious ones. As both the social character of the productive forces and the interdependence and scale of the economy have assumed increased proportions, so has the state taken on a growing range of functions. Not only does it appear as *Gesamtkapitalist* (total capitalist), legally regulating the system as a whole, managing internal conflicts and providing a common infrastructure; it now actively participates on the labour, commodity and capital markets as a *supercapitalist*, contributing to the supply-and-demand of investment capital, of goods and services produced by capitalist enterprise, and of labour power (through its manpower policies). To a more and more significant extent, the state supplements competitive private capital in the dynamics of the development of the productive forces, through direct and indirect financing and organization of research and development. In some cases, such as that of Britain in the sixties and seventies, the state has taken over the main responsibility for the creation and maintenance of an industrial reserve army, as part of a hitherto rather unsuccessful effort to depress wages and raise the international competitiveness of industry. The state as supercapitalist – as the most important actor on the capitalist market – is not, however, an altogether novel phenomenon. The Japanese state largely assumed this role in the development of a national capitalism during the world conjuncture of the late 19th and early 20th century.[61]

As a super-subject, the state appears as the only capitalist with sufficient resources to tackle many of the problems raised by the enormous scale of advanced technology industries. But its importance does not end here. From the point of view of the capitalist corporation, the national state and its local units are increasingly being transformed into an *object* of market calculations, rather than simply a territory to be secured as a profitable base or area of penetration. The systems of management and communication which have been developed within the big corporations make it possible for them to treat political-territorial units as calculable options in

[61] A. Maddison, *Economic Growth in Japan and the USSR*, London 1969, Ch. 2.

the location of different types of corporately-integrated production and administration. Thus, the new and important feature of 'multinational' corporations seems to lie in their ability to bind together productive units scattered through a number of countries into a single productive process, and thereby to profit from calculated mobility of location – rather than in the simple existence of a multi-local and multinational sphere of company activity, which is an old phenomenon of imperialist expansion. Private management has also shown a considerable capacity to adapt to the changed character of the productive forces.

Thirdly, the form of the expansion of state expenditure should warn us against facile functionalist interpretations of the relation between the state and monopoly capital, and thus against neglect of the dialectics of the class struggle. For, even though such expenditure enters into the reproduction of capital, monopoly sectors have, to put it mildly, never been enthusiastic advocates of social welfare. Nevertheless, this is the type of spending which has increased most rapidly, in recent years even in the United States.[62]

[62] Cf. the figures for Britain presented by I. Gough in 'State Expenditure in Advanced Capitalism', *New Left Review* No. 92 (1975), p. 60.

US public expenditure (federal, state and local) as a percentage of gross domestic product.

Year	Total	Welfare, social insurance, health (excl. veterans' benefits)	Education	Military and police
1902	7	0.4	1.1	0.9
1922	13	0.8	2.3	1.4
1932	21	2.0	4.0	1.8
1940	20[1]	3.0	2.8	1.9
1950	25	4.4	3.4	4.6
1957	28	4.3	3.4	9.2
1974	38	12.0	8.2	5.8[2]

Source: Calculations from *The Statistical History of the United States* (Stanford, Conn. 1965) Series F1–5, Y412–445 (L902–57), and *United Nations Statistical Yearbook 1975* (New York 1976) tables 195 and 201 (1974).

1. The fact that the proportion of public expenditure declined during the New Deal is explained by its relative rigidity in the trough of the Depression, when total production fell. The 1940 figure of 20% should be compared with the 1927 one of 12%.

2. Excludes state and local expenditure.

The character of the growth of public expenditure, as well as the adoption of Keynesian employment policies, must be understood as effects of the strength of the working class and labour movement. However, this third aspect of the expanded role of the state, while among the explicit demands of the working classes, corresponds neither to the logic of capital accumulation nor to the manifest ideology of the business community; in fact, the actual historical dialectic lying behind it is still rather obscure.[63] The problem is highlighted by the instance of the United States, where the achievements of the turbulent thirties and the New Deal appear quite modest when compared to the soaring expenditure of the sixties and seventies.

Now, it should be realized that the reproductive link between state and economy is one of mutual interaction. The economic base determines the political superstructure by entering into the reproduction of state power and the state apparatus. We have seen in the essay on the state apparatus the manner in which the economic division of labour patterns the organisation of the state. It shapes the character of state power by, among other things, providing the basic parameters of state action and structuring the population into classes. Below we shall go more closely into the modalities of class rule; for the moment we must confine ourselves to a mere hint of how the economy intervenes in the reproduction of state power.

State power is wielded in a field composed of two institutionalized relations. The state *represents* class society, above all the ruling class, and it *mediates* social relations between ruler and ruled. To reproduce the state power of a given class (fraction or alliance) is to reproduce its representation in state leadership and the mediation of its supremacy over other classes. Representation and mediation are specific institutional patterns which are generally irreducible to the relations of production. For instance, no political form – whether a

[63] A Swedish Marxist economic historian, Bo Gustafsson, is directing a large research project on the expansion of the public sector. An interim report, which is mainly descriptive in character, has already been published: B. Gustafsson (ed.) *Den offentliga sektorns expansion*, Uppsala 1977.

system of estates, in which clergy, burghers and, occasionally, peasants, are represented, or absolutist monarchy, parliamentarism, military and fascist dictatorship, or party government – may simply be reduced to feudal, capitalist or socialist relations of production. Indeed, by definition, mediation of social relations by the state involves the addition of a new component to the class relations of the economic mode of production.

However, the relations and forces of production impinge upon the functioning of the specifically political processes of representation and mediation, (re-) producing or undermining the political rule of a given class. For example, the general, basic reason why parliamentary or presidential democracy, contrary to the expectations of classical social democrats and liberals alike, has been able to reproduce the representation of the tiny bourgeois class is that the sphere of political representation is not independent of economically determined social relations. The way in which the working classes vote, organize, acquire their leaders, and put forward demands, is crucially affected by their submission and subjection to the bourgeoisie at work and in everyday life. (This subjection to the wealth, expertise and employer control of the bourgeoisie appears to be a much more important determinant than commodity fetishism.)

The bourgeois state typically mediates between the ruling and the ruled classes in formally universalistic (i.e., not overtly class-specific) terms. This appearance is clearly expressed in the motto: 'Equality before the law.' But since this mediation takes place in a social web woven by the relations of production, this formally universalistic intervention tends to reproduce the power of a particular class. Two illustrations will suffice here. During a strike, it is only one side which finds it necessary to disturb 'law and order' by mass meetings and picket lines. Similarly, when programmes of economic reconstruction or modernization are put into effect, big capital and big farmers are in the best position to benefit from them.

Once pronounced, all this is obvious to the point of banality. But very often the mutual reproduction of state and economy is disregarded in favour of a unilateral perspective, in which the sole visible object is either the role of the state in capital accumulation, or else the power constellations appearing on and behind the political stage.

One final point, which was already clearly grasped by Lenin, should be made in discussion of the reproductive interrelation between state and economy. From a political point of view, social reproduction (and revolution) must always be accomplished and secured in an endless chain of concrete situations. The state intervenes not in generalized processes and crises, but in this or that moment and crisis; the relations and forces of production, with all their peculiarities, impinge upon every moment of representation and mediation. Politics as a science has to comprehend the momentous determinations of politics as an art. Lenin's leadership of the victorious October Revolution proved in practice the conjunctural character of revolutionary politics. We shall see presently that success in reproductive politics is based on the same features.

The Three Modes of Ideological Interpellation

Another important aspect of social reproduction, which calls for a number of remarks, is the relationship of ideological reproduction to state power. The frequent emphasis on legitimation of a particular form of rule in the eyes of the ruled masses – a problematic largely issuing from the Weberian and Frankfurt traditions – appears to be seriously misplaced and should be discarded once and for all. This focus on production and maintenance of legitimacy stems from an unwarranted rationalist assumption that the ruled do not rebel only, or mainly, because they consider the rule of their rulers to be justified. But, economic and political constraints apart, there are a number of other reasons why people do not revolt. They may be broadly ignorant of and disinterested in the form of rule to which they are subjected. They may not be aware of alternative modes of social organization, and, even if they are, they may feel powerless to affect the existing state of affairs. However, this ignorance, disinterest or lack of confidence is not simply given, as a psychological characteristic of individuals and groups. It is generated by definite social processes, and forms part of the overall process of social reproduction.[64]

[64] Cf. the distinction between pragmatic and normative acceptance made by Michael Mann in 'The Social Cohesion of Liberal Democracy', *American Sociological Review*, Vol. 35 (1970), pp. 422–39. Exclusive concern with legitimation is often related to the normative conception that every form of rule *should* be based on the true and knowing consensus of the ruled which renders it legitimate. See, for example, J. Habermas, *Legitimationsprobleme im Spätkapitalismus*, Frankfurt/ Main 1972, esp. pp. 162 ff. But that is another question. Interestingly enough, Habermas and Offe both accept Max Weber's ideal type of competitive capitalism.

Ideology functions by moulding personality: it *subjects* the amorphous libido of new-born human animals to a specific social order and *qualifies* them for the differential roles they will play in society.[65] In this process of subjection-qualification all ideology, both revolutionary and conservative, proletarian as well as feudal or bourgeois, interpellates individuals in three basic ways.

1. Ideological formation tells individuals *what exists*, who they are, how the world is, how they are related to that world. In this manner, people are allocated different kinds and amounts of identity, trust and everyday knowledge. The visibility of modes of life, the actual relationship of performance to reward, the existence, extent and character of exploitation and power are all structured in class-specific modes of ideological formation.

2. Ideology tells *what is possible*, providing varying types and quantities of self-confidence and ambition, and different levels of aspiration.

3. Ideology tells *what is right* and wrong, good and bad, thereby determining not only conceptions of legitimacy of power, but also work-ethics, notions of leisure, and views of interpersonal relationships, from comradeship to sexual love.

Contrasting it to modern capitalism, they argue that the enormous increase of state intervention has made necessary a greater degree of ideological legitimation. (Habermas, op. cit., Ch. II; Offe, op. cit., pp. 27–63.) This view tends to mask the important role played in the era of competitive capitalism by such ideological phenomena as human rights declarations, the ascendance of bourgeois nationalism, and the maintenance of powerful established and dissenting religions. It also obscures the economic and political mechanisms of crisis and revolution in the contemporary period – a period which has witnessed the shattering of the economic foundations of Britain's position as a major capitalist power, at least the shaking of US supremacy, and the current politico-economic crisis of bourgeois rule in France and Italy.

[65] Cf. L. Althusser, 'Ideology and Ideological State Apparatuses (Notes Towards an Investigation)', in his *Lenin and Philosophy and Other Essays*, NLB 1971. For reasons which remain unconvincing, Althusser talks of ideological *state* apparatuses, thereby obliterating the peculiar apartness of the state from the rest of society, which has always been regarded as a distinctive feature of the state in the theory of historical materialism. It is precisely because of the cleavage of society into a separate state body and other social institutions that the state is bound up with the division of society into classes. Another weakness of Althusser's important contribution is the manner in which he models his exposition of ideological interpellations exclusively on the operation of conservative, ruling-class ideology. Revolutionary classes, too, are propelled by ideological interpellations.

In spite of the authors' sectarian Maoist leftism, the little book by Alain Badiou and François Balmès – *De l'idéologie*, Paris 1976 – represents another significant addition to the scanty Marxist literature on ideology.

All ideology contains these three modes of interpellation, but one or the other of them may receive greater emphasis in a given ideological discourse, or play a more important role in the process of social reproduction. For example, in the 1930's the leading circles of Swedish monopoly capital engaged in a long and intensive discussion over where to place the emphasis in relation to the Social Democratic government. The 'big five' of the engineering industry wanted to finance an aggressive propaganda campaign on the theme that 'free enterprise' (i.e., capitalism) was right, whereas the leaders of the Employers' Confederation and the Industrial League thought that the new situation called for an offensive according to what was possible – that is to say, presentation of apparently 'neutral' and 'factual' information on the needs of the economy and on the measures which would or not meet them – rather than proclamations of the blessings of free enterprise. The second, more 'objective' line was carried and proved to be eminently successful. Thus, when the government, during the short post-war radicalization, decided to investigate the possibilities of state planning, and even nationalization of a number of branches, the members of the relevant committees were selected from Industrial League experts, who, needless to say, came to the conclusion that nothing should be done.[66]

The Mechanics of Reproduction

We are concerned here not with the processes and problems of reproduction *per se*, but with the way in which they are determined. What, then, maintains social reproduction in the face of social crisis and challenge? There is a widespread tradition, both Marxist and non-Marxist, which answers this question by reference to coercion and/or consent. But that is a quite inadequate approach. 'Consent' masks crucially different forms, while the term coercion is either too undifferentiated or too exclusive.

The process of social reproduction is a totality of economic, political and ideological processes. Each of these contains sanctions, which come into effect if and when the process seems to be going off course. We may call these sanctions, *mechanisms of reproduction*. In class societies they function in and through the class struggle. Conversely, the class struggle is fought out, and the rule of the ruling

---

[66] S. Söderpalm, *Direktörsklubben*, Stockholm 1976.

class is exercised and maintained, in and through these reproductive mechanisms. We may give the names *economic constraint, violence and ideological excommunication* to the mechanisms involved. They are all situated within the context of the four axes of reproduction presented above.

Economic constraint operates at a number of levels, by means of the threat or actuality of ruin, bankruptcy, dislocation, unemployment, poverty or outright starvation. Development of the productive forces renders certain relations of production unviable or uncompetitive. For instance, the concentration of capital restricts the space of small commodity production and small capital. The international post-war boom has been the principal stabilizing pillar of bourgeois rule in the developed capitalist countries, whereas the current weakness of, say, the Italian bourgeoisie is significantly affected by the constraints of the end of that boom.

Economic necessity forced the Russian Bolsheviks to reproduce capitalism and petty commodity production in the 1920s. Various forms of international economic blackmail, such as the attachment of conditions to much-needed loans, has been an important, though seldom decisive, element in the reproduction of capitalism – from Morgan's telegram to Ramsay MacDonald in 1931, which split the Labour Party[67], through the monetary crisis which brought down Blum's Popular Front government[68], to the American refusal of credits to *Unidad Popular* in Chile. The existing relations of production also place restrictions on the way in which production can be organized within a particular economic enterprise, and they largely determine where and how even the most revolutionary peasant or worker can support himself or herself.

The use or threat of physical violence may similarly be deployed on many different levels, ranging from the beating of pickets and union organizers to foreign military invasion, and from the jailing of 'agitators' to extermination camps and terror bombing. Violence functions as both midwife and abortionist of history. But the means

---

[67] R. Miliband, *Parliamentary Socialism*, London 1961, p. 178; and R. Skidelsky, *Politicians and the Slump*, Harmondsworth 1970, p. 420.

[68] N. Greene, *Crisis and Decline. The French Socialist Party in the Popular Front Era*, Ithaca 1969, pp. 102–3. The immediate cause of the fall of the left-wing socialist Hornsrud government in Norway in 1928 was also the threat of a flight of capital. See further below.

of violence as well as their effectiveness are circumscribed by the four axes of structural determination. A mode of production is at the same time a mode of destruction and defence. Thus, no non-socialist society could have withstood the US invasion of Vietnam. The outcome of the Vietnamese war was further decided by the level of development and strength reached by the socialist part of the world, particularly the Soviet Union, but also China; by the solid popular anchorage of the NLF and Lao Dong; and by an international conjuncture marked by internal contradiction and conflict in the West – so different from the context of the Korean War.[69]

All three mechanisms of reproduction constitute mechanisms of expulsion – threatened or actual. In the ultimate forms of economic constraint and physical violence, they involve expulsion from the realm of the living; in less drastic cases, exclusion from the field of adequate material support and freedom of movement. In the ideological sphere, the procedure bears an old name: excommunication. This denotes refusal of a normal, sane, intelligible mode of discourse – relegation to madness or satanic depravity. The modest proposals of the British Labour Party at the 1931 elections, suggesting that it was possible to deal with the depression without cuts in the dole, were characterized by a former leader of the party, Philip Snowden, as 'Bolshevism run mad'.[70] From the outbreak of World War II until Stalingrad, and sometimes during the Cold War, when Communist MPs rose to speak in the Swedish *Riksdag*, the members of the other parties left the chamber. In Italian elections, particularly in 1948 and the fifties, Catholic workers and peasants were told by their pope and clergy that the Marxist working-class parties were against God and that consequently to vote for them was a sin.

The threat or risk that no-one will listen to a given discourse, except as a revealing symptom calling for therapy or repression, functions as a powerful pressure to accept what exists, what is possible, and what is right, as they are defined by a dominant mode of discourse resting upon the four-dimensional constellation of national and international forces.

[69] Cf. G. Therborn, 'From Petrograd to Saigon', *New Left Review* No. 48 (1968).

[70] Miliband, op. cit. 1961, p. 191.

Loss of State Power

State power is determined not only in the mode of reproduction, but also in those of loss and transformation. The mechanisms of reproduction may in fact function equally as ones of revolution. For example, violence and economic constraint undermined the position of the feudal ruling class in 16th–17th century England and mid-19th century Tokugawa Japan. The Russian soldiers, peasants and workers refused to listen to Kerensky in 1917 when he exhorted them to make war, not revolution. In conformity with the dialectics of history, the processes of social reproduction are *at the same time* processes of social revolution; revolutions occur when the latter become stronger than the former. The processes of revolution develop in two basic ways: as *internal contradictions* and as *disarticulating uneven development*. Contradictions refer to opposition and conflict between two forces which form an intricate, necessary unity.[71] Disarticulating uneven development denotes the growth of disjuncture and conflict between two or more forces which have become intertwined in an extrinsic, contingent reproductive totality.

Marx drew out the concept of contradiction almost exclusively in economic terms, locating the fundamental one in the unity of the relations and forces of production. The contradiction between these two gives rise to the application of economic constraint to the reproduction of given relations of production, entailing a change in the relations of size and strength between the two classes of the mode of production. It should be possible, however, to extend the analysis of contradiction to the state and ideological superstructure – areas never systematically treated by the founder of historical materialism. Two such contradictions may be suggested as a hypothesis: that between *domination and execution*, and that between *qualification and subjection*. In their political and ideological specificity, these correspond to, but are in the last instance determined by, the contradictions of the forces and the relations of production, respectively.

Our use of the terms 'domination' and 'execution' is more provisional than our identification of the political contradiction to which they refer. Every state apparatus has a specific class character, which expresses the rule of one class, fraction or alliance over others. At the same time every state has to perform or execute the general functions of rule-making, rule-application, rule-enforcement, etc. Domination and execution are linked to each other in a relationship

---

[71] Cf. Therborn, *Science, Class and Society*, op. cit., pp. 391 ff.

analogous to that which exists between the forces and relations of production. A particular form of domination presupposes certain means of execution, and conversely the form of domination determines the way in which the functions of the state are executed. But domination and execution may also come into contradiction with each other. For example, the feudal monarchies were obliged increasingly to rely upon non-noble secretaries, intendants and tax-farmers. Similarly, in order to execute the domination of the bourgeoisie in the stage of developed monopoly capitalism, the present-day state has had to enrol large masses of state employees and groups of intellectuals, no section of which may easily be controlled by the classical means of bourgeois bureaucratic hierarchy. Administration of the socialist state has, in varying degrees, necessitated employment of bourgeois experts. Similar contradictions have evolved historically in the organization of the military and the police. The incapacity of the feudal Tsarist state to wage a modern capitalist war, and to supply the population of Petersburg in a time of full-scale mobilization, was probably the contradiction which most directly led to its downfall in the February Revolution.

This contradiction in the state between domination and execution has been justly noted by many 'Euro-communist' writers. However, it is a general political contradiction, which manifests itself in all types of state during certain historical periods and at precise conjunctures. It does not by itself indicate, then, that the form of rule now typical of state monopoly capitalism is of a less repressive character than its predecessors.

Within the ideological sphere, subjection and qualification form an intrinsic unity. Subjection to a determinate reality principle and to internalization of a particular type of superego denotes the process whereby individuals qualify for membership of a class at a given point in the development of society. But the two aspects may also enter into contradiction. This is perhaps most evident in the case of the intelligentsia – particularly in the latter stages of feudalism, from 18th century France to Russia at the beginning of the 20th century; in the dependent capitalist societies of the Third World; and the university explosion of advanced capitalism during the 1960s. The growth of capitalism in the first two instances involved the qualification of a new intellectual stratum which could be subjected only with great difficulty, if at all, to the prevailing feudal or dependent capitalist regime.

Contemporary monopoly capitalism has generated immense

strata of subaltern intellectual employees, who tend to send their children for academic qualification; at the same time, rising employment opportunities for intellectual labour have attracted young people to higher education in far greater number than previously. As a result, the huge wave of qualification disintegrated the traditional means of bourgeois academic subjection – instruments which, in the imperialist countries, had functioned so successfully since the time of the bourgeois revolutions, preparing students for their future roles as members or hangers-on of the ruling class, and providing a pool of militant strike-breakers and, at certain times and places, dedicated Fascist storm-troopers.

However, the contradiction between qualification and subjection may also operate within the ruling and ruled classes themselves. The logical inconsistencies of the Christian religion – which qualifies the poor as those fully capable of attaining the true faith and salvation while subjecting them to the dues of Caesar – drove forward the rebellion of Thomas Münzer and the German peasants. Despite the constant efforts of capitalist management to promote dequalification and degradation of labour, the development of the productive forces under the sign of capital accumulation gives rise to a qualified labour force, which cannot easily be subjected to unrestrained managerial command. Sometimes, longer-established members of a ruling class may display an indifference born of privilege towards the newly-acquired spoils of fresh entrants to their ranks, even disqualifying them from the role of ruler. Under capitalism, where institutionalized channels of mobility exist, this phenomenon is largely confined to individual families, like Thomas Mann's Buddenbrooks; but in the case of feudal and pre-feudal dynasties and aristocracies, the contradiction has on occasions significantly contributed to the decline and fall of a ruling class as a whole.

Contradictions proper refer to the economic, political and ideological instances of a mode of production – both national and international. But a mode of production is always enmeshed in relationships with other modes, in the framework of a historical social formation which is in turn entangled in an international system of social formations. At any given time, these modes of production and social formations are articulated with one another in a specific way – through patterns of exchange and parameters of economic constraint; through violent relations of force and forms of political representation and mediation based on subordination; and through patterns of communication and intertwined ideological interpellations. As a reproductive process, this totality is in constant flux, whether slow or rapid. There is thus a constant tendency to uneven development and disarticulation of the previous totality. This may be illustrated by a number of examples.

In the transition from feudalism to capitalism in Europe, the development of capitalism overtook that of feudalism, leading sooner or later to the overthrow of feudal domination over the social formations. Similarly, the fact that the resolution of the issue of state power was different in Angola in the mid-seventies from its resolution in Spain in the thirties is attributable to the much-changed international situation – to the weakness of the West European capitalist powers, the at least temporary weakening of the United States after its defeat in Vietnam, and the greatly increased strength of the USSR. Sometimes the elements of this uneven development may be fairly smoothly re-articulated in a new totality, as happened in 1947 when the USA took over from Britain the 'white man's burden' of imperialist oppression in Greece. At other times it may result in wars and revolutions, as did the German challenge for Western supremacy in 1914 and 1939.

It is this constellation of multiple contradictions and dis-articulating uneven developments which constitutes what Althusser has called 'the overdetermination of contradiction'.[72]

---

[72] L. Althusser, 'Contradiction and Overdetermination', in *For Marx*, NLB, London 1977.

4.

Wielding State Power I: Formats of Representation

So far, we have tried to do two things. First, we have defined, as rigorously as possible, the class character of state power and the ruling class, and provided some instruments with which to assess and analyse them empirically. Secondly, we have presented a framework for explaining how the existence, viability or fall of the ruling class and a particular class state are determined, together with an overview of the place of the state in the overall process of social reproduction. Now that we have defined and identified the state power of the ruling class, explained its basis, and located its role in the functioning of society, we must go on to pose a third question: How is this power actually wielded and exercised?

A number of general points have already been made. Thus, we know that class rule is exercised in constantly ongoing processes of social reproduction or transformation governed by the inherent dynamics of the mode of production and its relationship to other modes co-existing with it. However, this is only part of the answer. For class rule is also wielded in the thick of a continuous class struggle. The dynamics of the structures and processes of the relations and forces of production – of the state apparatus and ideological system, on the one hand, and the class struggle, on the other – are in fact two sides of the same coin. But they may be distinguished in analytical exposition, in order to confront the enormous complexity of social life.

The Ruling-Class Problematic

We may begin our outline of the problematic of the exercise of class rule by listing its four basic components. These are: the ruling class itself, the ruled classes, the state as a special institution intervening in the societal process, and the structures and processes to be reproduced, of which the ruling class is in its essence the bearer. By definition, the ruling class exercises its ruling power over other classes and strata through the state – through holding state power. Consequently, two relationships must be ensured. The state, particularly its commanding personnel, must *represent*, that is to say, promote and defend the ruling class and its mode of exploitation or supremacy. At the same time, the state must *mediate* the exploitation or domination of the ruling class over other classes and strata. In other words, it follows from the irreducible material specificity of the class state that it is simultaneously both an *expression* of class exploitation and domination, and *something more* than a simple expression – something other than the non-state ruling-class apparatuses necessary to support these relations. The problems of representation and mediation encountered by the ruling class are rooted in the need to harmonize the sameness and otherness of the state within and between the two relationships. This sameness-otherness further underlies the basic political contradiction, which we have provisionally described as the one between domination and execution.

Though empirically simultaneous and intrinsically intertwined, the two relationships of representation and mediation may be analysed separately. Moreover, as we shall see, each poses its own characteristic problems. Representation denotes a relationship between ruling class and state, whose specific problems centre on the links of unity-division manifest both between different fractions of the ruling class and between the class of economic agents and its specialized political personnel. Mediation is a three-cornered relationship among the ruling class, the state and the ruled classes, in which the main problem concerns the strength of the ruled classes.

The so-called relative autonomy of the state, or, to be more precise, the specific irreducibility of the state to extra-political exploitation and domination, is governed by the problems of the relations of representation and mediation. Generally speaking, the greater the internal divisions of the ruling class, the sharper are the problems of representation, and the more pronounced is the specific irreducibility or 'relative autonomy' of the state. Similarly, the problems of mediation and the 'autonomy' of the state vary accordingly with the strength of the ruled classes.

In the class struggle, the ruling class must ensure such representation in and such mediation through the state, that the latter successfully contributes to the reproduction of its economic, political and ideological positions within the complex reproductive totality presented above. This ruling class problematic may be expressed in the following schema:

The Ruling Class Problematic

Relations to be ensured in the state:	Structures and processes to be reproduced:		
	Rel. and forces of production	State apparatus	Ideology
	(of a given mode of production superordinately articulated to those of other modes in a social formation, which is functionally articulated to an international system of social formations)		
Ruling class to top state personnel: representation	I	2	3
Ruling class to ruled classes via the state: mediation	4	5	6

In practice, the reproductive or revolutionary interventions of the state are circumscribed both by the problems of representation and mediation arising out of the class struggle, and by the structural dynamics of the mode of production as a four-dimensional determining totality.

Thus, state economic policies will further or maintain the positions of the ruling class in a given conjuncture, only if it is adequately represented in the state, and if efficient processes of state mediation are employed. Conversely, where these conditions are satisfied, the substantial content of what is effected by the state is determined overall by the ongoing processes of the determinant structural totality – that is to say, by the stage of development, the interrelationships and the internal contradictions of its parts in the given conjuncture. Ruling class representation and mediation between ruling and ruled classes, then, do not exhaust what actually happens in and through the state. They do, however, constitute crucial analytical aspects of the latter. A full-scale empirical analysis of the exercise of state power in a concrete case would therefore have to address both the problems examined in this and following chapters and those raised in the previous one. In this context, we shall directly touch upon only general questions of representation and mediation – particularly as they affect developed capitalist countries – and not their relationship to the specific structures and processes which form the object of reproduction.

Formats of Representation

Every state has a system for the selection of political leaders. From the point of view of the ruling class problematic, this constitutes the means by which the reproduction of the economic, political and ideological positions of the ruling class is given representation by state leaders. Therefore we shall call systems of leadership selection : *formats of representation*. This term will suggest that the concept does not refer directly to how representation is secured, but rather denotes the context within which the ruling class ensures, by numerous different means, that the reproduction of its positions is represented.

Owing to limitations of time and space, the exposé will concentrate mainly on formats of bourgeois representation and the problems they raise for the bourgeoisie as a ruling class. Only in order to gain the elements of a comparative overview will a few initial remarks be made about feudal and socialist formats.

From a very broad perspective, we may distinguish three general types of class format of representation – derived from the basic class character of the state apparatus. The socialist format is one of explicit class representation : the state openly represents the working class, or the working class and its allies. In the general bourgeois format, on the other hand, representation of the ruling class has to be expressed as *national representation* (however the legal nation may be defined). The supreme principle of the feudal format, finally, is lack of any representation. In practice, of course, representative and represented may become alienated from each other in a number of ways. But representation as a constitutional principle involves their intrinsic unity in a process of delegation upwards and accountability downwards. The feudal monarchy, however, from the *Lehensstaat* of the Middle Ages through Absolutism to the 19th-century constitutional monarchies, was based upon an inbuilt dualism of king and aristocracy, as well as of king and people. This was the case even of relationships in electoral monarchies – for example, that between the Emperor of the German-Roman Reich and his Electors.[73] But the relationship of the king to the aristocracy and to the rest of the people was not a completely unilateral one, even under Absolutism. While not representing his subjects in a strict sense, the king owed them certain obligations – usually expressed at his coronation in the form of an oath and referring to religion, justice and privileges. (This is indicated by the classical feudal phrase: 'noblesse oblige'.) Moreover, both before and after the era of Absolutism, this *obligation format of representation* was combined with forms of constitutional representation, such as noble councils and assemblies, or estates.

Any concrete format of political representation makes use of one or a number of general principles of leadership selection. Leaders may be *elected*, they may be *institutional*, or they may be *self-enforced*. Institutional leadership is bestowed upon persons holding a certain position within a given institution – a position which they may have either inherited or achieved through promotion. The main examples of the application of this principle are the dynastical monarchy, many variants of the aristocratic *magnum consilium*, and the modern army dictatorships of Argentina, Brazil, Chile, Peru, and so on. They should be distinguished from 'usurpation' of power by a leader or group – the manner in which many feudal dynasties were founded (for instance, the Swedish Vasa dynasty in the 16th century) and the pattern of innumerable bourgeois coups d'etat since the 18th Brumaire of Napoleon I. The principles are quite often combined. Thus, although German Fascism came to power by electoral means, its supreme principle was the self-enforced power of the *Führer*.

The main selection principle of the existing socialist countries is the institutional one. State leadership is automatically conferred upon individuals who are promoted to high positions within the

---

[73] The great German constitutional historian of medieval times, Heinrich Mitteis, has written: '. . . thus the dualism of Emperor and princes remained in force until the end of the Empire (1806).' H. Mitteis, *Der Staat des hohen Mittelalters*, Weimar 1940, p. 405.

party – a norm which is now to be enshrined in the new Soviet Constitution. It should be noted that whereas the Cuban revolution may be characterized as a self-enforcement of the Fidelista *guerrilleros*, rather similar in kind to the abortive 19th-century republican uprisings before the unification of Italy, this description cannot really be applied to the October Revolution. The insurrection was in fact conducted by a party which, in previous debates, struggles and elections, had acquired the most representative position among the Russian working class. By contrast, the strategies of the major West European Communist Parties adhere to the electoral principle, as did the *Unidad Popular* in Chile; according to this conception, the working class and its allies are not to be represented exclusively through one party, but through an open electoral process in which several parties organize and seek the support of the working population.

Main Bourgeois Formats of Representation

Given the role of national unification and independence in the bourgeois revolution and system of power, the leading political spokesmen of the bourgeoisie have to put themselves forward as representatives of the nation. They may enter positions of state leadership by election, institutional position, or more or less violent forms of self-enforcement. The general principle of national representation – which does not preclude effective representation of foreign classes by a satellite comprador bourgeoisie – as well as the corresponding mechanisms of leadership selection, are embodied in a number of concrete, conjunctural political settings, in which the ruling capitalist class struggles for and asserts the representation of the reproduction of its positions. Rather than group the main variants under the rubrics of institutional, electoral and self-enforcing leadership, each with its own sub-headings, we shall list them in ascending order of apparent complexity.

1. Capitalist institutionalization
State leaders may be drawn from members of capitalist economic apparatuses, on the simple basis of the positions they occupy within the latter. Such direct political institutionalization of the bourgeoisie as the ruling class appears to be the most convenient way in which to ensure ruling-class representation. Why then has it been so rare?

It has functioned only in some, but not all[74], of the city republics of early mercantile capitalism, and even there it was seldom the exclusive form.[75] In the United States, national and, above all, local political matters are sometimes delegated to a committee of important businessmen, but the corporation has never been able to impose itself as the guardian of the 'national interest', as the army has done in many countries.

The solution to the problem is fairly evident. Nevertheless, the question is an important one, since it highlights the role of the electoral principle in the politics and pre-history of bourgeois democracy. First, direct political institutionalization of capitalist rule was impossible in the age of competitive industrial capitalism because of the anarchic relations obtaining within the bourgeoisie itself. (By contrast, trade in the Hanseatic cities of the pre-industrial epoch was largely organized under guild or guild-like auspices.) Secondly, of course, such institutionalized representation of a tiny minority class, if applied beyond the narrow confines of a mercantile city, raised formidable difficulties of mediation – of political rule over other classes, including an exploited class which was much less captive than the peasants of the aristocracy. This was already revealed in the 18th-century Dutch bourgeois republic, which, governing more by corrupt 'elections' than by capitalist institutionalization, proved unable to maintain itself against the rural aristocracy and Orange dynasty when the latter, with the considerable support of rebellious Amsterdam carpenters, acquired in 1747 the hereditary right to the supreme political position of *Stadhouder*.[76] In the era of industrial monopoly capitalism, with its large proletariat, it is quite clearly impossible to ensure that the ruled will accept and contribute to a regime of direct, institutionalized capitalist representation.

[74] Venice, for instance, was ruled by a hereditary nobility. See F. Lane, *Venice*, Baltimore 1973.

[75] According to the Census of 1669, the council of Lübeck consisted of jurists and unspecified merchants as well as three members each of the two main mercantile companies. See J. Asch, *Rat und Bürgerschaft in Lübeck 1598–1669*, Lübeck 1961, p. 170.

[76] L. Leeb, *The Ideological Origins of the Batavian Revolution*, The Hague 1971, pp. 58 ff. For the background, see P. Geyl, *The Netherlands in the Seventeenth Century*, 2 vols., London 1961, 1964.

2. Notables

The classical format of bourgeois representation is one whereby political leaders emerge as outstanding individuals out of an informally organized bourgeois public, composed of members of the ruling class and allied strata, lawyers and sometimes bureaucrats. These persons appear as candidates for leadership in various non-institutionalized ways during the everyday social intercourse of the ruling class. Originally, they were then elected by other members of that class. This was the prevailing pattern in the Dutch Republic, in England until at least 1832, and in France under the Restoration and the July Monarchy. It even managed to survive radical extension of the suffrage. Thus, a notables format has characterized the French Third and (after 1947) Fourth Republics, and, in significant though modified ways, the still unstable bourgeois party system of the Fifth Republic[77]; it largely marked British politics before 1945 (it was not until 1965 that a Conservative leader – Edward Heath – was formally elected[78]); and, on the whole, it prevails in the United States to this day.

However, since candidates are also elected by members of other, numerically more significant classes, this format has had to undergo a number of adaptations. Campaign committees and loose parties of notables have been formed, and money has been used for the purposes of mass communication rather than personal bribery.

Two other new devices have played a highly important role. One has been the use of *imagery* to project a non-ruling-class aura on to the candidate. This careful monitoring of the areas of popular vision and blindness has for the most part been remarkably successful. It has a long ancestry, moreover. In 1824 the US Democratic presidential nominee, a merchant, land speculator and cotton-planter named Andrew Jackson, was effectively presented as a rustic frontier democrat. In 1840 the Whig Henry Harrison, of old Virginian

[77] The ruling Gaullist party, for instance, has operated over a twenty-year period under three different forms and appellations: the UNR, UDR and now, under Chirac, the RPR. To these should be added the loose grouping of 'Independents', from whose ranks Giscard d'Estaing rose to the presidency, and the endless permutations and transmutations of the formations of the 'Centre'. This system presents a striking contrast both to that of other contemporary West European countries and to the loyalty shown by all generations to the ideologically empty labels of the US Democratic and Republican parties.

[78] *Keesing's Contemporary Archives, 1965–66*, Bristol, p. 20879.

landowner stock, could appear with equal results as the 'log cabin' candidate. We could extend the list a great deal further.[79]

There are, however, also limitations to the use of imagery. Andrew Mellon, one of the real magnates of US capitalism, was selected to head the Treasury in the 1920s, and Nelson Rockefeller became Vice-President after the Nixon–Agnew gang had to resign; but none of their kind, the *crème de la crème*, has ever managed to be elected President. In 1952 André Boutemy, a former Vichy prefect and the main political spokesman in the Fourth Republic for the French Employers' Confederation, won an election to the Senate in the guise of a farmer candidate(!). But his entry the following year into the cabinet of René Mayer was too much for even the strong stomach of post-1947 public opinion to digest: Boutemy was forced to resign.[80]

A second, and more significant factor has been the existence of *captive populations*. This concept should be reserved for voters who are relatively free from a formal point of view and distinguished from that of participants in state-rigged elections where the whole people is held in subjection.[81] It should also be differentiated from that of groups which are simply influenced by other classes than their own. A captive population denotes a group of people who are personally dependent upon, and excluded from independent political participation by, members of another class. The latter are then able to deliver the votes of the former. Four such populations have been of importance in the modern history of bourgeois rule.

First, rural communities of workers, tenants and small peasants may be so organized by more or less de-feudalized landowners, often linked to the local clergy. Bismarck was one of the first modern

[79] E. Roseboom, *A History of Presidential Elections*, New York 1958, pp. 81, 120 and *passim*.

[80] H. Ehrmann, *Organized Business in France*, Princeton 1957, pp. 225–6.

[81] Napoleon III introduced this system and applied it with great skill. (See T. Zeldin, *The Political System of Napoleon III*, London 1958.) Perhaps the most shameless use was made of it in Romania in the 1920s. The composition of government was decided by cabals of the Bucharest financial community and by the court *camarilla*; and those who were selected for government had a free rein to rig elections. Thus, in 1926, when Averescu and his People's Party held office, the elections gave him 1,366,160 votes against 192,399 to Bratinau's Liberals. But when the latter returned to government the following year, they were supposed to have received 1,704,435 votes as against Averescu's total of a mere 53,371. (J. Rothschild, *East Central Europe Between the Two World Wars*, Seattle and London 1974, p. 299.)

statesmen to see the great potential of such a structure.[82] It has also played a very powerful role in Belgian Flanders, western France, southern Italy, Spain, Brazil, Japan and many other countries.

A second case is that of workers in early industrial company towns and areas: for example, the Le Creuzot concentration in France around the Schneider steel works; the German Saar region in the age of von Stumm; the Du Ponts' state of Delaware in the USA to this day[83]; and, more generally, workers in small patriarchal family businesses. The structure of dependence is here provided by the employer and his all-embracing relationship to his employees.

In the United States, where no landowning aristocracy existed outside the South and where the farming population has been more a base of radical populism than a reservoir of reaction, a third captive population has been of enormous significance: namely, the ethnically divided working-class immigrants, gathered in the big cities and remaining for long ignorant of the language and workings of their new country. Political machines such as the Tweed Ring and Tammany Hall organizations – created more or less explicitly to capture control of the local state apparatus for the personal enrichment of their bosses – mediated between the strange new state and the fresh immigrants in exchange for their votes. The machine bosses are then linked in a similar relationship to the national politicians of the more 'respectable' bourgeoisie. The northern Democratic city machines were crucial to Roosevelt's victory in 1932; but, when, in 1936, the coalition of New Deal interest groups necessitated a campaign of more political mobilization, their role began to decline.[84] Although this process has since then been sustained by unionization, social services and immigrant absorption, the machines have by no means disappeared; despite the recent death of its old boss, the notorious Daley machine has so far continued to rule the city of Chicago.

A fourth category has been constituted by state and municipal employees, whose jobs depend on political allegiance to their superiors. This forms part of the American 'spoils' system, usually superintended by the Postmaster-General. It is also important in

[82] See note 67 of the essay on the state apparatus.
[83] J. Phelan–R. Pozen, *The Company State*, New York 1973.
[84] Schlesinger, *The Age of Roosevelt*, op. cit., Vol. III, Chs. 22–23.

contemporary Italy. Work there is scarce, particularly in the centre and south of the country, and lower and middle-ranking state posts are considerably better paid than equivalent ones in the private sector.

Political use is made of these captive populations in a number of ways: exchange of petty favours for obedience; inculcation of deference by means of isolation from the wider class and nation, coupled with local displays of wealth and power; and outright intimidation. It is a quasi-feudal pattern which has thus been harnessed to bourgeois rule. The many variants of such political clientelism have acquired telling names in different countries: from *caciquismo* in Spain, *coronelismo* in the Brazil of the Old Republic, *sottogoverno* in contemporary Italy, to machine politics in the United States.

As long as it is not challenged by strong organization of the ruled, this is an excellent format of ruling class representation. Nevertheless, it too has its problems. Principal among these is the phenomenon of corruption and graft. For it must be ensured that the elected members of the ruling class really represent the class (fraction or alliance) as a whole, and not just themselves and their immediate entourage. Various 'corrupt practices acts' – regulating campaigning methods, access to the media, and techno-bureaucratic specialization – as well as investigative bourgeois journalism, civil service reform and professional city management, have all been adopted in an attempt to deal with this problem. Sometimes, sectors of the ruling class have, with varying success, striven to disenfranchise populations held captive by other sectors. Thus, the French Radicals and Belgian Liberals opposed extension of the suffrage to women, whom they held to be under the sway of the church. Having seen the way in which the French Second Empire functioned, the German Liberals opposed for similar reasons the introduction of a general franchise, while Bismarck advocated universal (but not equal) male suffrage.[85]

3. The Bourgeois Party

Now, the bourgeoisie, like every ruling class, has to assert itself in struggle, in what is far from always the best of possible worlds. In the face of organized opposition of the working class, and perhaps

---

[85] W. Gagel, *Die Wahlrechtsfrage in der Geschichte der deutschen liberalen Parteien 1848–1918*, Dusseldorf 1958.

also the petty bourgeoisie, it is hardly viable to resort to a format of notables, parading as the political representatives of the nation. The bourgeoisie, then, may have to make do with merely a good world: that is to say, rule through an organized bourgeois party (or coalition) with a large dues-paying membership, and through specialized functionaries and formally elected professional politicians. The Italian Christian Democracy, the Japanese Liberal-Democratic Party, the West German CDU, the modern British Tory Party, and even the French UNR-UDR-RPR are the most conspicuous examples. Such parties not only maintain a hold over the numerically declining captive sections of the ruled classes; utilizing to the full their greater scope for professional manoeuvre, they may also rally the petty bourgeoisie, the middle strata and parts of the unionized working class.

Neither Marx and Engels nor the Marxists of the Second International ever expected bourgeois mass parties to prove capable of the degree of longevity and tenacity which they have in fact exhibited. The strength of these organizations rests upon three basic factors – of which one was analysed in too summary a fashion, and the other two were gratuitously dismissed by the founders of historical materialism. First of all, these parties have a *potentially broad class base*, arising out of the fact that social polarization, while in the main conforming to Marx's prediction, has proceeded at a much slower pace than he forecast. Capital and labour have undergone considerable concentration, at the same time as the middle strata have been increasingly proletarianized, coming to resemble the working class proper in terms of pay, working conditions and union organization. But this has been a long and gradual process; and it is still possible to play upon a variety of distinctions between the middle strata and the working class. Except in the United States, the development of agriculture has largely maintained the family farm and brought about an exodus of the rural proletariat, instead of agro-industrial concentration. Altogether, then, the bourgeois parties could towards 1970 find, among the middle strata and petty bourgeoisie, a potential class base of 45–50% of the active population in Britain, France, Italy and West Germany, and 60% of that of Japan.[86]

---

[86] Compilations from *Yearbook of Labour Statistics 1975*, Geneva 1975, Table 2. Included are employers, self-employed, family workers, and employed professional, administrative, clerical and sales workers.

Of course, the overwhelming majority of these layers also constitute a possible base for working class parties. But hitherto, the anti-socialist bonds of property and delegated managerial authority have, on the whole, proved much stronger than anti-capitalist or anti-monopoly solidarity. The French Communists have attracted a number of southern vinegrowers and other farmers away from the old left-republican tradition, and the Communist Parties of Yugoslavia, Greece, Albania, China, Indo-China and Indonesia acquired a mass peasant base in their struggle for a national-democratic revolution. However, working class parties have generally been able to rally only semi-proletarian sections of the petty bourgeoisie, such as the Finnish crofters, Norwegian fishermen-farmers, Malayan rubber-tappers or Emilian tenants.[87] With the possible exception of parts of the Third World, this pattern seems unlikely to change significantly. Regarding the middle strata, on the other hand, the prospects are quite different. Since the late fifties, the Swedish Social Democrats have made heavy inroads into these sections, while the education explosion and student movement of the late sixties have in most countries deposited enduring left-wing traces among the middle strata. The flamboyant rebirth of the French Socialist Party is the clearest indication of this.

Bourgeois parties have also been able to capitalize on *nationalism* and *religion*. In the leading imperialist countries – the United States, Germany, Japan, France, Britain – nationalism has lost virtually every progressive connotation. (The only instance where this was perhaps not fully so was the rise of French anti-Americanism in the period following the Algerian war.) Once an intrinsic aspect of the bourgeois revolution, it has become a potent weapon of capitalist rule and has also had a certain appeal to sections of the working class. The bourgeois parties have as a general rule managed to pose as *the* national party. The recent upsurge of regional nationalism – in Britain, France, Belgium, Spain, Canada – has complicated the situation, however. One way or another, this very real phenomenon must be seriously tackled, and not simply denounced by the working-class parties.

Where it has been successfully employed, religion has proved an even weightier means of enlisting the support of ruled classes. The Lutheran and Anglican state churches have not been very effective

---

[87] Cf. the fascinating study by Jeffrey Paige, *Agrarian Revolution*, New York 1975.

in this respect. But dissident Protestant denominations, such as Methodism and Baptism, have often served as vehicles of Liberalism in Protestant countries, while Calvinism, Catholicism and Islam have all sponsored explicitly denominational parties and trade unions with a broad mass base, but a bourgeois class character. All the same, the advance of secularization slowly continues. In Britain and Sweden, dissenting Liberal workers have all but disappeared; the confessional French trade union, the CFTC, has, save for an insignificant minority, been transformed into the left-wing social democratic CFDT; the Italian CISL is now a class union, co-operating with the Communist-Socialist CGIL; and the political tide turned in Italy with the defeat of clericalism in the 1974 divorce referendum.

A certain price has to be paid, however, for the advantages of the bourgeois party format. The political leadership, circumscribed by both party elections and the weight of party considerations in general elections, grows less accessible to and malleable by the ruling class. A trade-union wing, however moderate it may be, must be given some consideration even in an organization like the West German CDU. The big capitalists of the Italian Confindustria are rather unhappy about the influence exerted within Christian Democracy by the archaic clerical integralism of Catholic Action, not to speak of socially-minded Catholic politicians and trade unionists.[88] Above all, a bourgeois mass party may lay undue stress – from the point of view of monopoly capital – on the small and petty bourgeoisie. In particular, obstacles may thereby be erected in the way of modernization, rationalization and concentration of the state and economy; or the intransigence of small bourgeois layers may threaten the mediation of power over the working class – a danger which, for example, the City of London glimpsed when, according to reports in the serious British bourgeois press, it met with sinking heart the success of Margaret Thatcher's Tory party in the spring 1977 by-elections.

These difficulties have to do with the fact that the role of parties in the exercise of bourgeois power is quite different from their function under the rule of the proletariat. The task of the working-class party and trade union is to unify and give direction to the class. Indeed, individual subordination of the workers to the capitalists and managers makes their collective self-organization a necessary pre-

[88] J. LaPalombara, *Interest Groups in Italian Politics*, Princeton 1964, pp. 403–4.

condition of working class power. The organizational basis of the bourgeoisie, however, is not self-organization but the organization of others in the capitalist enterprise and state. Its party is thus above all a vehicle for the organization of other classes around the bourgeoisie, on an apparently equal footing with the latter. Working-class parties have typically been rooted in trade unions, enterprise cells and workers' districts – the very bases of working-class power. Bourgeois parties, by contrast, have normally emerged from parliament – which is hardly the source of capitalist power – when groups of politicians went out to organize support for themselves.

The class character of a party is here defined neither in terms of ideology or 'objective interests' represented, nor in terms of constituency and composition, but essentially according to its organizational effect. A bourgeois party organizes the population around capitalist enterprise and the capitalist state, on the basis of various ideologies. A working-class party organizes the working class as a class apart from the bourgeoisie, even though its ambitions are not necessarily higher than protection of the workers within capitalism. Petty-bourgeois parties may be characterized in a similar way. This definition is theoretically congruent with the one we gave of the class character of the state, and it catches an important aspect of the historical development of parties. In several current contexts, it will require further precision, but it should be sufficient for the purposes of this analysis.

All things considered, of course, the inconveniences of the party format are not very great. Though they may take a more sophisticated view, bourgeois party leaders see essentially the same world as the leading agents of capital – a world in which capitalism is the natural economic system, in which class antagonism does not exist, and socialism poses a mortal threat. The parameters within which professional bourgeois politicians act are defined by their similar formative milieu they share with owners and managers of capitalist enterprise. Often this is complemented by more specific personal ties: a common education at Oxbridge, the Parisian *grandes écoles*, or Tokyo university; high society intercourse; family connections; various kinds of personal clique, particularly important in Japan where strong feudal characteristics have survived.[89] In spite of

[89] C. Yanaga, *Big Business in Japanese Politics*, New Haven and London 1968. Each of these types of patronage clique bears its own name in Japanese – a circumstance which points to their semi-institutional character.

membership dues and, in some cases, state support, bourgeois parties finance their election campaigns and organizational structures very largely out of contributions from capital. The bourgeois state, for its part, relies heavily on the expertise of big capital for the economic information and programming resources it requires. The ruling class may think that its professional party politicians do not always serve it well; but it can on every occasion count on their anxiousness to serve.

The basic problem posed by the party format and that of notables is not so much to secure ruling class representation *in* them, but to ensure maintenance *of* them. We have already noted several acquisitions and devices which are used by the bourgeoisie for this purpose: imagery, the clienteles of captive populations, class bonds of property and managerial authority, the attractions of nationalism and religion, funds necessary to sustain campaigns and appeals of all sorts, and surviving pre-capitalist vehicles of domination. A more general feature should be added.

The conjunctural character of all politics creates innumerable different ways in which the central issue of the day may be defined as *in* but not *of* the existing society. Employment, prices, social services, growth, income distribution, peace and war all appear as immediate problems of the here-and-now. As society is never completely static but always in process, several concrete options are available in every case. Often there are also a number of possible leaderships: Müller, Brüning, von Papen, von Schleicher and Hitler, in the death agony of Weimar Germany; Hoover and Roosevelt in the USA of the thirties. Of course, appeals are not tenable by themselves: they must to some extent be affirmed in practice, as is shown negatively by the instances of Brüning and Hoover, and positively by those of Roosevelt, and Adenauer-Ehrhardt and De Gasperi in the years of Marshall Aid. But as it is unlikely that capitalism will simply collapse, there exist many possibilities of effective affirmation of capitalist ideology and leadership.

The strength of advanced bourgeois rule probably lies above all in its polity – its political organizations and administrative machinery – rather than in the casemates of civil society as Gramsci thought. These states will not, it seems, disintegrate in the way that the Kerensky regime did in Russia. Socialist transformation of advanced capitalism will, for this and many other reasons, look very different from the Russian October.

4. Statism

A statist format denotes the principle according to which political leaders are recruited from incumbents of positions within the state apparatus. The bureaucracy, sometimes including a crowned head, and above all the military have been the suppliers of statist leadership. Interestingly enough, this has never been true of the police (although Ionnides, the leader of the last, short-lived Greek junta, was chief of the military police). If a police state in the above sense has never existed, this is essentially because, in peaceful times, the police are allotted a subordinate position, and when the chips are down and the opposition must be crushed, the repressive force they are able to provide is not sufficient. The stronger arm of the military then has to intervene. Statism may be either institutional, that is to say, derived from the institutionalized social position of the throne, bureaucracy or military, and exercised by the institution as such even against the will of the population; or it may be self-enforced by a particular Leader and his entourage. Although the one may be no less undemocratic or brutal than the other, the two types differ significantly in respect of governmental form, future viability, and problems of representation.

In rough weather, a statist format is often a good haven for the ruling class. Its adequacy crucially hinges upon the class character of the state apparatus. While the latter need not be entirely bourgeois, and may perfectly well bear the significant imprint of an allied class, nevertheless, if it is open to the influence of non-allied and inherently alien classes, or if it is so divided and lacking in institutional structures that it is unable to maintain ruling class representation in a unified manner, then serious problems and threatening developments may arise.

In modern history there have been several types of context in which a statist format has appeared. Examples of the first of these are: Wilhelmine Germany (where a notables format played a supplementary role); Japan from the Meiji Restoration to 1945; and present-day Iran (where a different pre-capitalist past has resulted in certain peculiar features). In these cases, a combination of internal and external forces and events – ranging from Napoleon I and Commodore Perry to the growth of industrial capitalism – led to the formation of a strong national-bureaucratic state, in which the bourgeoisie was, however, too weak to eradicate the remaining feudal elements. The outcome was a bourgeois-feudal class alliance[90], which on the whole remained stable and harmonious until military defeat sealed the fate of its feudal component. In the international stage of monopoly capitalism, the late feudal class depended on rapid industrialization for the pursuit of its military ambitions and turned to the strong state to provide it with the necessary means. Such a policy promoted above all the development of monopoly capital, whose imperialist strivings coalesced with the more traditional military-territorial politics of the feudal class. The *haute bourgeoisie* seems never to have encountered serious opposition to its economic demands on the part of the Emperor and the upper bureaucratic and military echelons. (It was these latter who furnished the political leadership in, for example, Japan – although some consideration should also be paid to the parties and elections which existed until 1937.) In addition, big capital received the support of a formidable repressive apparatus, which was quite adequate to its political needs.

Another classical form arises out of regroupment and change in the balance of forces between various fractions and sectors of a weakened bourgeoisie – one which, while secured against the feudal aristocracy, is in an exposed position vis-à-vis the popular classes, and usually, if not necessarily, international capital. This variant of statism has emerged where a notables format has failed either to structure the masses or to achieve unified representation of the ruling class, or both, and where disunity and underdevelopment of the latter has excluded recourse to the party format. Though often erected after the smashing of working class rebellion, this kind of regime is neither one of triumphant counter-revolution nor the expression of catastrophic equilibrium between different classes. In these cases, the rebellion has already been crushed by a previous government, belonging to one or another type of the notables format. Moreover, the state power of the new regime is as bourgeois as that of its predecessor. The fact that leadership selection and

[90] On Germany, see the two splendid volumes by T. Hamerow: *The Social Foundations of German Unification 1858–71. Ideas and Institutions*, Princeton 1969; and *Struggles and Accomplishments*, Princeton 1972. Meiji Japan explicitly modelled itself on Prussia and Germany: its constitution was directly inspired by the teachings of Lorenz von Stein and Rudolf Gneist; and a German scholar, Hermann Roesler, was among the drafters of the Japanese Constitution of 1890. (See G. Akita, *Foundations of Constitutional Government in Japan 1868–1900*, Cambridge, Mass. 1967, Ch. 4. Cf. Beasley, op. cit.)

political representation of the ruling class is ensured through the state apparatus should in no way be equated with state autonomy of classes. A state apparatus may be at least as bourgeois in character as a political party.

Like the bourgeois-feudal alliance, this bourgeois statism has in peacetime a predominantly civilian composition, although the army occupies a very strong place. In relation to the ruled classes, the state functions as does a supernotable to his clientele, holding it in check by means of petty favours, ideological isolation and physical intimidation. If elections are held at all, they are rigged by the state apparatus rather than by private bosses. To the bourgeoisie the regime presents itself as a form of unified representation, offering a fresh solution to economic and political crisis under the aegis of a changed balance of power within the ruling class.

The pre-eminent instance of this variant is the Second French Empire, which was established by Louis Bonaparte's 18th of Brumaire. The rule of Napoleon III may be said to constitute the first modern bourgeois regime, or, perhaps more precisely, the first transition to one. The country whose bourgeois revolution reached a peak of political radicalism was also the one where the notables format of bourgeois rule first broke down; this happened under the combined impact of the February Revolution, which advanced demands for widespread male suffrage, and of the division within the *haute bourgeoisie* between agrarian and financial fractions. The modernity and originality of *Bonapartism* lay in its utilization and manipulation of mass franchise and support, by means of a statist format of imperial power, prefectural pressure, and public appeal.[91]

Later, under the Third Republic, it became possible to re-establish the notables format as a result of the growth of small bourgeois and urban petty-bourgeois forces, and the abdication of a now re-unified *haute bourgeoisie* from the political arena in the wake of the failed coup of 16 May 1877. Both in France and in Italy (where the system of landowner and *haut-bourgeois* clientelism collapsed in 1876), the lawyer-politician came to play the role of broker between the ruling bourgeoisie, the state and the masses.[92]

[91] Zeldin, op. cit. In a letter to Marx of 13 April 1866, Engels called Bonapartism 'the true religion of the modern bourgeoisie' (*Marx-Engels Werke*, Vol. 31, p. 208). He was wrong, however, to dismiss the viability of notables and bourgeois party formats and to assume that a 'Bonapartist semi-dictatorship' would be the 'normal form' of modern bourgeois rule.

[92] These lawyers were often both important political leaders and legal representatives of capitalist enterprises. Such was the case, for example, of Millerand,

Bonapartism is, of course, the subject of one of Marx's most famous political analyses. However, in his major writings on this theme – *The Class Struggles in France 1848–50, The Eighteenth Brumaire of Louis Bonaparte, The Civil War in France* – Marx's polemical thrust against the bourgeoisie's abandonment of its own parliamentarism, as well as the fresh complexities of a hitherto unknown form of bourgeois rule, led him to indulge in a number of equivocal formulations, which subsequently formed the basis of an erroneous interpretative tradition. Marx played on the ambiguity of the word representation by saying that Bonaparte represented the peasants, whereas Orleans represented money and finance. Marx was, of course, fully conscious of the fact that Bonaparte did not actually further the positions of the peasantry in the way that the July monarchy promoted those of the financial bourgeoisie; he was simply referring to the peasantry's support for Napoleon III. When the term representation was used in the latter sense, the concept of political power underwent a similar change of meaning. In saying that the bourgeoisie lost its political power to Bonaparte, Marx did not mean that Bonapartism had ceased to represent the class positions of the bourgeoisie – just as the Restoration regime had been the state power of the newly-bourgeois landowners, and the July Monarchy that of the financial bourgeoisie; he was merely indicating the fact that a parliamentary system of bourgeois notables had been replaced by an authoritarian state. These equivocations culminate in the dictum that Bonapartism 'was the only form of government possible at a time when the bourgeoisie had already lost, and the working class had not yet acquired, the faculty of ruling the nation.'[93] In the very next sentence Marx goes on to talk of the prospering of bourgeois society under the Second Empire!

In reality, *Bonapartism expressed not an equilibrium or vacuum of classes, but the power of the big bourgeoisie in a new political conjuncture.* Before the advent of Bonaparte, the working class had been decisively defeated in June 1848 by the bourgeois republic. Bonaparte's presidential candidacy and later *coup d'état* were supported

---

Poincaré and Waldeck-Rousseau (Ehrmann, op. cit., p. 212). On the intermediary role of the lawyer-politician in Italy after 1876, see *inter alia* L. Graziano, 'La crise d'un régime libéral-démocratique: L'Italie', *Revue française de science politique*, No. 2 1977 – an essay which also provides valuable insights into subsequent forms of Italian clientelism.

[93] K. Marx, *The Civil War in France*, in *The First International and After*, op. cit., p. 208.

by the big bourgeoisie; the top political personnel of the Second Empire were largely recruited from its ranks; and the imperial state actively furthered its development. The Bonapartist imperial state was, in fact, less distanced or 'autonomous' from the big bourgeoisie than the Third Republic.[94]

Examples abound in the twentieth century of such a statist re-groupment of bourgeois forces. It characterized a large part of Eastern Europe, from Bulgaria to Estonia, after the blows of the world depression[95]; the Salazar regime in Portugal[96]; that of Vargas in Brazil between 1935 and 1945[97]; and the rule of the Greek Right from 1952 to 1963.[98] In each case, a breakdown of traditional rule by notables occurred in the midst of economic crisis and ruling-class division; in each case, too, the masses were beginning to recover from a previous crushing defeat: the repression of the Baltic revolution of 1918; the overthrow of Stamboliski's radical peasant government in Bulgaria, and the smashing of the Communist uprising of 1925; the violent repression of strikes in the Portuguese Republic; the rapid suppression of the ANL insurrection in Brazil; and the victory of the Right in the Greek Civil War. It should be noted that the same format of representation may be used by different fractions of the bourgeoisie – which does not imply that the above-mentioned regimes manifested the same constellation of bourgeois power or internal hegemony.

The fact that the crises which issued in statism could not be over-come by reassertion of the notables format or introduction of a party one is an expression of ruling class weakness and under-development; this is clearly shown both by the early date of the Bonapartist *coup d'état* and by the internationally dependent character of the 20th-century cases. However, the new regime also overcomes the crisis and largely reunifies the bourgeoisie, thus testifying to a position of relative strength. Those fractions of the

[94] J. Lhomme, *La grande bourgeoisie au pouvoir (1830–1880)*, Paris 1960. In spite of his non-Marxist focus on forms of power and control, Lhomme's very substantial empirical study firmly situates the Bonapartist Empire within the period of the exclusive exercise of power by the big bourgeoisie.

[95] For an excellent overview, see Rothschild, op. cit.

[96] H. Kay, *Salazar and Modern Portugal*, London 1970; A. de Figueiredo, *Portugal: Fifty Years of Dictatorship*, Harmondsworth 1975. A peculiarity of the Portuguese regime was the fact that both dictators, Salazar and Caetano, were called in from university chairs by the governing junta.

[97] T. Skidmore, *Politics in Brazil 1930–1964*, New York 1967.

[98] C. Tsoucalas, *The Greek Tragedy*, London 1969, Ch. 10.

ruling class which are regrouped under the sign of statism no longer have to face serious disturbance to their representation.

The problems of real importance here are twofold. First and foremost, statist regroupment institutionalizes a form of conjunctural crisis politics which may later prove to be dangerously rigid in a changed political situation. A realignment which resolves one particular crisis is frozen into the structure of the polity as a pack of solid ice; in a new crisis, however, this tends to crack up and melt away. Nevertheless, the relative strength and adequacy of the format is indicated by the fact that breakdown has usually followed upon external blows: from the Battle of Sedan to the holocaust of World War II and the African wars of liberation.

Secondly, although this type of regroupment has characteristically involved all important fractions of the ruling class, it has varied considerably in breadth and invariably omitted at least some sectors of the bourgeoisie and their political and intellectual personnel. Reunification is never complete, and divisions may reappear with a change in the conjuncture. Thus, Vargas had to withdraw in 1945 after the war victory of US liberalism; and in Greece, right-wing rule by the king, the army and their conservative premiers, presiding over a system of rigged elections, began to disintegrate in the early sixties in the face of a fresh challenge from reinvigorated liberal forces. Both regimes had a significantly narrower class base than did those of Bonaparte or Salazar – either too nationalist-progressive (Vargas), or too reactionary (the Greek Right).

A third type of statist format encountered in the history of bourgeois politics is the counter-revolutionary military dictatorship. The Chilean junta, the regime in power in Brazil since 1964, the Suharto dictatorship in Indonesia, and Franco's Spain are the most notorious examples. The relationship of the ruling class to these regimes is above all based on the firm cement of a counter-revolutionary union, formed with the express purpose of defending its own positions and privileges against threat from workers, landless peasants and radicalized middle strata. Although opinions may differ about the level of repression necessary, the ruling class stands united behind the dictatorship; the bond of counter-revolution smooths over even the inconveniences of centralization.

Still, such a dictatorship is a rigid machinery, strongly marked by conjunctural imprint. Even more than Bonapartism it is an expression of weakness. This becomes very apparent if we consider the range of options normally, but not in this case, available to the bourgeoisie.

First, the threat, if not the reality, of revolution may be contained by non-violent methods. Neither in Spain nor in Brazil did the bourgeoisie confront an actual attempt at socialist revolution. The Spanish Popular Front government, formed out of the electoral majority of February 1936, was a completely bourgeois regime, in which no Socialists or Communists participated. (However, social polarization was developing against a background of individual killings on each side.[99])

Although the Indonesian bourgeoisie had had to endure Sukarno's free-wheeling populism and co-operation with the strong Communist Party, it had successfully averted a PKI land-reform campaign in 1964. What triggered off the armed forces of counter-revolution was not a move by the President or the Communists, but a misfired coup attempted by a number of junior officers, with some CP youth involvement and passive approval by the party leadership and possibly Sukarno himself. This action threatened the delicate balance of power within which the army was by far the most important guardian of the positions of capital. But it did not signal an imminent danger of socialist revolution.[100]

In Brazil, Goulart's actual promises referred to nationalization of the oil refineries, a very limited land reform, and support for soldiers' organization in the army; the leaders of the military coup were essentially responding to the threatened establishment of a radical presidential regime over the heads of the conservative political bosses and their clientele, who had curtailed the powers of the president before allowing Goulart to take office.[101]

By contrast, Chilean capital was, of course, immediately exposed to direct attack. But even here a peaceful way out was not in-

[99] R. Robinson, *The Origins of Franco's Spain*, Newton Abbot 1970.

[100] To my knowledge, the best account of this obscure and fatal attempted coup is that made by Rex Mortimer in two appendices to his solid *Indonesian Communism under Sukarno*, Berkeley 1970. It is fairly clear that the coup was an internal army affair, of which Aidit and the top PKI leadership and possibly Sukarno himself had advance knowledge. The master of the counter-revolution and future dictator, General Suharto, had personal links with several of the conspirators; and it is possible that the coup was in part a provocation. (The bloodless and less catastrophic 25th of November 1975 in Portugal exhibits a number of apparent similarities.)

[101] Skidmore, op. cit., Ch. VIII.

conceivable in August–September 1973. Hit by strong domestic and international economic pressure, Allende and important sectors of *Unidad Popular* were prepared to call a halt and even a retreat, while awaiting new elections or possibly a referendum which the bourgeoisie stood a good chance of winning. If this policy had been pursued, the labour movement would not have been crushed so completely; but it would have been fatally demoralized and split, since more intransigent sections of *Unidad Popular* were unlikely to have backed down.

Secondly, a violent counter-revolution may very well succeed without the installation of a military dictatorship. Apart from the counter-revolution in Spain, all the bloodiest waves of repression in Europe (Finland, Hungary, Greece between 1949 and 1952) ended in a party or notables format of civilian rule. Nor did the German counter-revolutions of 1919–1923 endanger the Weimar party coalition.

When the bourgeoisie recovers strength and the crushed revolution fades away, frictions and pressures for 'liberalization' are therefore liable to develop. But since the bourgeoisie is represented by the dictatorship, it will hardly move into direct opposition to it. How far it is prepared to accept liberalization will depend on the availability of modes of transition to other, equally good or better, formats of representation. The full story of the end of the Franco dictatorship has yet to be told, and that of the replacement of the Indonesian, Brazilian and Chilean ones yet to be enacted.[102]

[102] An interesting analysis is Poulantzas's *The Crisis of the Dictatorships*, NLB 1976. However, the empirical grounding of his key distinction between 'interior' and 'comprador' bourgeoisies seems slippery, and evidence presented in support of it is rather flimsy. For a critique on this point, see N. Mouzelis, 'Capitalism and Dictatorship in Post-War Greece', *New Left Review* No. 96 (1976). The same issue contains a very good journalistic report on Spain by Ronald Fraser, 'Spain on the Brink', which covers the period up to March 1976. The unexpectedness of later developments – the emergence of Suaréz, the marginalization of Fraga and the inglorious defeat of Arías and the bunker – is highlighted by Fraser's conclusion of 1 March: 'the splitting of a fraction of the bourgeoisie from Fraga's reform project seems unlikely.' (p. 31) In the Portuguese case, emphasis on the comprador bourgeoisie seems to fit badly with the fact that Salazar came to power as a reaction against the surrender of the Portuguese customs as security for foreign loans (Figueiredo, op. cit., p. 61) and that, in comparison to the old republic and the late monarchy, Salazar's Portugal was less dependent on foreign capital until the disastrous colonial wars began to take their toll. The financial oligarchy was, it is true, intertwined with more powerful sectors of foreign capital in the exploitation of the colonies, but it had developed in the thirties and forties from traditional

The statist format includes a number of military regimes which represent not unity or reunification, but division of the bourgeoisie – often of the state apparatus as well. Their links with the capitalist class are therefore considerably more precarious. Examples of this variant range from the classical Latin American *caudillo* dictatorships to the reformist institutional rule of the army in contemporary Peru; from the party-military regime in Syria and Iraq to the amorphous armed cliques which govern many African countries; from the short-lived putsches of the first Portuguese Republic to the MFA regime of 1974–1975; and from Pilsudski in inter-war Poland to the Greek junta. Indeed, such forms of rule are so diverse and widespread, both in time and in space, that even to cover their most immediate origins, structures and modes of functioning would necessitate a special analysis.

From the standpoint of the bourgeoisie of a given society, they involve, in various ways, more or less temporary repressive institutionalization of a critical economic or political impasse. At least three serious problems of representation are actualized within them.

The classical Latin American military coup, and its current replications on the three continents of the Third World, tended not to interfere with the ongoing processes of exploitation. Moreover, whatever the name of the dictator, the repressive apparatus was normally available to put down the workers and peasants. But little positive could be expected from the state in respect of infrastructural development or protection of domestic business. In fact, the state represented more the local enclaves of foreign capital than the native bourgeoisie, thus condemning the latter to perpetual underdevelopment and subservient dependence.

Secondly, to the extent that the dictatorship not only rested upon division within the ruling class but also was based on only a fraction of a disunited repressive apparatus, the stage was set for a cyclical pattern of coups and counter-coups and resultant dislocation of the administration and, in more serious cases, of the conduct of business.

Thirdly, a particular form of disruption occurs when a politicized

internal bases rather than as middleman of foreign capital. (See R. da Costa, *O desenvolvimento do capitalismo em Portugal*, Lisbon 1975, pp. 76 ff.) I have attempted a different analysis of the fall of the dictatorship and the swift radicalization of the revolution up to Autumn 1975 – a course which was unlike the outcome of the collapse of the Greek junta or, as we can now see, the death of Franco: 'Portugal: Revolutionens dialektik', *Zenit* No. 44, 1976.

military turns to social forces which are neither part of nor allied to the bourgeoisie. Directly anti-capitalist measures may then sometimes be undertaken. In such a case, bourgeois representation is ensured mainly by foreign imperialist blackmail, both economic and military – a form of pressure to which these dependent regimes are eminently vulnerable.

The external dependence and internal divisions and underdevelopment which give rise to these types of rule also protect them from serious challenge as long as they retain full control of the means of repression. But once they lose command, then, like the last Greek junta, they crumble swiftly and completely. They lack the firm social base which alone could support them in such a crisis.

5. Movement-Statism

Although it is a clumsy neologism, the term movement-statism at least has the advantage that it immediately conveys the two essential components of this format of representation. It denotes a regime which rests upon the agglutination of two different forces: a bourgeois state apparatus, deployed in an authoritarian or terroristic manner, and a predominantly non-bourgeois mass movement. The latter provides the former with a peculiar dynamism. But while the mass movement may act as a vigorous defender and promoter of capital accumulation, and in no event comes forward with a non-capitalist alternative, it also generates disruptive and destructive effects, arising out of its social composition. The problem facing the bourgeoisie, then, is to harness the movement-state to the wagon of capital, while minimizing its disruptive intrusion into the running of capitalist enterprise.

The movement-states may be analysed into two broad categories according to their relation to the main enemy of capital: the working class and the labour movement. One of these originates in a process of struggle and restructuring wholly internal to the bourgeoisie and its different fractions, the petty bourgeoisie, and, sometimes, a peasantry lying outside the sphere of commodity relations. Examples of this type are the short-lived reign of Stamboliski's agrarians in Bulgaria; Peronism in Argentina; the polity of the Mexican Revolution, particularly under Cárdenas, before it was increasingly submerged under statism; and a number of other regimes in Africa and Asia, both past and present, such as the Ghana of Nkrumah and the CPP, and Sukarno's Indonesia. As the cases of Sukarno and

Perón demonstrate, however, this restructuring may involve significant mobilization of working-class support against other bourgeois
fractions and sectors. The other variant entails both internal re-
shuffling within the bourgeoisie, petty bourgeoisie and middle strata,
and reorganization of the mode of containment and repression of
the working class. Italian and German Fascism is the prototype of
this.

It would be presumptuous to seek, in a couple of pages, to strike
an analytical path through the almost impenetrably dense and highly
controversial literature on the class character of the Mexican Revolution, Peronism and Fascism. We shall confine ourselves here to a
sketch of certain general contours. How, first of all, was bourgeois
representation ensured in these movement-states, which owed their
mass base to a powerful, if diffuse, antagonism to capitalism or big
capital? The absence of a practicable political alternative was undoubtedly the essential factor, as is most strikingly illustrated by the
heroic and tragic experience of the Mexican Revolution. When the
revolutionary armies of Zapata and Villa met up in Mexico City in
1914, they had all power in their hands. Nevertheless, they shrank
away from power, since they had no clear notion of what to do with
it. After the revolution, then, there developed a process of regeneration and re-staffing of capitalist positions and social relations which
was able to withstand even the radical presidency of Lazaro
Cárdenas.[103] For their part, the Fascist petty-bourgeois radicals and
labour organizers were all frustrated in their anti-monopolist and
corporatist strivings, because the regime depended, for the pursuit
of its supreme political and military goals, upon the active co-
operation of big capital. The latter successfully preserved its independence of state and party commissars and labour trustees, blocking
both anti-monopoly discrimination and medievalist utopias.[104]

[103] An excellent introduction to the epic of the Mexican revolution is John
Womack's biography, *Zapata and the Mexican Revolution*, London 1969. For an
English-language survey of the reign of the enigmatic Cárdenas, together with an
extensive bibliography of works on the period, see W. Cornelius, 'National-
Building, Participation and Distribution: The Politics of Social Reform under
Cárdenas', in G. Almond et al. (eds.), *Crisis, Choice and Change*, Boston 1973.
Subsequent developments have been analysed by H. Cline in *Mexico. Revolution
to Evolution*, London 1960. The standard Mexican work on national politics is:
P. Gonzalez Casanova, *La democracia en México*, Mexico D.F. 1967.

[104] A. Schweitzer, *Big Business in the Third Reich*, Bloomington 1964; M.
Broszat, *Der Staat Hitlers*, Munich 1969, Ch. 6; R. Sarti, *Fascism and the Industrial Leadership in Italy 1919-1940*, Berkeley 1970; F. Adler, 'Italian Industrialists
and Radical Fascism', *Telos* No. 30 (Winter 1976-77).

In this case, of course, the lack of an alternative had different roots. While consciously imitating certain working-class forms of organization, Fascism was largely, though not exclusively, an anti-working-class movement. Arising in the age of imperialism, its big power ambitions had to rely on the industrial capacity of monopoly capital. In the underdeveloped countries, moreover, there was never a strong, independent working class on the political arena. The social cataclysm of the overwhelmingly agrarian Mexican Revolution, equalled only by those in China and Vietnam, took place before the October Revolution had made its mark on history and spread the influence of revolutionary Marxism among the Third World intelligentsia. In spite of earlier, not insignificant anarchist and communist efforts, the Argentinian working class was in its mass organized only under the confused populist auspices of Perón. The small but combative Bulgarian labour movement was no real match for Stamboliski's Orange Guards, while the PKI was held in check by a powerful army which had emerged from a victorious anti-imperialist war.

One interesting and intriguing problem concerns the asymmetrical impact of Fascism and the other movement-states upon the leading fractions of the bourgeoisie. Although Fascism was by far the best organized and the most violent and dynamic of such formations, it rested upon a remarkable continuity. Identical companies and roughly the same personnel stood at the apex of capital before, during and after the period of Fascist power: Fiat, Pirelli, Falck and others in Italy, Krupp, IG Farben, Siemens, etc. in Germany. But the Porfiriate bourgeoisie of Mexico was annihilated, and in Argentina, the previously mighty landowners and cattlebreeders of the Sociedad Rural were largely marginalized under Perón.[105] Whereas the 'populist' movement-regimes signalled total internal restructuring of the bourgeoisie, Fascism involved a political reorganization of monopoly capital in its confrontation with the domestic labour movement and foreign competitors.

Strictly speaking, however, Fascism was never a representative of monopoly capital. Though hatred of the labour movement united it with the whole bourgeoisie, the seizure of power was not a counter-

---

[105] Concerning the dominant role of the rural cattle-raising fraction of the Argentinian bourgeoisie prior to the rise of Perón, see Peter Smith, *Politics and Beef in Argentina*, New York and London 1969. For some indications of the fate of the Sociedad Rural under Perón, see Waldmann, op. cit., pp. 216 ff.; after 1950 the relations changed somewhat (ibid., p. 244 n.).

revolution. As De Felice, the great Italian historian and biographer of Mussolini has suggested[106], Fascism was rather a challenge by the rising 'middle classes' to the old bourgeois oligarchy. The available evidence is still somewhat flimsy. But De Felice's thesis is supported by the fact that, among those countries where bourgeois democracy collapsed, only the two most developed ones witnessed the victory of Fascism. In Italy and Germany, the strongest new petty bourgeoisie and small bourgeoisie had been combined with the weakest palaeo-capitalist or quasi-feudal establishment. Elsewhere, the Spanish JONS, the Romanian Legion of Archangel Michael (more notorious under the name of the Iron Guard), the Hungarian Arrow Cross, the Latvian Thunder Cross all succumbed to the equivalents of Victor Emmanuel, Salandra, Hügenberg, von Papen or von Schleicher, that is to say, the leaders of the traditional Right.[107]

The Confindustria and the Reichsverband (later Reichsgruppe Deutsche Industrie) were able to preserve their internal autonomy and 'self-regulation': bourgeois managers from IG Farben and Hermann Göring Werke (Krupps)[108] staffed the apparatus of the German four-year plan, as did IRI (Beneduce) experts the corresponding Italian ones[109]; private big capital profited enormously from rearmament and such spoils of military victory as captive markets and slave labour; and the interference of the *ras* and the SA was successfully averted. Prevented from implementing its constructive utopias, Fascism kept up its destructive war-like momentum on the fuel of the Versailles trauma. Thus, towards the end of the war, the Fascist movement reasserted its independence in the Salo Republic and the Götterdämmerung of Hitler's scorched earth

[106] R. De Felice, *Intervista sul fascismo*, Bari 1976, pp. 30–31.

[107] At the last hour, when they could be of brief value as last-ditch henchmen of Nazi Germany, some of these movements were able to form governments. Thus, an Arrow Cross regime was installed in Hungary in the last months of 1944, and an Iron Guard government-in-exile was created in Vienna (!) after the liberation of Romania. See H. Rogger–E. Weber (eds.), *The European Right*, Berkeley and Los Angeles 1965.

[108] W. Manchester, *The Arms of Krupp*, London 1969, p. 426. The Hermann-Göring Werke had started production for military reasons in order to exploit low-grade Salzgitter iron ore – an operation which was unprofitable to private capital.

[109] Sarti, op. cit., pp. 119–20. After a pre-Fascist career as a Social Democratic politician, Beneduce had made a rapid rise in the business world as the protégé of some of its established leaders. The financial organisation of IRI as a state holding company involved a complex intertwining of private and public capital.

tactic.[110] In the moment of truth, then, it was the capitalist character of the Allied victors over Fascism which ensured the reproduction of monopoly capital in Italy and West Germany.

6. The Party of Labour

Finally, we must consider the format defined by a working-class party. The bourgeoisie has been able to function as the ruling class even where a party rooted in the working class provides the elected government, either alone or as the main component of a coalition. To the founders of historical materialism such a circumstance would have been absolutely inconceivable. How, then, has it happened?

This variant appears all the stranger if we bear in mind that most of these working class party governments have not even tried to bring about a socialist transformation. The only cases to the contrary are the Communist-dominated governments of Eastern Europe after World War II and the Chilean *Unidad Popular*. It is true that the 1945 electoral manifesto of the British Labour Party reaffirmed that the party's 'ultimate purpose at home is the establishment of the Socialist Commonwealth of Great Britain'; and the majority of party activists undoubtedly regarded the Labour government as a start to the realization of that goal. But, however important the innermost convictions of these militants may have been, the party leadership and the government clearly had no concrete ambition to move towards the establishment of a socialist society. The list of nationalizations (which was later put into effect) had been included in the party platform against the wishes of the leadership and could not, in any case, have been said to form a coherent programme of socialist transition.[111]

Labour governments have not been without problems for the ruling class. It has remained on its guard throughout, prepared to react with counter-moves whenever necessary. The bourgeoisie exerts constant pressure on reformist labour governments by three principal means. First, it maintains an ongoing public ideological campaign, orchestrated by well-financed mass media, parties and propaganda organizations. Usually of a high-pitched and unscrupulously demagogic nature, this campaign is combined with

---

[110] On the relation of Hitler's tactics to capital, see A. Milward, *Die deutsche Kriegswirtschaft*, Stuttgart 1966, pp. 160 ff.

[111] R. Miliband, *Parliamentary Socialism*, op. cit., Ch. IV; D. Howell, *British Social Democracy*, London 1976, Chs. 4–5.

seemingly more factual memoranda and declarations of business organizations and leaders concerning the imperative needs of the 'economy'. Thirdly, the ruling class normally keeps open a number of highly informal, private and semi-secret channels, through which its spokesmen gain backdoor access to individual labour leaders on a fairly amicable plane. Such activity is intended to outweigh the links of these leaders with the working-class party. All three forms have also an international dimension – that of foreign media campaigns, OECD and IMF reports, and international conclaves like the infamous Bilderberg group. The mechanisms of reproduction generally employed are various kinds of economic constraint – flight of capital, whether real or threatened, attachment of conditions to credit, etc. – and ideological smears serving to excommunicate opponents as 'communist', 'tyrannical', 'foreign', and so on.

The most puzzling aspect, however, is not the ease with which the bourgeoisie has been able to maintain its representation, but the fact that its power has only rarely been threatened within this format. How capitalist resistance to serious challenge failed in Eastern Europe and succeeded in Chile is sufficiently well known in broad outline.

The viability of government by a working class party as an instrument of bourgeois rule seems to be circumscribed by at least three basic co-ordinates. One lies in the very nature of capitalism – a system characterized by equivalent exchange on the labour, commodity and capital markets, and corresponding formal equality of citizens of the state, as well as by expansion of the productive forces. The first of these features implies a differentiation between formal equality and practical subordination, and thus the possibility of disjuncture between formal political position and real social position. By contrast, no feudal social formation could conceivably function under a peasant government – and indeed, none ever has. The second aspect points to a zone of possible compromise and co-operation between capital and labour. For capitalist exploitation is quite unlike a zero-sum game: unionization, shortening of the working-day, higher wages and introduction of social services have all proved compatible with not simply the maintenance, but also the expansion of capital accumulation. The contingency of a non-socialist labour party and labour government is thus inherent within capitalism. The post-war boom in the advanced capitalist countries has sustained and broadened the scope for this kind of class collaboration.

The old concept of a labour aristocracy seems much too crude or narrow to account for the widespread phenomenon of working-class reformism. But in its way, it points up a very important aspect. The sustainment of reformism hinges upon the solidity and elasticity of capitalism – features to be found only in the imperialist centre of the world, and not in the dependent periphery of the international capitalist system. Nevertheless, the mechanisms linking the strength of the former with the poverty of the latter are often very complex, even if this relation has deep historical roots in the full-scale plunder of three vast continents at the dawn of European capitalism.

The encounter of capital and labour in the twilight zone of class collaboration explains a notable difference between the effects upon the bourgeoisie of, on the one hand, reformist labour government, and, on the other, non-Fascist movement-states. The precise impact of the long period of Social Democratic rule on the development and world position of Swedish society is the subject of a collective research project which I am currently directing. But this much seems fairly clear from the outset: Social Democracy has not only maintained capitalism – something which a party may do while pushing back the front-line between capital and labour; it has also left the basic internal structure of the bourgeoisie intact. The power structures of banks, industrial groups and capitalist families all exhibit a striking continuity with those of the period before the thirties. The changes that have occurred in this respect have been the result of capital concentration, mergers and absorptions, and problems of succession internal to certain dominant finance families.

Four decades of Social Democratic rule in Sweden, and three decades in Norway, have had much less effect on inter-relations between the various fractions of the bourgeoisie than, say, the half-dozen or dozen years of Cárdenas in Mexico and Perón in Argentina. Although the Scandinavian Social Democratic governments originated in a political deal with the agrarian petty and small bourgeoisie for state intervention in the Depression, this never developed into an anti-monopoly alliance. The basis of sustained class collaboration was the high profitability of big capital, whose expansion was then actively furthered by both state and trade unions. Recently, however, this pattern has run into crisis. In the early seventies, the

Norwegian petty bourgeoisie revolted over entry into the Common Market – a measure promoted by Social Democrats and big capital alike; while today the onset of a structural crisis of Swedish monopoly capital makes necessary a drastic internal reshuffle and the closedown of many plants.

But this is not the whole story, or even its most important part. The contradictions and class struggles of capitalism generated mighty socialist movements and brought about a union of working-class organization with revolutionary Marxist theory. These processes are currently regaining importance, firstly because of the end of the post-war boom, and secondly because the traditional formats of party politics and bourgeois notables have been considerably weakened by the evaporation of reservoirs of captive populations and by the proletarianization of the middle strata. Nevertheless, the history of the labour movement has largely been shaped by long years of bourgeois pressure.

A second major determinant of the adaptation of labour movements and governments to the bourgeoisie has been the tenacious strength of the latter's popular influence. The vision of classical Marxism, as expressed by Engels in his 1895 introduction to Marx's *The Class Struggles in France*, looked forward to a totally different development. Speaking of the massive electorate of German Social Democracy, Engels wrote: 'Its growth proceeds as spontaneously, as steadily, as irresistibly, and at the same time as tranquilly as a natural process . . . To keep this growth going without interruption until it of itself gets beyond the control of the prevailing governmental system . . . that is our main task. There is only one means by which the steady rise of the socialist fighting forces in Germany could be temporarily halted, and even thrown back for some time: a clash on a big scale with the military, a bloodletting like that of 1871 in Paris. In the long run that would also be overcome.'[112]

Engels here summarized the experience of what may be called, with great simplification, the first two phases of the working class movement. In the first stage, the working class evolved defensive organizations within the new capitalist society: solidarity insurance, trade unions, and groups of varying importance linked with or appended to bourgeois and petty-bourgeois movements and politicians. The sharpening and increasingly visible contradictions of

[112] F. Engels, *Introduction* to Karl Marx, *The Class Struggles in France: 1848 to 1850*, Moscow 1968, pp. 23-4.

capitalism subsequently led to the formation of an independent working-class party, and the adherence of the labour movement to some kind of socialist theory and programme, whether Marxist, *marxisant*, or predominantly non-Marxist. In the following years, this movement grew in both electoral and organizational terms. Quite soon, however, the 'natural process' of growth came to a halt at a point far short of a majority position within society, in many cases falling back to previous levels for a certain length of time. *In none of the leading capitalist countries have working class parties ever yet won a majority of the votes*: not, of course, in the United States, nor in Britain, France (although the SFIO and PCF came very close in October 1945), Germany, Italy and Japan. There has never been a working-class parliamentary majority in Benelux, Canada, Denmark, Greece, Iceland, Ireland, Spain, Eastern Europe before the Communist seizures of power (except Czechoslovakia in 1946) or Latin America or elsewhere in the Third World. Where a majority has been achieved, it has been a late and often short-lived phenomenon: Austria experienced its first working class party-majority in 1971; Czechoslovakia in 1946; Finland in 1966; New Zealand in 1938; Norway in 1945; Portugal in 1976; and Sweden in 1936. Only in Australia was it attained early in the history of the political labour movement – in 1914. The workings of parliamentary representation have sometimes yielded quite a large labour majority of seats: in New Zealand in 1935, Britain in 1945. But nowhere save Sweden (from 1936 to 1956 and from 1960 to 1973) and Norway (from 1945 to 1973) have working class party-majorities been sustained over a long period.[113]

In its own way, the Fisher government of the Australian Labour Party (1910–1913) also fits into this general electoral pattern. Though by no means a government of socialist transformation, it did put forward proposals for constitutional reform, which would have made possible central regulation of business and even federal nationalization of private monopolies. But these plans were rejected in the two referenda of 1911 and 1913.[114]

[113] This information has been drawn from official electoral statistics. For good but incomplete surveys, see S. Rokkan–J. Meyriat (eds.), *International Guide to Electoral Statistics*, of which only the first volume pertaining to Europe appears to be available (The Hague 1969); and R. Rose (ed.), *Electoral Behavior*, New York 1974. By working-class parties we refer to Social Democratic and Communist Parties and socialist parties and groups to the left of Social Democracy.

[114] F. K. Crowley (ed.), *A New History of Australia*, Melbourne 1974, pp. 307–8.

The massive and enduring weight of bourgeois political influence is undoubtedly one of the most significant roots of right-wing opportunism and reformist class collaboration. These postures can now, in fact, be understood as an accommodation to seemingly unshakeable bourgeois predominance.

Of course, socialist options were also available: a Bolshevik-type insurrection; alliances around a transitional programme, as distinct from a fully-fledged socialist one; utilization of a parliamentary majority for anti-capitalist ends – a constitutionally legitimate course even in the absence of a majority of votes. Given the aforementioned stability of the advanced capitalist polity and the international constellation of military forces, a Western equivalent of the October uprising seems to have had a clear chance (although by no means a certainty) of success in only two cases: Germany after the collapse of the Empire, and Finland after World War II. In particular, German Social Democracy, which held the crumbling state in its hands but chose to restore order in alliance with the army high command and the *Freikorps*, must bear an exceptionally heavy historical responsibility.[115] A socialist transformation of this most central capitalist country would have altered the whole course of 20th-century history, and would almost inevitably have prevented the immense tragedies of Fascism, world war, death camps, and Stalinism – although the Communists bear a responsibility of their own for the latter. The German Social Democrats instead placed their confused hopes on the election of a Constituent Assembly. But once bourgeois order had been forcefully reimposed, this failed to yield a Social Democratic majority.

An insurrection in Finland, where the proletariat had already fought and lost one civil war, would probably have been successful only with more or less active Soviet support. By contrast, the outcome of the wars in Spain and Greece shows that revolution was unlikely to have been victorious in France in 1936, or in Western Europe after World War II. As we know, the legal Spanish Republic, supported by sectors of the bourgeoisie and petty bourgeoisie, was finally defeated. An uprising of the French working class in June 1936 would have met a unified bourgeois front, probably including

[115] Two good, calm academic accounts are: V. Rittberger, 'Revolution and Pseudo-Democratization: The Formation of the Weimar Republic', in Almond et al., op. cit.; and, in particular, F. L. Carsten, *Revolution in Central Europe*, London 1972.

its share of SFIO Eberts and Noskes, and receiving aid not only from the Fascist powers but from Britain as well. The Greek Communist resistance, which, together with those of Yugoslavia and Albania, was by far the strongest in Europe, was also severely beaten – even if bad political leadership after the Liberation was partially responsible for this. It has to be remembered, too, that Greece was more peripheral to British and US imperialism than France or Italy. In either of these latter cases, an attempted revolution would have prompted massive armed intervention.

Nor is it likely that a French Communist insurrection in 1968 would have escaped crushing defeat. The French army, backed by the United States, was still intact, and in the event of an unconstitutional uprising, it would probably have been supported by most of the population, as is indicated by the results of the June elections which followed de Gaulle's show of force.

We are left, then, with the option of a non-Bolshevik revolutionary strategy in the stable capitalist countries. The fact that such an alternative was completely lacking until the quite recent elaborations of the Italian, French and Chilean Communist Parties and their Socialist allies is the third fundamental determinant of bourgeois representation in labour governments.

The strategy of the Second International was based upon the assumption that inexorable advance on the electoral and organizational fronts would automatically bring about a socialist revolution. When that advance stopped, even the most left-wing classical Marxist leaders (with the exception of Leninists) found themselves completely at a loss. Listen, for example, to this exposition by the leader of the Italian maximalist socialists, Serrati. Writing in 1919, he said: 'We Marxists interpret history, we do not make it . . . We do not attribute powers of transformation either to principles or to barricades. We think that there is more revolutionary content in the transformation of the means of production than in all abstract proclamations.'[116]

The most interesting case in this respect is that of the Norwegian Labour Party. As we have seen, it retained a parliamentary majority for a long time after World War II. Moreover, it had a very left-wing tradition, in contrast to the Swedish Social Democrats, who

[116] G. M. Serrati, 'In vista del Congresso di Bologna', *Communismo* Vol. 1 No. 1 (1919), quoted from P. Spriano, *Storia del Partito Communista Italiano*, Vol. 1, Turin 1967, p. 31 n.

succumbed to revisionism at a very early date, even though they had adopted a socialist programme in 1920. Alone among the parties of the Second International, the Norwegian one adhered to the Comintern nearly in its entirety, incurring only a small split to the right. Although the party refused in 1923 to accept the harshly centralized discipline of the Comintern, it still embraced the dictatorship of the proletariat as its revolutionary goal and regarded itself as part of the post-October revolutionary movement. Its youth organization was characteristically called Left Communist Youth.

A minority government, formed by the party in 1928 on a demonstrative anti-capitalist basis, was very soon toppled. The 1927 reunification with the Social Democrats was bought at the price of certain concessions, of which the most notable was the abandonment of the term, the dictatorship of the proletariat. However, in 1930, the programme was revised in a radical direction in order to correct any opportunist dilution which might have resulted from reunification and the attraction of new members and supporters in the electoral advance of 1928. Then in the trough of the worst economic crisis in the history of capitalism, the party was rapidly and organically transformed into an ordinary Social Democratic one; it headed a cautious minority government between 1935 and the German invasion of 1940, and after 1945 it set about the reconstruction of Norwegian capitalism. What had taken place?

Essentially, two things. The anti-revolutionary mobilization of the bourgeoisie led to a decline in the proportion of the labour vote at the 1930 elections. Then the Depression forced the party to act. It faced not only massive unemployment, but also, and even more menacingly, the prospect of a fascist-type reaction to the industrial and agricultural crisis. The party which had previously been characterized by its intransigence and narrow proletarian base went to the country in 1933 under the slogans: The Whole People at Work and Defence of Popular Government. The fresh appeal was successful, and the party was able to preside over the end of the crisis. After the war, its main preoccupation became national reconstruction and avoidance of the expected new slump.

Once the most immediate and urgent post-war reforms had begun to be implemented, the Norwegian Labour Party, like its British and Swedish counterparts, had no perspective of further advance. Lacking a coherent strategy of gradual socialist transformation, all these parties were trapped by their own success, relative and modest though it was, in the administration of capitalism. Their absorption with day-to-day problems of bourgeois society and recurrent electoral tests was closely related to other lacunae of Social Democracy, both left and right. Capitalism was seen not as a mode of production which constantly generates new and old forms of exploitation and inequality on the basis of market relations, but as a static set of arbitrary powers which could be curbed and abolished by nationalizations, administrative controls, or policies of redistribution. Nor were their leaders in any way conscious of the class character of the state administrative apparatus, of its function in the reproduction of working class subordination. This was most blatantly manifested by the bureaucratic nationalizations of the British Labour Party.

Thus, the need to *conquer* political power and *break* the ongoing processes of reproduction – even via one or more intermediary stages – was never posed as a serious problem. It is impossible to say with any degree of assurance whether a gradual strategy of socialist transformation would in fact have succeeded in Norway, Britain or Sweden, or whether it would have met the same fate as the Chilean *Unidad Popular*. Here we are only concerned with the reason why such a policy was never even earnestly contemplated, let alone attempted. Clearly it was not fear of a Pinochet.

One further characteristic of Social Democracy must be considered, since the reactions of the Norwegian Labour Party (DNA) were not all that dissimilar to those of the PCF at the time of the Popular Front. The crucial difference between the two is the following: whereas the PCF kept its' commitment to socialism, the DNA lost its own so completely that it became during the Cold War a party of rabid anti-communism. In those countries where protracted guerrilla warfare was out of the question, the Communist Parties also had no concrete socialist strategy, except one that depended on the shield of the Red Army. But through their unshakeable commitment to the October Revolution and the USSR, they alone had a concrete idea of a socialist society – a vision which, while contorted and naively idealized, was nevertheless *real*. The Communists were firmly conscious of the actual historical presence of socialism as a concrete alternative to modified capitalism. The engulfing Stalinist juggernaut had wiped out this awareness even among most left-wing socialists. (Long before the rise of Stalin, Western Social Democrats – from Branting to Blum – had been overawed by the Bolsheviks' *making* of history and filled with contempt of Russian 'primitiveness'.) With some spectacular exceptions – Italy, Chile, Japan – the international polarization of the Cold War sealed the fate of left-wing Social Democracy. In the choice between Stalinism and US imperialism it sided with the latter, with all that it implied. The fact that it regarded the alternative as one of 'dictatorship or democracy' does not significantly affect the matter.

In Norway, the national front which had been formed under Nazi occupation entered into the programmatic basis of the post-war DNA government. Nevertheless, serious negotiations with a view to unification of the DNA and CP reached quite an advanced stage in 1945. As elsewhere outside Eastern Europe – where the Communists could force the issue – the discussions ended in failure; but until the outbreak of the Cold War, strong unitarian tendencies persisted even at the top of the party. But then the leadership committed the organization and the country to the Marshall Plan and NATO. From that time, although the Norwegian bourgeoisie may have grumbled about state controls, it knew that it had nothing to fear from these committed allies of the Pentagon.[117]

[117] E. Bull, *Arbeiderklassen i norsk historie*, Oslo 1947, pp. 274–337; H. F. Dahl, *Fra klassekamp til nasjonal samling*, Oslo 1969; idem., *Norge mellom kriegene*, Oslo 1971; E. Lorentz, *Arbeiderbevegelsens historie*, Vol. II, Oslo 1974.

5.

Wielding State Power II: Processes of Mediation

From the perspective of the ruling class problematic, state mediation of relations between the ruling class and ruled classes involves ensuring that the latter both submit to the established social order and contribute to its functioning. The special apparatus of the state provides two material means for the accomplishment of these tasks.

First, the state effects a centralization of the resources of the ruling class – although the degree to which this is done varies greatly from the medieval feudal state to modern dictatorships. Those who belong to the ruled classes have to face not only a local individual member of the ruling class, but a formidable apparatus in which the acquisitions of that class have been pooled.

But the state is more than a centralized external power confronting the ruled classes. In another sense it also comprises them. Thus, the peasants as well as the lord were subjects of the feudal king; members of all classes are citizens of the state in a capitalist or transitional socialist society. Secondly, then, the state is based upon a totalization of social relations. Through it are effected intermediary interventions between different classes and between individual members of different classes.

Mediation, like representation, is traversed by the class struggle; how it functions in practice is determined by the constellation of forces arising out of the class struggle. But the state is never a neutral or passive mediator. Its fundamental class character is determined by the class character inscribed in the material rule-making, rule-applying, rule-adjudicating and rule-enforcing apparatuses, as well as by the reproductive mechanisms of the ruling class which circumscribe the radius of state intervention. Mediation here signifies not arbitration, but exercise of class power through the state. The class state does not go between the classes in order to separate fighters, but to connect them, in an asymmetric relationship of domination and exploitation.

However, asymmetry does not entail unilaterality. The relationship is not one-way, and the mediation processes involve the demands and protests of the ruled classes as well.

Submission and contribution are thus ensured by means of state centralization and totalization as expressed in a number of processes. The most important of these may be charted as follows:

Means	Processes of Mediation	Primary Effects	
	Submission	Submission-cum-contribution	Contribution
Centralization	Repression	Displacement (Canalization)	Extraction
Totalization	Co-optation	Judicature	Support

We should now briefly clarify some of these terms and spell out certain implications of the processes concerned. Attention should also be paid to the contradictions inherent within them: both the overall one between centralization of ruling class resources and totalization of all classes in the state, and ones specific to each process. In general, these contradictions may be seen as manifestations of the basic political contradiction between domination and execution. Centralization thus involves both pooling the resources of domination and establishment of a certain distance between domination and execution; while totalization entails both global domination over the ruled and inclusion of the latter in its execution. In order to succeed, not only revolutionaries but also counter-revolutionaries have to master the dialectics of social life.

1. Repression

The repressive apparatuses are the ultimate guardians of the pre-vailing social order – the mailed fist which strikes when the ongoing process of reproduction breaks down and the ruled classes revolt. But, of course, no guarantee is completely reliable. The exactions and ravages of centralized repressive apparatuses may also provoke rebellions: desperate peasant risings, like the *jacquerie* in the Paris region in 1358 and the Tuchin movement somewhat later in central France during the Hundred Years War[118]; or working-class agitation for democratic and social demands.[119] Sometimes, these apparatuses may, like the Russian army in 1917, be rent by the contradictions of the whole society.

In fact, besides the need for repressive mediation, a second factor has played a major role in the development of a centralized repressive machinery, namely, the striving for undivided representation of the ruling class. Important as a background to the formation of a unified repressive state were feuds among various magnates, each with his own armed retinue: for example, the War of the Roses between York and Lancaster, or the struggle among the houses of Guise, Montmorency and Bourbon, during the French Huguenot Wars and at other times; clashes between enterprising *condottieri*; and rivalry among modern army cliques and *caudillos*. Another propelling force has been conflict between the ruling classes of different societies.

Although a strong and reliable repressive apparatus is indispensable at the decisive hour, as de Gaulle recognized by making his secret tour of crack military units in late May 1968, a class society also exhibits non-state forms whereby the means of repression are concentrated in the hands of the ruling class. Indeed, in the everyday system of oppression, this local might is often more significant than that of the state. The feudal lords had their courts, bailiffs, henchmen and prisons; the modern capitalist corporation has its armed guards, undercover networks and, where necessary, local town vigilantes. The big automobile companies – General Motors, Ford, Citroen and Fiat – have acquired the greatest notoriety in this respect. It is not surprising, then, that state centralization of the means of repression has often been advanced as a defensive popular demand.

However, the state repressive apparatus intervenes also in more routine control of the ruled classes. This is true not only in dictatorships, but, to take what is probably the significant case, in the United States. Here, union organizers, strikers and pickets quite normally have to reckon with intervention by the courts and police. This

---

[118] R. Hilton, *Bond Men Made Free*, London 1977, pp. 112 ff.

[119] On the important role of external war in the rise of bourgeois democracy, see my 'The Rule of Capital and the Rise of Bourgeois Democracy', *New Left Review* No. 103 (1977).

system, which reached its peak in the 1920s, was patterned by the US Supreme Court and its Chief Justice, ex-President Howard Taft – a man who had a quite explicit view of his task as supreme judge of a bourgeois state. In 1922, Taft explained in private correspondence what was to be done: 'That faction [labour] we have to hit every little while.'[120]

In the normal exercise of class rule, repression functions in four modes: *prohibition* of opposition, *restriction* of intra-systemic opposition, *harassment and terror*, and *surveillance*. If official prohibition of organizations of the ruled classes has gained importance only in the 20th century, this is essentially because under feudalism these classes were as a rule too weak and geographically isolated to pose a concerted threat, and because in the 19th century whole classes, rather than just their organizations, were constitutionally barred from political influence.[121] Trade unions were made legal at quite an early date – 1824 in Britain, 1884 in France, 1890 in Germany (the date when the last restrictions were lifted following the repeal of anti-Social-Democratic emergency legislation) – and they have remained so in non-dictatorial bourgeois regimes. With one important exception, the parties of the Second International in Central and Western Europe were all permitted.

Modern dictatorships, however, have proscribed both unions and reformist parties. In addition, Communist parties have been banned several times by non-dictatorial states, particularly in the period of the ascendancy of Fascism, from the Depression to Stalingrad. Together with Japan, where the labour movement was severely repressed before 1945, Germany stands out among leading capitalist states in this respect: it was the only one which banned a party of the Second International (1878–1890) and the only one which proscribed the Communist Party after World War II (1956–1968), not to speak of the period of Fascist rule. (The CPUSA was not formally illegalized, although in the fifties it was largely driven underground as a result of its definition under the Smith Act as a foreign agency.)

In capitalist states, restriction of intra-systemic opposition has above all taken the form of limitations on the right to strike – a practice which has a tradition going back at least to the modified

---

[120] I. Bernstein, *A History of the American Worker*, Vol. 1, *The Lean Years*, Boston 1960, p. 191. Bernstein devotes a chapter, the fourteenth, to the workings of this judicially framed system of repression.

[121] This thesis is developed to a certain degree in Therborn, op. cit. 1977.

British Combination Act of 1825. At various times, picketing has been repressed; particular strikes have been proscribed; all unofficial stoppages have been forbidden, as is currently the case in Sweden; or else internal trade-union organization and decision-making have been subject to state regulation and supervision. The policies have been many. Except under dictatorships, the old institution of censorship has generally disappeared (although it re-emerged in France during the Algerian war). Local state authorities often hampered the early labour movement by denying access to places for meetings and demonstrations, and the actions of the West German and US Communist Parties are still restricted in this way. Where the old practice of disbarment of oppositional individuals from state employment is still broadly applied, it has greatly increased in significance as a result of the enormous expansion of this sector. Once again West Germany has taken the lead with the widest and strictest *Berufsverbot*. The ban covers all kinds of tenured state employment – from ordinary teaching posts to postmen and engine-drivers – and is applied also to Social Democrats who have at any time worked with Communists in the same organization.

Police harassment and violent intimidation are not a characteristic of dictatorships alone; they have occupied a conspicuous place in the arsenal of methods employed by the US state to handle opposition. The numerous examples include: the smashing of the Pullman strike and the repeated use of anti-strike terror before the second New Deal; the Palmer Raids conducted against all kinds of radicals in 1920; police raids on Communists and harassment of suspect ex-Communists during the Cold War; the clubbing of demonstrators against the Vietnam war; and the physical liquidation of the Black Panthers in the 1960s. The violence of riot squads, particularly the Italian police and carabinieri, is today a matter of notoriety in most bourgeois democracies.

Finally, we should consider the role of surveillance and compilation of dossiers on the activities of the ruled classes. These preparations for a showdown, which have long been practised and which provide invaluable source-material for labour historians, have during recent years grown immensely in both scope and efficiency. The traditional system, involving the use of informers and undercover agents, eavesdropping and infiltration, and submission of oral or handwritten reports, has been supplemented by highly specialized agencies furnished with computerized files and the most advanced photographic and microphone equipment. Watergate and its after-math have revealed the almost unbelievable extent of police sur-veillance in the United States. Even in the more peaceful and peripheral Scandinavian countries, a high level of operations has been disclosed. Thus, crucial links have been built between, on the one hand, the secret police and, on the other, anti-communist net-works within the unions and Social Democratic party (Sweden), company personnel departments (Norway) and right-wing extrem-ists (Denmark, Sweden).

Repression and preparations for repression, directed against economic, political and ideological opposition, form an inherent part of the everyday activity of the democratic class state. It is also worthy of note that, among the non-dictatorial states of advanced capitalism, the two most powerful – the United States and West Germany – have been, and remain the most repressive. (Of course, Germany also produced the most ferocious Fascist dictatorship.)

It is true, however, that all the above-mentioned forms of state repression may also be found in abundance in each of the existing socialist states. Moreover, they are applied not only against the bourgeoisie, but equally against dissident sectors of the working class and the Communist Party.

2. Displacement (Canalization)

State centralization of the ruling class may bring with it condensa-tion of the contradictions of the social formation, widened exposure of oppression and exploitation, and unification of the ruled classes. More often, however, the opposite aspects are dominant. Through the interventions of the state it becomes possible to displace contra-dictions, gloss over private exploitation, and play off different classes and sectors of classes against one another.[122] The satisfaction of popular demands may be delayed and, if they prove too costly to be resisted, channelled into non-disruptive institutions and processes. The success of every ruling class crucially depends on, among other things, its ability to displace, and find safe channels for, the welter of contradictions amid which it exercises its rule. The centralized and thoroughly politicized socialist states – particularly those which, like the USSR in the twenties and thirties and certain East European regimes in the post-war period, rest upon a rather restricted social

---

[122] Cf. L. Althusser, 'On the Materialist Dialectic', in *For Marx*, p. 216.

base – have great difficulty in displacing contradictions and pre-venting their condensation into dangerous ruptures. They have thus often employed repression as an alternative.

There are a number of general displacement processes. First of these is *isolation* of grievances and conflicts. A local landlord or boss may be seen in his true, dark, light, but the state which represents the class of this particular enemy may appear as a protector of the ruled. Precisely because of its centralization, the state and its leaders are frequently supposed not to know of or be responsible for imme-diate class exploitation. This pattern is exhibited both in the rela-tionship of the Russian peasant masses to the Tsar, and in that of the working class to bourgeois-democratic governments.

Extroversion of aggressive frustration is another ancient device of displacement. Pogroms, external wars, hunts for foreign agents and spies have repeatedly served as powerful instruments with which to divert class conflict and rally the ruled behind their rulers. Just as old, but rarely as effective, is the creation of *scapegoats*, that is to say, the purge of selected leading personnel who are made responsible for unpopular state policies.

Another means employed to prevent the explosion of accumu-lating pressure is: *pre-emptive canalization*. The importance of this policy owes much to the fact that the implications for social repro-duction of a particular measure are often determined more by its form and timing than by its intrinsic content. The most striking historical illustrations of this circumstance are: the abolition of serf-dom from above, out of a position of strength and within the frame-work of existing institutions, and the similar manner in which suffrage rights were extended, and workers were granted a certain say in the enterprises of capitalist societies.

Displacement and canalization also include *provision of intra-systemic alternatives*. Contradictions *of* the system may be displaced into contradictions *within* it, provided that alternative forms of the same state (i.e., class rule) or even simply different leading personnel are available. For instance, the serious contradictions which had been developing within the foremost capitalist country after the collapse of the jubilant business boom of the 20s were successfully displaced by the Roosevelt administration into a conflict between supporters and opponents of the New Deal.[123] It should be noted that not only electoral formats of representation function in this

---

[123] The story is told, eloquently and admiringly, by Schlesinger, op. cit.

way. The peasants and burghers of feudal societies often found themselves placed before an alternative – whether it was constituted by rivalry between two dynasties, or by the contradiction between decentralized and royal-absolutist forms of feudalism. Opposition to a dictatorial bourgeois state is also faced with a choice of direction: either socialism, or a regime led by another bourgeois dictator, or a bourgeois democracy.

In fact, provision of intra-systemic alternatives may be regarded as part of a broader process of canalization. Every state offers the ruled a system of institutionalized *channels for the presentation of grievances*. These may become blocked as a result of malfunctioning of the state, and they may be burst by a rising flood of discontent. Nevertheless, to the extent that they are in service, they involve petitioners in the existing structures; people who present claims, keeping to the established forms, times and spheres of competence, thereby perpetuate the system of domination, against aspects of which they are themselves protesting.

In systems marked by relatively free elections and a broad suffrage, the notables and party formats of bourgeois representation are largely sustained by displacement processes – isolation and sectoralization of issues; imperialist or chauvinist extroversion; pre-empting initiatives; presentation of alternative images; well-managed arbitration and electoral outlets; delimitation of the boundaries of class alliance in order to prevent a union of popular forces.

Displacement entails preservation of submission; but it also harnesses popular energies to the expanded reproduction of the system by channelling them into the existing political, economic and ideological processes.

3. Extraction

In the specific dynamics of the production process, the working classes of every exploitative mode of production have to yield surplus labour and surplus product to their exploiters. But, in addition, they have to finance the rule of the state over them. The forms of such contribution range from the judicial fees delivered to the early feudal kings (who generally owned their own peasants) to modern systems of taxation. Centralization of the state is associated with extraction of higher payments from the ruled in two respects. Pooling the services, goods and money extorted from the ruled produces a quantity which is greater than the sum of its parts. For it may be used to undertake large-scale operations – such as the military exploits of the feudal state and the promotion of economic growth – which would not otherwise have been possible.[124] Moreover, the greater the effective centralization of the state, the less will be the waste arising out of the extraction process, corruption, tax-farming profits, and avoidance.

Furthermore, owing to the distance of the state from both the immediate exploitative process and local traditions of a 'just rent' or 'fair wage', it is usually easier to increase the amount extracted for 'public' purposes than it is directly to raise the profits of individual members of the ruling class. A rise in state taxation has tended to encounter less resistance than rent increases or wage-cuts.

However, development of the state does require higher levels of taxation, and this may generate resistance and fiscal crisis. The great French medieval historian, Georges Duby, has concluded: 'There is no doubt that of all the ills which afflicted them, the peasants suffered more painfully and less patiently from the burdens of war and remote taxation.'[125] Still, even if rebellion should break out, the state's resources of counter-insurgency are mightier than those of the individual landowner or employer.

In keeping with the increasingly social character of the forces of production – the social scale and interdependence of the production process – extraction has assumed greater significance in state mediation of the private character of the relations of production. This growth of extraction provides the resources with which the state carries out a more and more important task: namely, public underwriting of private capital accumulation.

It will be remembered that mediation, while asymmetric, is not unilateral: a growth of tax levels and requirements has also affected the ruling classes, giving rise to opposition, obstruction and conflict. The furthering or maintenance of the positions of the ruling class by no means always coincides with short-term maximization of its individual members' wealth. Taxation and other forms of state extraction are therefore often the source of clashes within the ruling class, as well as between classes.

---

[124] Japan and the USSR provide the two most important examples of massive state extraction from the peasantry for the purposes of economic accumulation: of capital, in the first case, and collective use-values in the second. Cf. Maddison, op. cit.

[125] G. Duby, *Rural Economy and Country Life in the Medieval West*, London 1968, p. 333.

4. Co-optation

Like all other processes of mediation, co-optation functions both through the state and through non-state apparatuses. Like them, too, it is an old phenomenon, in no way peculiar to bourgeois democracy. The feudal lord frequently tried to co-opt his peasants by making them feel that he was 'their' lord: indeed, under feudal law, he protected against external forces all the inhabitants of his estate.[126] This patriarchal pattern was carried over into several early capitalist firms, and was later replaced by company unions or institutions, or work-force consultation and 'participation'. But, of course, the state has far greater means of co-optation, since it stretches beyond the immediate nexus of exploitation.

The feudal pattern of co-optation first of all involved a conception of society and social relations as a totality of *non-market exchange* and *mutual obligation*, in which every estate had its proper place – a conception which was reinforced by the all-embracing catholicity of the *Church*. It further employed the imagery of the *family* to present the king or emperor as the father of his peoples. (Familial legitimacy was a central component of feudal formats of representation.)

The bourgeois state substituted fresh patterns of co-optation for the feudal ones. The organic unity of orders and estates, each with its specific range of mutual obligations, gave way to the *legal equal opportunity* of all citizens. Neither idea is mere ideology. Both are inscribed in material institutions and practices – franchises, privileges and charters, in the former case, *laissez-faire* legislation, legal procedures and court practices, and (much later) universal suffrage, in the latter.

The divine order, while lingering on in many bourgeois countries, was progressively replaced by the *national community*. Patriotism first demonstrated its tremendous political force in the *levées en masse* which were introduced at a time when the French Revolution was mortally threatened by feudal and (in Britain) conservative bourgeois enemies. Nationalism has also functioned as an important co-optative process in socialist countries: in the USSR during the 'Great Patriotic War' (World War II), and in China, Korea, Indo-china, Cuba, Albania and Yugoslavia. Its relative in-

---

[126] This system is unfolded in rich detail, although rather apologetically, by O. Brunner, *Land und Herrschaft*, Brno-Munich-Vienna 1943.

applicability in the rest of Eastern Europe – with the recent exception of Romania – has made the regimes there comparatively fragile. Nor is nationalism reducible to a simple ideological appeal; it, too, is materialized in a new, non-dynastic unification of the state, manifested both in the conduct of foreign policy and in cultural institutions.

Although the family has largely lost its ideological role on the state level of co-optation, it has on occasions been quite effectively utilized in ideological discourse. For example, in Sweden in the 1930s, the Social Democrats coined the slogan 'A good home of the people', thus presenting the society they wished to attain as a nice family home governed by 'equality, concern, co-operation and helpfulness'.[127]

In the twentieth century, co-optation by *economic growth* has constituted an original and increasingly important process, the function of which is to rally all classes behind policies and institutions of quantitative economic expansion. It probably first became prominent at a state level in the Soviet variant of socialist industrialization – a campaign which co-opted a large number of engineers, managers and other technocratic intellectuals to the brutally authoritarian Stalinist pattern. After World War II, the effectiveness of the Marshall Plan and the (for a time) well-managed growth of the advanced capitalist economies projected with considerable success the vision of a multi-class community based on an unprecedented level of wealth. Since then, victorious anti-imperialist struggles and the crisis of the seventies have to a great extent uncovered the exploitative foundation of that pseudo-community. But the latter may be revived in fusion with nationalism, to be turned against new anti-imperialist challenges in the Third World. A further variant of co-optation through growth – one which worked very well in Brazil for some years at least – is the ideology and practice of developmentalism within the stronger capitalist states of the Third World.

Last but certainly not least, we should mention a highly complex form of co-optation which is of crucial significance for the labour movement in the contemporary advanced capitalist countries. I am referring, of course, to *bourgeois democracy*. A certain number of initial specifications and qualifications should be made at this point.

---

[127] G. Fredriksson, 'Per Albin och folkhemmet', in G. Fredriksson et al., *Per Albin linjen*, Stockholm 1970, p. 26.

From a historical point of view, bourgeois democracy emerged not as a mode of co-optation of the popular masses by the bourgeoisie, but rather as a conquest of popular struggle *against* the bourgeoisie.[128] However, it could be converted into a process of co-optation, because bourgeois resistance everywhere proved sufficiently skilled and powerful to prevent a direct or complete victory of the popular democratic struggle. The bourgeoisie was thus largely able to determine the timing and modality of democratization, fitting universal suffrage, free elections and government responsibility to the electorate into the bourgeois state apparatus, the process of capitalist reproduction, and bourgeois mechanisms of reproduction. The working class was thereby integrated into a democratized *bourgeois* polity. In the chapter on formats of representation, we observed the way in which the bourgeoisie has been able to rule by means of democratic party and notables formats. Here we shall consider the functioning of democracy as a co-optive mediation of bourgeois class power.

Co-optation through democracy denotes the process whereby the loyalty of the working class – both submission and contribution to its own domination – is secured by virtue of the fact that the bourgeoisie rules in democratic forms. This clearly goes beyond simple neutralization of the disruptive effects of democratization upon the power of a tiny minority. Has such co-optation really occurred? If so, to what extent?

As we emphasized in the section on ideology, the acquiescence of ruled classes is ensured in a very complex manner, and there is little firm evidence with which to weigh up the various components in the accomplishment of their submission and contribution. We later indicated other basic reasons for the strength of bourgeois parties and labour reformism. It would be wrong to regard bourgeois democracy as the all-important integrative institution of contemporary advanced capitalism. But the recent declarations of a number of Communist Parties testify to its major significance. They also, of course, constitute a strenuous effort to prevent ruling-class ideological manipulation of an institution which arose out of bitter workers' struggles against the bourgeoisie. Allegations that socialism and communism are undemocratic or non-democratic have formed a crucial part of the arsenal of anti-communism; there can be no

---

[128] See further on this Therborn, op. cit. 1977.

doubt about that. They have served to rally non-bourgeois layers around the bourgeois regime, and against the socialist states and revolutionary working-class movement.

Although the co-optive function of democracy is undeniable, its precise significance has still to be defined. Let us then look at its determining co-ordinates. The fact that the proletarian democracy of soviets turned into a grim authoritarianism, and under Stalin into massive terror, has not been as decisive as may appear at first sight. The French petty-bourgeois Radicals, as well as the Social Democrats, were co-operating with the Communists in the Popular Front against the bourgeois Right just at the time of the Moscow Trials and the bloody purges in the Soviet Union. The Chilean Communist Party could realize a broad front for democratic socialism while openly declaring, in the words of its popular General Secretary, Luís Corvalán: 'We are Soviet fans.'[129]

I would suggest as a hypothesis that bourgeois democracy has functioned as a major process of co-optation mainly since the outbreak of the Cold War – since the time, that is, when the first determinant was affirmed anew and supplemented by three others. For democracy to work in this way, the bourgeoisie must itself believe in its efficacy; and this faith did not develop until quite a late stage. Only a few peripheral capitalist states were democracies prior to World War I. After a short-lived conversion, the inter-war crises once again made the bourgeois world unsafe for democracy. Thus, by 1939, only a minority of the most advanced capitalist countries exhibited a democratic regime, and sympathy for Mussolini and Franco (if not so much for Hitler) had been widespread in the thirties among even the non-Fascist bourgeois. This situation then changed drastically as a result of war with, and often occupation by, Fascist powers, and above all after their disastrous military defeat. Both vanquished and victorious bourgeoisies rallied to democracy following their experience of World War II.

Secondly, the necessity and possibility of a functioning co-optive democracy requires the exhaustion of reservoirs of captive populations able to serve as objects of manipulation for the ruling class. The ruled classes must then be effectively, though always only partially, brought into the political process. Rural exodus, industrialization,

[129] L. Corvalán–E. Labarca, *Kommunistische Politik in Chile*, West Berlin 1973, p. 92. (Original edition: E. Labarca, L. Corvalán, *27 Horas*, Santiago de Chile 1972.)

full-employment policies and industrial mobility, national integration of immigrants and a limited new inflow in the United States,
growth of the labour movement – all these phenomena fostered mass
contribution to the system in the developed centre of capitalism.

It is not clear to what extent mass support for the Social Democrats' adherence to bourgeois democracy (rather than proletarian
dictatorship) explains the failure of Comintern parties to win and
retain a majority of the organized working-class in the twenties and
in the Depression. It seems likely that the inexperience, internal
division, sectarianism, adventurism and unrealistic expectations of
imminent revolution which marked the early Communist movement were much more powerful factors. Moreover, Fascism bestowed upon the idea of dictatorship concrete and sinister connota-
tions which did not fail to impress even the already harshly exploited
and oppressed proletariat. It was, after all, through their resolute
and combative defence of democracy that the Communist Parties of
France, Czechoslovakia, Spain, Portugal and Italy became mass
parties and acquired their leading position among the workers. Only
in a few cases was this not true: in Bulgaria, where the Communist
Party's mass base was rooted in revolutionary traditions similar to
and contemporary with those of the Bolsheviks; in Germany, where
the left-wing Social Democrats of the USPD, disenchanted by the
Weimar restoration, rallied to the KPD in 1922. In Finland, too, the
Party had grown out of the revolutionary Social Democracy which
had been defeated in the Civil War of 1918. But it won its mass
character only with the establishment of bourgeois democracy in
1944 following the defeat of Finnish and Nazi troops by the Soviet
Union. (If the notorious notion of 'social fascism' ever had any contact with reality, it would have been during the wartime alliance
between Finnish Social Democracy and Nazi Germany.)

We come now to the third co-ordinate of democratic co-optation.
When the Cold War set in, the developed capitalist countries
appeared to stand in continuity with this democratic anti-Fascist
struggle, whereas the socialist states were embarking upon heavy-
handed unifications of the labour movement and a new wave of
show-trials and massive police repression. This resulted in effective
isolation of the revolutionary workers' movement, whether it was
large or small, and incorporation of the rest of the non-bourgeois
masses into a democratic pseudo-community under bourgeois command. The democratic continuity was in fact both apparent and

real: real to the extent that democratic forms were retained (even though the decimated West German CP was banned); apparent in the sense that Fascists and former collaborators were rehabilitated. Violent repressive measures were taken against strikes and other forms of working-class opposition; strict police surveillance was instituted over the revolutionary movement; lavishly financed undercover operations were mounted – for example, in order to split unions and parties; and imperialist violence was unleashed in Greece, Madagascar, Malaya, Guatemala, Algeria, and so on.

The close connection between CP strength in Europe and in Chile,[130] and the defence of democracy; between the influence of Asian CPs and the struggle for national independence – these simple correlations eloquently indicate the political, non-economistic character of the dialectic of class struggle. All the same, it is the revolutionary working class nature of these parties which accounts for their endurance, perseverance and combativity in the fight against Fascism and imperialism.

A fourth co-ordinate, though probably minor, should be added to the others. In the developed capitalist countries, the fate of a system combining isolation of revolutionary forces with bourgeois-democratic co-optation was eventually sealed by the high level of employment sustained in the long post-war boom. Contrary to Communist predictions, the Marshall Plan had the intended effect. Only the end of the boom, the fresh crises in the polities of advanced monopoly capitalism, and the Twentieth Congress of the CPSU with its delayed and uneven impact on the Communist movement, have made it possible to loosen the grip of the bourgeoisie and anti-socialist reformism. In the new crisis affecting the capitalist centre, the revolutionary labour movement is beginning to regain its vanguard role in the defence and development of democratic rights and freedoms. Whether this will lead to a socialist breakthrough remains to be seen. More clearly, however, we are now witnessing the end of the post-war period, in which, through a twist of historical irony, a privileged minority was able to sustain its domination of the people through democratic co-optation. But there exist other co-optation processes and other means of mediation. Co-optation, then, should be seen as a large-scale social process, involving more than incor-

[130] The Chilean situation is distinguished by the fact that bourgeois democracy stood in much sharper and more immediate contrast with US imperialism than with Stalinism.

poration of a handful of political leaders into the traditional elite. Whole classes, or large sectors of them, may be more or less temporarily co-opted into the system.

The ideological process of political *legitimation* functions within the material dimension of co-optation. The legitimacy of a regime is based on one or another form of unity between ruler and ruled, within which the latter consider the superordinate position of the former to be justified. The effect of co-optation is precisely to bring about such unity. In a class society, this unity is always asymmetric: it is both a reality, and an appearance concealing fundamental antagonisms. It is for this reason that we have chosen the term co-optation – which carries the connotation of asymmetry – instead of, say, inclusion or incorporation.

Co-optation is a contradictory phenomenon. Entry of the ruled classes into unity with their rulers provides both a means to secure their active and willing submission and a platform for their demands and opposition. The peasants tried to bend feudal laws and customs to serve their ends, while the existence of an all-embracing religious community repeatedly fostered and inspired movements against oppression and exploitation. Similarly, nationalism has supplied an important rallying-point against the comprador bourgeoisie, and the creation of institutions of citizenship and suffrage has stimulated working-class demands for economic democracy. Under socialism, emphasis on economic growth has also had a contradictory effect: among not insignificant sections of the population, the public campaigns and propaganda have thrown an attractive light on the even more fully 'grown' countries of advanced capitalism, or, at least, on their technocratic aspects and levels of private consumption.

5. Judicature

The significance, in the present context, of state totalization of social relations is perhaps most clearly demonstrated by the judicial process. The judicial apparatus of the state mediates relations between rulers and ruled by providing institutions of appeal to which conflicts among individual members and collectives of the various classes may be brought for settlement. Under medieval feudalism, where administration proper was still rudimentary and laws were more interpreted than made, the king's supreme judicial rights constituted his most weighty prerogative. He too was bound by the feudal laws; but his subjects had the right to petition, and royal power could be used against the claims of individual noblemen.

In capitalist states laws are made – by legislation and prejudicate. They are established in a universal and abstract, rather than class-specific form, even though their content is circumscribed, with varying degrees of rigour, by capitalist relations of production. The way in which laws are applied to conflicting claims is largely determined by the practice of the judiciary itself. While constrained by the formulations of the legal system, judges' decisions are broadly shaped by their own formation within or on the periphery of the social milieu of the ruling class.

The judicial process tends to put a check on arbitrariness or idiosyncrasy which sections of the ruling class may exhibit in the exercise of power. The legal apparatus may indeed be used by the ruled classes to assert the rights they have won within the existing society – as a result of which they may be provided with reasons for submission and contribution to the system. The courts of a class state do not function exclusively as organs of repression against the ruled classes. When the employers facing them have been too powerful, unions and political labour movements have also fairly frequently appealed for state intervention, and sometimes even for court arbitration.[131]

Several contradictions may arise out of the bourgeois courts' independence of the legislature and executive, and the wide range of judicial discretion. In certain circumstances, this autonomous domain may become the site of conflicts within the ruling class – as is illustrated by the struggles between the New Deal administration and the Supreme Court in the United States. The fact that bourgeois law is not class-specific whereas bourgeois political rule is, may also lead to a number of contradictions. Sometimes, the judiciary may stick to the law rather than to the practice of its social milieu. The first major crack in official US racism, for instance, was the 1954 Supreme Court ruling against segregation. When judges are no

---

[131] The demand for industrial arbitration was advanced and realized at an early stage of the Australian labour movement, after the defeated strikes of the 1890's (Crowley, op. cit., pp. 279 ff.); a similar development occurred in New Zealand in response to wage-cutting during economic depression (B. Brown, *The Rise of New Zealand Labour*, Wellington 1962, pp. 153–4). On the appeals made by the French labour movement to the state, see E. Shorter–C. Tilly, *Strikes in France*, London 1974, pp. 30 ff.

longer solidly formed within the ruling class, the application of bourgeois law may in some cases be quite embarrassing to the bourgeoisie. Recent occurrences in France are an indication of the threat created by the education explosion and student movement of the sixties to the class composition and reliability of the judiciary.[132]

In the existing socialist states, formal legality has been heavily subordinated to the substance of politics and ideology. Although, in practice, the judiciary has become clearly subservient to the repressive apparatus, this outcome is hardly intrinsic to such a political system of law. The latter may, in contrast, be deeply enmeshed in non-state institutions and movements of the popular masses.

6. Support

It would be false to equate emphasis on the class character of the state and on ruling class determination of state politics with a denial that the state can and does also materially support the ruled classes. Indeed, this very phenomenon was already well known in ancient Rome. Under feudalism, the king was often the official legal protector of orphans and widows[133], and a system of charity was normally operated by both the crown and the church. We have noted above, in another context, that the state was responsible for provision of the Parisian population with grain. At times, royal justice restricted aristocratic exploitation of the peasantry. The English ten-hours bill and factory legislation, and Bismarck's social insurance were not, then, as novel measures as they may seem. In the advanced capitalist countries, of whatever political coloration, this welfare support has since increased to an enormous extent.

But can support of the exploited classes really be called a mediation of class rule? Is it not rather a concession extracted from the ruling class, a mitigation of its rule – or even a manifestation of the benevolent neutrality of the state? Now, social policies have developed for a number of different reasons[134], and of great impor-

---

[132] Cf. D. Charvet, 'Crise de la Justice, crise de la Loi, crise de l'Etat?' in N. Poulantzas (ed.), *La crise de l'Etat*, Paris 1976; and R. Canosa, 'Alcune contradizzioni negli apparati di stato: magistratura, polizia, esercito', *Quaderni Piacentini* No. 57 (1975).

[133] Concerning the French case, see R. Holzmann, *Französische Verfassungsgeschichte von der Mitte des 9. Jahrhunderts bis zur Revolution*, Munich and Berlin 1910, p. 244.

[134] There is no materialist, economico-political history of social policy. How-

tance has certainly been the exertion of such strong pressure from below that the ruling class deemed further resistance to be too costly. Nor should diffuse ideological tendencies, of a humanitarian and charitable kind, be *a priori* denied all causal significance. In the early stages of industrial capitalism, quasi-feudal sectors frequently manifested paternalistic concern for the fate of the workers of the upstart bourgeoisie. Even reactionary monarchist opponents of German national unification had some such feeling[135]; and the pioneering British factory legislation was shepherded through Parliament in the 1840s by a Tory aristocrat, Lord Ashley, who, according to the rules of British aristocratic succession, was later to become Lord Shaftesbury.[136]

Upon a moment's reflection, there need be nothing surprising in the thesis that support of the poor and weak may be an expression of the rule of the rich and strong. Feudal ideology and law were, as we have seen, permeated by such conceptions. *Noblesse oblige!* Anyone who has ever been the object of charity, whether material or psychological, has already felt in his or her bones the condescending superiority which it embodies. The urge to exhibit (a small part of) one's appropriated wealth and lofty character – this has been a powerful factor in the spread of humanitarian ideologies among well-established ruling classes.

But where does state support of the ruled classes fit into the reproduction of ruling class power? It involves mediation of class rule in at least three areas. First, it strengthens the connection between rulers and ruled by increasing the latter's contribution both to the prevailing system of exploitation and to that of political domination. Secondly, as we indicated in our discussion of judicature, it links the ruled classes to the global system of rule by going against the personal idiosyncrasies of members of the ruling class. Thirdly, it may mediate between individual members of the ruled classes, solving their conflicts and problems for them.

In order to deliver surplus-value, the working class must be able to reproduce itself, both from day to day and from generation to generation. This process was directly endangered by the appalling

---

ever, a useful overview is provided by G. Rimlinger in *Welfare Policy and Industrialization in Europe, Russia and America*, New York 1971.

[135] Hamerow, op. cit. 1969, pp. 211 ff.

[136] G. D. H. Cole–R. Postgate, *The Common People 1746–1946*, London 1961, pp. 313 ff.

sanitary situation of the early British industrial towns and by the widespread occurrence of child labour. (The former also threatened to lead to epidemics, which could evidently affect the ruling class as well.[137]) The introduction of children's allowances often formed part of an explicit attempt to increase the population (of wage-labourers and soldiers).[138] Similarly, free or subsidized education has been expressly conceived as a means to broaden the pool of talented individuals capable of occupying positions within the system – to tap the 'talent reserve' as Swedish educationists have put it. Much modern welfare policy is also geared to labour market requirements – to regulation of labour mobility according to the needs of the economy (i.e., capital accumulation). Socialist states have supported agrarian petty-commodity production in order to heighten the peasants' contribution to socialist construction.

Although the above kind of state intervention is often implemented against the opposition of sectors of the ruling class, and although it usually plays a subsidiary role in the totality of measures oriented towards maintaining or increasing the rate of exploitation, nevertheless its importance may be gauged by an extreme historical case. In 1942 Hitler ordered that Russian forced labourers in German industry should be better fed and no longer kept behind barbed wire. The instruction was, of course, motivated by considerations which were far from humanitarian. But it was still ignored by Krupp.[139]

Distribution of welfare also serves to secure contributions to the prevailing system of political domination, both internally and against external enemies. A Japanese statesman of the Meiji period, Itagaki Taisuke, expressed this aspect in a memorandum: 'After all, the people's wealth and strength are the government's wealth and strength.'[140]

Bismarck set the modern pattern when he introduced his famous social insurance schemes in 1881 as part of an overall policy of domination which had recently inspired the banning of the Social

[137] Ibid. p. 338.
[138] This was the case in Sweden, for instance, where the public debate and state commissions preceding the introduction of children's allowances after World War II originated in a booklet by Alva and Gunnar Myrdal: *Kris i befolkningsfragän* (Crisis in the Population Question), Stockholm 1934.
[139] Manchester, op. cit., p. 553.
[140] Beasley, op. cit., p. 385.

Democratic party. In the twentieth century, bourgeois parties and politicians have retained and expanded this instrument of enlisting popular support for their rule. Thus, the British Beveridge Reports, which advocated, during World War II, a comprehensive programme of welfare policies, are permeated by admonitions that such measures are essential to the survival of a 'free society' (by which the Liberal author referred to capitalist democracy).

But Beveridge also developed the rationale for a crucial feature of modern social policy, namely, redistribution overwhelmingly *within* the working classes and between different periods in the life of the individual: employed/unemployed, sick/well, old/young, child-rearing/childless. Beveridge found that 'two causes between them accounted for practically all the acute poverty existing in Britain; the two causes were interruption or loss of earning power and failure to relate family income to family needs.' Thus, 'poverty could be abolished by a redistribution of income within the working classes, without touching any of the wealthier classes at all.'[141] The ruling class could, then, restructure the internal situation of the working classes at the same time as it continued to organize their exploitation. The two aspects were brought into inter-relation with each other.

State support of the exploited classes implies totalization in the following sense: the state takes a *total* view of the need for efficient maintenance and expansion of the global system of exploitation and domination, thereby overriding narrow and myopic perspectives of individual members and sectors of the ruling class. But totalization is also implied in another sense. State support partially associates the working classes and their demands in disposal of the fruits of their labour, even though other mechanisms of reproduction ensure that it threatens the appropriation of surplus labour by the ruling class as little as does private charity. Finance ministers and state creditors keep an ever watchful eye on expenditure.

Nevertheless, decisions concerning state support, however 'rational' they may appear to the ruling class, are not as smooth and harmonious as the argumentation of a functionalist sociologist. The Beveridge Reports, for example, were written for the wartime coali-

[141] W. (Lord) Beveridge, *Power and Influence*, London 1953, p. 306. Beveridge adds in his memoirs that he did not mean that the wealthy classes should not be affected at all. But he also deplores the fact that the Labour government financed the implementation of his scheme with greater taxation and fewer direct contributions than he had recommended. (p. 332)

tion government at the request of the TUC, and Churchill and the Conservatives could not bring themselves to endorse them unequivocally. It befell the post-war Labour government to implement the proposals, while in the 1945 elections Beveridge lost his Liberal parliamentary seat to a Tory.[142]

State welfare policies should be regarded neither as an expression of supra-class benevolence nor as a shrewd ruse of the ruling class. They are rather a manifestation of the inevitably contradictory and conflictual character of class rule.

[142] Ibid., pp. 296, 323 ff., 348.

Summing-up

In a sense this has largely been a methodological essay, whose purpose was to present a means of analysis of class rule and political power. We have tried to spell out the radically different analytical problematic of historical materialism, as compared to other approaches to the question of political power. It has been argued that the scientific superiority of the former resides in its more general and inclusive character – its ability to tackle problems which cannot be solved by other methods, as well as to incorporate their non-ideological contributions.

Historical materialism we regard not as a special language for the re-interpretation of events, but as an instrument of empirical investigation of men's social conditions and possibilities. Within this perspective, we have put forward an analytical schema, and certain definitions and research procedures for study of the class character of state power and the ruling class. To be sure, the degree of precision attained by them would hardly conform to the canons of the exact sciences. But in the social field, the precision of science cannot serve as substitute for the art of qualitative judgment – whether exercised by the political cadre in the midst of struggle or by the historian in serene retrospect. We have simply proposed a number of tools with which such judgments can be made. For in politics, analytical schemas are synonymous with schematic analyses.

To the extent that it proves fertile, the above presentation will have cleared a path through the narrowly subjectivist or personalist debate which is conducted between 'pluralists' and 'elitists' on the questions of political power; it will also have lifted discussion out of the quagmire of objective and subjective, short-term or long-term, 'class interests'. The result is an empirical scientific basis for study of the strategically crucial phenomenon of ruling-class power and class rule in general.

In this essay, we have also offered a range of explanatory theoretical propositions relating to the existence, maintenance and loss of the state power of a given class. Having defined this power for the purposes of empirical research, we have sought to explain its significance and describe the modalities according to which it is exercised. We have regarded state power and class rule as determined by, and wielded within, an ongoing process of societal reproduction and transformation. We have further elaborated the multiple determination and conjunctural nature of the exercise of political power – features which were indicated in hints by Marx, forgotten by the Second International, and developed and practised by Lenin. We have emphasized that state power functions within a dialectical process of internal contradiction and uneven development. Both the retention and capture of state power are dependent upon mastery of these contradictions and disarticulating processes of uneven development.

What then does the ruling class do when it rules? Essentially, it ensures that its dominant positions in the economy, state apparatus and ideological superstructures are reproduced by the state in relation both to the other modes of production present within the social formation and to the international system of social formations. These reproductive state interventions are enmeshed in the structural dynamics of the mode of reproduction, but they also have to be secured in the thick of the class struggle.

It has been argued that the modalities of class rule cannot be pressed either into the straitjacket of force-and-consent or into that of the structural dynamics of the economy (under capitalism, accumulation) combined with political legitimation. The concepts of consent and legimation do not embrace the complex functioning of ideology. In reality, the latter tells us not only what is right but also what exists and what is possible, thus structuring identities, knowledge and ignorance, ambitions and self-confidence. Moreover, force is too crude a concept to cover the alternatives to consent or acquiescence.

We have described three sanctions or reproductive mechanisms: economic constraint, violence or physical coercion, and ideological excommunication. The ruling class problematic, as it is exhibited in the class struggle, is primarily characterized not by the need to secure legitimation of its rule, but by the attempt to ensure representation in the special apparatus of the state together with state mediation of its rule over other classes. This has to be done in various institutionalized formats of representation and through certain processes of mediation, whose function is to master the specific manifestations of the fundamental political contradiction: that between class domination and the execution of the societal tasks of the state. In this way, we have sought to make a theoretical contribution to what seems to be the most urgent task of Marxist political analysis: namely, disclosure and elucidation of the complex base and functioning of bourgeois rule in the advanced capitalist countries.

The purpose of this essay has been largely methodological and theoretical, and empirical references have, as a rule, been introduced only for the sake of illustration. However, a number of hypotheses have also been presented, concerning the character of state power prior to the bourgeois revolution in Britain and other countries; the nature of Bonapartism; the tenacious strength of bourgeois popular support; the reasons for the development of reformism; the effects of bourgeois democracy, and so on. Although these hypotheses have been motivated, their validity can be decided only by direct investigation.

The state power of the ruling class is exercised within a contradictory and complex totality which is in constant flux and development. The class struggle is pursued in and through these contradictions and developments, while the latter function in and through the class struggle. A social revolution occurs when these contradictions and disarticulating processes of uneven development reach the point at which the three reproductive mechanisms, under their dominant aspect, turn into revolutionary mechanisms of a new ruling class.

It has been a basic assumption of both essays of this book that historical materialism has to break out of a traditional capitalist-centric mode of analysis in order to grasp the specificity of capitalism in relation to other modes of production. This explains our constant effort to analyse feudal and socialist states as well as capitalist ones. In our final remark, however, we should stress the originality of socialism and the socialist revolution.

From both a scientific and political point of view, socialism has to be seen not as an ideal millenium, but as a historical form of society, immersed like others in the concrete problems and contradictions of real development. Socialism is still a class society, because the working class exists as an entity distinct from other classes and strata. But it is also unique in that provides a possible way out of the dialectics of the rise and fall of ruling classes. A socialist revolution does not exclude the contingency of the re-emergence of exploitative class society, whether in new or old forms. The power of the working class, in other words, may be undermined and ultimately lost. But socialism is not itself an exploitative society: the working class as the ruling class has no class to exploit, and the growth of its power is co-terminous with the dismantling of remaining class differentials. If it succeeds, then, socialist revolution opens up the road to classless communist society.

Taking State Power from Advanced Capitalism

Some Reflections on Socialism and Democracy

The History of the Present

The current debate on the Left in the advanced capitalist countries focusses above all on problems of socialism and democracy. I hope that I shall be able, in the near future, to undertake some real research into the development of the strategic theory and practice of the revolutionary labour movement. The present essay, however, is merely a rough sketch, containing a number of reflections of relevance to the discussion.

Socialism and democracy can be, have to be, and are being tackled from many different angles: theoretical and conceptual, ideological and programmatic, practical and pragmatic, historical and experiential, and so on. Here we shall attempt to situate contemporary discussion on the democratic-socialist strategy for the conquest of state power within the historical evolution of the labour movement, raising at the same time certain problems that will have to be faced in the future. Our ambition is to offer neither a history of the labour movement nor a recipe for socialist revolution in the societies of advanced capitalism, but rather a small contribution to scientific and political understanding of the present situation, as well as to awareness of a number of difficulties lying ahead.

In the first mass political organization of the working class, generated by the union of Marxist theory with the labour movement, democracy and socialism were related to each other in a wholly unproblematical manner. The Second International fought for equal and universal suffrage and elected government, as well as for collective appropriation of the means of production and the development of a classless society. Democracy and socialism were thus intrinsically connected in the consciousness of both the labour movement and the bourgeois theorists and politicians who resisted their advance. Democracy was seen as the instrument which would bring the working class to power and secure the realization of socialism.

At first sight, socialism and democracy do appear to be inter-related in a simple and straightforward manner. Democracy means popular rule, and socialism specifies this with regard to the relations of production. Democratic political institutions – government elected by equal and universal suffrage – have been part of the Marxist conception of socialism since the very beginning. Conversely, democratic rule by the people of its own life presupposes that it owns the means of production and plans their deployment for collective use.

In the real history of classes and the class struggle, however, the relationship is rather more complex. State power is wielded by the ruling class in many forms and with diverse means; distinct social relations provide the content of constitutional forms; and the organization of the state apparatus exhibits specific effects. In short, the wide range of possible variation between legal form and social content crucially complicates the ideal simplicity of the democracy-socialism relationship and calls for political analysis and strategic elaboration of a materialist and dialectical kind. This must simultaneously take into account: the specificity of the political and the legal; the socio-economic context of struggling classes; and the interaction of these two aspects. Marx and Engels never developed a fully-fledged political theory, while the Second International closed its eyes to a number of serious problems affecting both its strategic conceptions and its future practice.

As was noted in the preface, the entire Marxist tradition has had enormous difficulty in coming to grips with the paradoxical phenomenon of bourgeois democracy – a regime in which the exploiting minority rules by means of a system of legally free popular elections. Of course, Marxists have only themselves to blame for the backwardness of their theory in this respect. But one important contributory factor was the very late stage at which bourgeois political theory announced its scientific pretensions. In Marx's time, the only discipline with any such claim was bourgeois political economy, in the critique of which historical materialism developed as a systematic science. The major classic of Marxism is called not *The State* or *Classes and Class Struggle*, but *Capital* – and although a volume on the state was to be included in this *magnum opus*, it never even reached the stage of a draft. These origins gave to historical materialism from the very beginning a strong tendency to economistic reductionism.

Marx treated the first modern form of bourgeois rule, Bonapartism, in a rather confused way. This basic analytical insecurity was then carried over into the fragile economistic and evolutionist premises of the thinking of the late Engels and the Second International. Anticipating steady growth towards a socialist electoral majority under conditions of universal male suffrage, they never understood, or even seriously confronted, the political modalities of bourgeois rule. When the predicted outcome failed to materialize and the labour movement underwent a deep split, the Social Democratic attachment to democracy came to function as a vehicle of accommodation to bourgeois rule and increasingly as an ideological cover for abandonment of the struggle for socialism.

Lenin is by far the greatest political analyst of historical materialism. It was he who made explicit and developed Marx's fragmentary and complex political thought, which had been ignored and deleted in the conceptions of the Second International. He pointed to the multiple determination of state power, the class character of the state apparatus, and the conjunctural specificity of politics. For Lenin, revolutions do not fall as the ripe fruit of economic growth; they have to be made. But his exposure of bourgeois rule in democratic forms was too crude and summary, too scorched by polemical heat, to constitute an adequate basis. Quite naturally, moreover, he had little experience of a firmly established bourgeois democracy. Nor did he ever elaborate a realistic theory of the revolutionary socialist state: the dictatorship of the proletariat. On this foundation, whose instability was only aggravated by the subsequent systematization of Marxism-Leninism, the Comintern came to combine offhand denunciation of bourgeois democracy with apologetic support for the increasingly authoritarian socialism being built in the USSR. The Comintern parties never won over the majority of the working class, and their insurrectionist strategy either suffered defeat in combat or failed to reach the stage where it could be applied.

The two most brilliant minds of the Comintern after Lenin – Antonio Gramsci and Mao Tse-tung – worked out their strategic conceptions in a process of reflection upon the defeats of the original Comintern line. Indeed, the components of their thought display striking similarities. Both regarded the socialist revolution as a protracted war, not as a single insurrectionary blow. Both considered that the problem of mobilization involved not only winning the majority of the working class, but, equally important, linking the struggle of the proletariat with that of other oppressed classes and strata. Gramsci used a military metaphor, 'war of attrition', to bring out the concern with ideology that was central to his strategy; while Mao's conception of people's war referred in non-metaphorical terms to a war of attrition waged by a proletarian technology of military organization. Both perceived the problem of the mass base of bourgeois rule with a clarity which Lenin never possessed, and for which his attention to the 'labour aristocracy' was a poor substitute. But neither Gramsci nor Mao had to wrestle concretely with the problems of bourgeois democracy – problems which will never be solved by even the most penetrating exegeses and elaborations of Gramsci's thought. Indeed, 'Gramscianism' can easily become an opiate of Western Marxism.

The traumatic experience of Fascism brought the material reality of bourgeois democracy to the fore. The Communist Parties became its most resolute defenders – in the Popular Fronts, the Spanish Civil War, and the Resistance. For this, they often came under attack from left-wing Socialists, who, from France and Spain to Chile, kept a dismissive disdain for bourgeois democracy.

Paradoxically, with the exceptions of Czechoslovakia, Germany after the KPD-USPD unification, and possibly Bulgaria, *Communist parties have only become mass parties* (or, where this had already been achieved, majority parties) of the working class, *in struggle for what Marxists regard as tasks of the bourgeois revolution*: for elected government and freedom of expression in Europe, Chile and Japan; for national liberation and land reform in south-east Europe and dependent countries of Asia. While it is true that the Bolsheviks grew at fantastic speed in the fight against the weak bourgeois state of the February Revolution, the party had developed in struggle against a late-feudal state. The land programme, which was an essential part of Lenin's revolutionary strategy in 1917, was, as he made explicit, a programme of bourgeois revolution, involving division of the landed estates into individual peasant plots.

Where democracy had been destroyed, the Communists fought not for mere restoration of the *status quo ante*, but for a 'new', 'progressive', 'advanced' or 'popular' democracy, which would

eradicate the roots of Fascism and terroristic dictatorship and prepare the road for advances towards socialism. The dictatorship of the
proletariat remained the long-term strategic goal, but it was no
longer the touchstone by which everything and everybody had to be
judged. In contrast to the secessionary foundation of a sharply-
demarcated Comintern – a policy which was applied with the utmost
rigidity even in relation to maximalist socialist mass parties such as
the Italian and Norwegian ones – the Communists now strove for
close co-operation and reunification with Social Democracy.

However, the great hopes of the period immediately following
World War II rested upon a deeply ambiguous and unstable foundation. Fascism was bourgeois and monopoly-capitalist in character, but so too was the United States, a major partner in the anti-
Fascist coalition. The outbreak of the Cold War very soon put an
end to 'national roads to socialism' in Eastern Europe, as well as to
progressive democracy and any form of socialism in the rest of the
continent. The labour movement split again – so deeply, this time,
that an iron curtain fell in all countries between Communism and
Social Democracy.

It is meaningless to speculate about what would have happened in
Eastern Europe and the USSR after Stalin's death had it not been
for the onset of the Cold War. The irreconcilable antagonism
between capitalism and socialism is a part of contemporary reality
which cannot be removed by thought. It is, of course, necessary to
combat bourgeois myths that the Cold War was the result only of
Stalinist bedevilment; or the argument that the post-war measures
– intervention in Greece; early restrictions on the whole labour
movement in the Western zones of Germany; the veto applied by
the US military authorities to socialization laws passed by regional
West German parliaments during 1946; the granting of economic
aid to Western Europe in winter 1947 on the condition that the
Communists were thrown out of (by no means socialist) governments of national reconstruction; the introduction of the Marshall
Plan and NATO – that all these were undertaken only to save the
freedom and prosperity of each and all. But it makes little sense to
allocate the major share of blame here or there. The primary responsibility lay with neither side, but with their antagonistic relationship to each other. We should, perhaps, mention the active involvement of the British Labour government in the restoration of
bourgeois reaction both in Greece and, to a lesser extent, in West

Germany. The fact that a Labour government with avowedly socialist aims was able to take this stand against the popular forces of another country – as early as 1945 in the case of Greece, and somewhat later, under heavy American pressure, in that of West Germany – is, indeed, a quite remarkable vindication of Lenin's theses concerning the crucial role of the character of the state apparatus.[1] Ernest Bevin and the Labour Cabinet embraced the traditional policies of the Foreign Office and the King's Army; while the hopes of masses of Labour militants that Britain would take international positions different from those of the USA and USSR came to nought.

The Cold War was a serious setback to both democracy and socialism. The democratic potentialities in Eastern Europe were cut short, and a new wave of show-trials and terror unleashed instead. Though much less drastically, democratic liberties were restricted in the West too: the Communists were driven into a ghetto, and Social Democracy swallowed the bait of booming capitalism hook, line and sinker.

The Cold War pushed the Communist movement onto the defensive, essentially because it was an unequal war made increasingly unequal by the fact that both sides fought with the same methods. It was an ideological war waged largely on the themes of democracy and economic development, and in both these respects the Communist side was weaker. The USSR was manifestly more authoritarian than the capitalist democracies. Entering the war from a much poorer starting-point, the Soviet Union had furthermore been seriously wounded by the German invasion: its national income in

[1] A British bourgeois journalist has aptly said that the position taken by the Labour Foreign Secretary, Ernest Bevin, in relation to Greece was 'pure Palmerston'; that is, it faithfully continued the work of the chief architect of mid-nineteenth-century British imperial policy. 'We cannot,' Bevin told the Labour Party Conference in 1947, 'afford to lose our position in the Middle East; our navy, our shipping, a great deal of our motive power for our industry, in the shape of oil, are there . . . The standard of life and the wages of the workmen of this country are dependent upon these things . . .' (D. Watt, 'Withdrawal from Greece', in M. Sissons–P. French [eds.], *The Age of Austerity*, Harmondsworth 1964, p. 118.) Thus, the interests of the British Empire, especially protection of the route to the spoils of the Middle East, demanded that Greece be prevented from 'going Communist'. For a survey of the actions of the British commander and ambassador after the liberation of Greece from the Germans, see: C. Tsoucalas, *The Greek Tragedy*, London 1969, pp. 61 ff.

As regards West Germany, the Labour government, including Bevin, did at first express support for socialization of the coal and steel industries; but the

1945 was 83% of that of 1940, as compared to the American figure of 212%![2] As regards population levels, the USSR lost about 20 million citizens, whereas the American losses totalled 400,000.[3]

Nevertheless, with the exception of West Germany where the KPD was largely demolished even before it was banned, the Communist parties generally withstood the tremendous onslaught of intimidation, isolation and mass consumerism with remarkable success. Taking the area as a whole (Western Europe, North America, Japan, Australia and New Zealand), the influence of the Communist parties, as indicated by the size of their electorate for instance, was broader during the post-war ebb of the fifties and early sixties than it had been at any time prior to World War II – although notable declines had occurred in certain individual countries, particularly Germany, Norway and Spain. The Finnish, French and Italian parties consolidated their newly won mass base, while the smaller ones retained considerable industrial weight, and the underground parties of Greece and the Iberian peninsula were engaged in building up their forces. The Soviet Union was no longer an isolated, exposed state, whose territories were coveted even by Finnish imperialists, but the second major power in the world, surrounded by a number of socialist states, including the immense People's Republic of China. This power of resistance was cemented with authoritarianism, dogma and apologetics, but it is the primary force behind the present actuality of the question of socialism and democracy. Without the strong Communist parties of Chile[4], France and Italy, these themes would not have become topical, either on the plane of principles or in relation to the practical strategy of the

---

British occupation authorities withheld their sanction throughout 1945 and 1946. After 1 January 1947, when the British and US occupation zones were merged because of British difficulties in financing their military presence, Whitehall followed the American anti-socialist line in West Germany. Probably the best recent book on the reconsolidation of capitalism in West Germany is U. Schmidt–T. Fichter, *Der erzwungene Kapitalismus*, West Berlin 1975. See also E. H. Huster et al., *Determinanter der westdeutschen Restauration*, Frankfurt 1975. The latter work contains a wide selection of documents.
   [2] K. Steinhaus, 'Probleme der Systemauseinandersetzung im nachfaschistischen Deutschland', in H. Jung et al., *BRD-DDR. Vergleich der Gesellschaftssysteme*, Cologne 1971, p. 409 n.
   [3] J. Elleinstein, *Histoire de l'URSS*, Vol. 3, Paris 1974, pp. 220 ff.
   [4] The strength of the Chilean Communist Party was built up underground between 1948 and 1958.

labour movement as a whole. Had the Communist parties succumbed, the struggle for socialism would have had to start anew with the small groups of the late sixties. If it had been confronted with them alone, the old French SFIO would probably have survived for considerably longer than it did. The Socialist parties of Chile, Italy and Japan – which also withstood the Cold War – were and are thoroughly divided; and in the sixties, the PSI was caught in a process of rapid social-democratization. In Chile, Allende's extremely narrow victory was made possible by inclusion of the Radical Party in the Unidad Popular – a measure which was suggested by the Communist Party and initially opposed by the Socialists. The French Union of the Left is also a Communist initiative.

Already, American and West German imperialism have on a number of occasions more or less explicitly threatened to intervene, above all through economic warfare, in the case of a development towards socialism in France and Italy; indeed, this type of blackmail is applied today in Portugal to considerable effect. It is, to say the least, unlikely that such dangers would have been less grave and imminent if the Communist post-war advances had been 'rolled back'.

Thus, *it is principally due to the Communist parties* and the international detente and balance of power assured by *the strength of the USSR that democratic socialism has become a serious possibility in the advanced capitalist countries.*

Now, this reunion of the perspectives of socialism and democracy has, of course, arisen out of a complex internal development of the Communist parties, and an even more intricate social dialectic. Compressing a highly elaborate chain of causation, we may say that the combination of two historical events, mediated by internal change within the CPs, has been of decisive importance.

We have already mentioned the first of these: namely, the experience of Fascism and of the real difference between democratic and terroristic-dictatorial forms of bourgeois rule. It should be emphasized that the classical Leninist strategy of armed insurrection cannot be simply counterposed to a 'democratic' strategy. Armed insurrection, where it expresses the will of the majority, may be at least as democratic as the wielding of a parliamentary majority. Lenin was no putschist, and he formulated two preconditions for insurrection: the revolutionaries must have won the majority of the working class; and there must be an objective crisis of the old state –

a revolutionary situation. However, from a democratic point of view, Lenin's conception suffered from two grave deficiencies. Since the working class nowhere constituted the overwhelming majority of the population, an insurrection could involve the action of a minority, as it did in Russia, despite the fact that the large mass of the non-proletarian layers were not exploiting capitalists and landlords but petty bourgeois and employees. Secondly, although Bolshevik strategy in 1917 accorded crucial importance to the slogan of land distribution and relied on a class alliance with peasantry, nevertheless, Lenin attached little strategic weight to other parties and organizations, except in the field of short-term tactics. The October Revolution was a purely Bolshevik action, and although a short-lived government was formed with the Left SRs after the discouraging results of the Constituent Assembly elections, Lenin was at first vehemently opposed to such a coalition.[5] It is clear, however, that a popular majority is always heterogeneous in character and comprises several organized political tendencies, which must be taken into account in the elaboration of a democratic strategy.

The struggle against Fascism and bourgeois terror led the Communist parties to make crucial corrections to their traditional view on these two points. Their new conception of progressive democracy as a stage towards socialism did not by itself bring together democracy and socialist revolution. For the dictatorship of the proletariat had been understood by Marx and Lenin as a democracy – an expression of the free will of the majority of the population. The decisive factor was rather the development, within the struggle against Fascism, of broad popular alliances and forms of unity with other, independent political parties and organizations.

The Chilean, French and Italian strategies of democratic socialism are all rooted in the unity of the anti-Fascist struggle. This continuity is particularly striking in the Italian case. It should be remembered that the Christian Democrats, who have formed the governing party of the Italian bourgeoisie ever since 1947, were once part of the Resistance coalition. It is this tradition that the PCI conception of a 'historical compromise' attempts to bring back to life.

However, the present situation has been created not simply by the

[5] E. H. Carr, *A History of Soviet Russia. The Bolshevik Revolution*, Vol. 1, Harmondsworth 1966, pp. 118 ff.

re-emergence of the post-war constellation from the ice-pack of the Cold War. The current strategic conception differs in essential respects from the previous version.

The second major phenomenon in the evolution of the forces of socialism and democracy has been the upsurge of the class struggle in the late sixties. Those events shook the very elements of the anti-Fascist coalition which had secured the restoration and renewed development of capitalism after World War II: namely, the US and domestic non-Fascist bourgeoisie. At the same time, they brought forward new and large anti-capitalist forces outside the core of the working class.

The dialectic of the Vietnam War was completely different from that of the Cold War. In both cases, a Communist-led movement was pitted against a liberal American government; but there the similarity ends. In the sixties, the United States did not appear as the rich protector of European elections and mass consumption against a harsh, austere socialism, but as an imperialist invader and enemy of a poor people's fight for national liberation and deliverance from the most blatant exploitation. The Vietnamese did not present an alternative social model to that of advanced capitalism, but their heroic combat was the source of tremendous ideological inspiration. The huge disparity between the wealthy American superpower and Vietnam was compensated by the superior methods of struggle available to the popular forces. The war had enormous reper-cussions all over the world, showing that imperialist war is a *natural* product of the *normal* regime of the *centre* of the world capitalist system. From that time onwards, the term the 'Free World' vanished as a designation of the US-led part of the globe; or else it was placed within ironic quotation marks by forces far beyond the ranks of the Communists. In Latin America, the blockade and attempted inva-sion of Cuba had earlier had a similar effect.

A parallel dethronement occurred within particular national formations. In Chile, where the Christian Democrats had succeeded the Radicals as the major reformist party, the 1964–1970 presidency of Eduardo Frei both aroused the masses with a programme of agrarian and other reforms, and thoroughly disillusioned them when it imposed limitations on these measures and met fresh demands with repression. In France, the post-war reconsolidation of capital-ism had, after the abdication of de Gaulle in 1946, been presided over by the reformist Centre or so-called Third Force, in alliance with the Social Democrats, bourgeois Radicals and Catholic MRP. Although it was barely noticed in the glaring light of the student movement, the most important consequence of the French May was the final and inglorious end of this Centre, the burial of the SFIO, and the split within what was left of the Radicals. (The MRP had already evaporated before 1968.) France was polarized between a Gaullist majority, soon to become a heteroclite conservative bloc without de Gaulle, and a strong socialist minority, on the verge of majority support. In Italy, another decisive political shift took place. The massive popular struggles of the late sixties sounded the death-knell of the 'centre-left' – that attempt of the Christian Democrats to regain the vigour of capitalist reformism (which had been one element in de Gasperi's post-war success) through a governmental marriage with the Socialist Party. The social-democratization of the PSI was stopped and reversed, and the PCI emerged from isolation to become the unifying and directing force of an increasingly wide-spread opposition.[6]

Out of the upheavals of the late sixties emerged fresh anti-capitalist forces, as well as a new generation of traditional forces. In the long run, the student movement has not proved as important as it appeared at first. However, the mass of students nowadays become subaltern employees; and the middle strata have experienced an intense radicalization which is manifested in, for example, the new and flourishing French Socialist Party. In Italy, the PCI, more intellectual than the PCF, has attracted the bulk of these layers. Other highly significant movements have appeared, particularly those directed against women's oppression and ecological disruption, and the movements of solidarity with the Third World. All these are largely based on the middle strata and exhibit, beside their particular dynamics, a common anti-capitalist orientation.

These occurrences of the late sixties affected the problems of socialist strategy most directly by making the Communist party a major participant in the strategic coalition. To say major is not the same as to say dominant. For the Socialist partner may have slightly broader electoral support and may provide the unifying figure of the coalition. Nevertheless, the present situation is significantly different from that of the Popular Front or the post-war period, when

[6] Cf. G. Napolitano, *La politique du parti communiste italien*, Paris 1976, pp. 48 ff.

strong bourgeois forces had the upper hand. In France and Chile, the CPs remained outside the Popular Front governments, which were based, respectively, on a bourgeois Radical-Socialist coalition and a Radical presidency and cabinet. The post-war governments, in which the Communists did participate, had strong bourgeois leaderships: Gonzalez Videla in Chile; de Gaulle in France – supplemented and later succeeded by MRP and Radical politicians who exerted significant influence over the Social Democrats; de Gasperi in Italy. The US army was always close by, watching.

The new situation not only signifies that the possibilities of advance towards socialism have increased. It also requires clarification of certain ambiguities in the post-war strategic conception of the Communist parties. Two major problems were then left hanging in the air. One concerned the internal functioning of the broad strategic coalition: the relationship between independence and unity, and the mode in which leadership was exercised. The second involved the character of the socialist state which would follow the stage of new democracy.

As a continuous process of opinion-formation and decision-making, democracy presupposes the possibility of different internal developments and changes, not merely the assertion of the will of the majority at a given point in time. In this respect, the post-war formulations were rather vague and evasive, and the actual practice was ambiguous. In the West, where they were weak, the Communists had to adapt themselves to superior forces, accepting their brusque expulsion from government and even, as in Chile, the imposition of a ban which drove them underground. In the East, where an opposite balance of forces prevailed, heavy-handed methods were employed to unify the labour movement, control and purge other members of the coalition, and manage elections by presentation of a single slate within which seats were allocated among member-parties in a pre-established proportion. Both in practice (*Unidad Popular*, the Union of the Left, and the PCI's dealings with Socialists, Catholics and leftists) and in explicit programmatic formulations, the Communist parties have now given straight-forward replies to questions concerning the functioning of a democratic process. Thus, it has been acknowledged that unity of the strategic coalition has to be based upon diversity, mutual independence and equality; and that its forms of direction must be adapted accordingly. These practical and theoretical answers have not referred merely to the top level of government, parliament and inter-party relations. They have placed equal stress on self-organization of the masses at the base, on the specification of what Pietro Ingrao has called a 'mass democracy' – not as a utopian-demagogic substitute for constitutional arrangements at the centre, but as their necessary complement.

Some early post-war formulations of a national two-stage road to socialism (including such authoritative East European ones as those of Gomulka in Poland and Dimitrov in Bulgaria[7]) envisaged a socialist state distinct from a proletarian dictatorship – a kind of workers' and peasants' state, or people's state. But as far as I know, the way in which this would actually differ from the form of the dictatorship of the proletariat existing in the USSR was never fully explained. In the special sense in which Marx and Lenin used the term, 'dictatorship' was not merely compatible with democracy; it actually designated the broadest form of democracy – a state in which the free will of the majority of the population is asserted. But neither Marx nor Lenin specified in a realistic and concrete manner how such a system would function. By the time of the Popular Front, the dictatorship of the proletariat had developed into a highly authoritarian regime in the USSR. However, the Communists did not then openly acknowledge this fact, and they suggested no other concretization of the socialist state. The result was a fundamental ambiguity: on the one hand, explicit presentation of a strategy for socialism that differed from the Bolshevik one; on the other, evasiveness concerning whether this would lead to a different kind of socialist state.

If the strategic conception is now considerably less ambiguous and indistinct, this is due primarily to the consequential logic of specifications of the democratic stage, and, in the French, Italian and

[7] A very interesting panorama of post-war strategic conceptions emerges from a collection of articles by CP leaders, East and West, published for the 30th anniversary of the Swedish Communist Party: *Det nya Europa*, Stockholm 1946. On Dimitrov, see Philip Mioche's article on the context in which Maurice Thorez gave his famous interview to *The Times* of 17 November 1946: *Cahiers d'histoire de l'institut Maurice Thorez*, No. 19 1976. As for Thorez, he simply evaded a question on the dictatorship of the proletariat. The Italian Giangiacomo Feltrinelli Institute has published an enormous and highly absorbing volume on Marxist social and political theory of the twentieth century. It contains, among other noteworthy contributions, a thorough exposition of Kautsky's political thought – M. Salvadori, 'La conception du processus révolutionnaire chez Karl Kautsky de 1891 à 1922', *Histoire du marxisme contemporain*, Vol. 1, Paris 1976.

several other cases, to demarcation from the Soviet state. Some major social questions have also been accorded new weight. Thus, the problem of sexism, which, in spite of Kollontai's work, was largely neglected in the highly masculine Communist tradition, has received a great deal of attention in recent years. However, the political content and modalities of the stage beyond the Common Programme or the Historical Compromise have, on the whole, been left extremely vague.

This lacuna is, quite naturally, of little concern to the Social Democrats and bourgeois politicians who are pressing the Communists to give proof of their 'democratic reliability' – as if such forces could ever serve as adequate judges of the matter. For their own reasons, they are much more interested in denunciations of the existing socialist countries. However, the latter are a poor substitute for a specification of democratic socialism. In particular, they suffer from two interrelated defects. A denunciation is only a negative demarcation – a statement which says, for example, that a socialist France will be very different from the USSR, without giving any indication of the precise character and mode of development of the new society. Secondly, unless they are based on a clear positive conception of socialism, criticisms of the non-capitalist states easily tend to tail behind bourgeois attacks, which are concerned above all with maltreatment of individual bourgeois and (in a case like that of Solzhenitsyn) pre-bourgeois intellectuals. Criticism of the authoritarian treatment of oppositional intellectuals is in my opinion justified; but Communist parties have a more important task. Critical assessment of existing forms of socialism from a clear socialist and proletarian standpoint constitutes an important duty of 'proletarian internationalism' – a contribution to the development of socialism and the working class in these countries.

This new democratic-socialist strategy has, with varying degrees of elaboration and consistency, been developed by a large number of Communist parties: not only those of Chile, France and Italy, but also, to take the most conspicuous examples, those of Japan and Spain, as well as smaller parties, such as the British and Swedish ones. Clearly, it has not just sprung out of the heads of a few wise Communists. Although originating in a Communist initiative, these conceptions are being worked out in common with Socialist parties and other sections of the Left. Moreover, they are the fruit of hard and often bitter experience.

The events of the late sixties provided the basic parameters of the learning process. The Communist parties were then prompted to rethink their positions – to speak and act, as the decomposition of capitalist reformism opened up possibilities of advance. In contrast to the post-war situation in Eastern Europe, the parties were now completely on their own: they had to discover by themselves how to deal with the bourgeois state apparatus and how to relate to other forces and movements, each with its specific base and store of experiences. The new generation of workers and radicalized middle strata, who largely accounted for the decisive shift in the constellation of social forces, had not grown up in the same context of struggle as the CP cadres. They had not known the October Revolution; the contrast between planned industrialization and the mass unemployment of the Depression; or the anti-Fascist struggle and the victory of Stalingrad. New answers and practices had to be developed in response to their queries and concerns.

Given the continuity in the development of the strategic conception, it is perhaps not so remarkable that this learning process has occurred within a basically unchanged party form. The orderly methods of succession now in force present a striking contrast to the drastic leadership changes that were common in the twenties and early thirties. All the same, the leadership did undergo modification, at a time which broadly coincided with the political turn of the late sixties and in a manner which normally facilitated the process of rethinking and reorientation. While the change is, of course, very uneven among the different parties, it seems to represent a general phenomenon. However, it is above all due to the chance meeting of social and biological laws.

The post-war leaders of many Communist parties, such as those of Chile, France and Italy, were shaped in the period about 1930. They were typically both very young and long-lived, but by the sixties biological time had overtaken them and made necessary a generational change. The new leaders that then came to the fore had not been formed at the time when the national parties were disciplined sections of the Comintern; they had not lived together in the sombre rooms of the rundown Lux hotel in Moscow; they had not organized the International Brigades in Spain; they had not been on secret Comintern missions to all parts of the world, nor had they been tutored by such plenipotentiaries. Instead, they had received their fundamental training within their own national parties and particular social contexts.

Their heightened sensitivity to new developments in the national social formation was further enhanced by the diminishing possibilities of unified international formation and direction. The large international party conferences of 1957 and 1960 were impressive only at a rather superficial level. Beneath the documents lay mounting diversity, crisis and schism within and among the ruling Communist parties. The unstable and non-statutory changes of the Soviet leadership were not conducive to an atmosphere of unquestioned authority. The 20th Congress of the CPSU had opened the cupboard of Stalin's corpses and the excommunication of Yugoslavia had been withdrawn in 1955. Full-scale conflict developed between Moscow and Peking, while crises recurred in Eastern Europe at the precise moment when the Western parties were beginning to reorient themselves. It was against the not so dissimilar redirection of the Czechoslovak Communist Party that the USSR launched a military intervention.

Apart from the Chinese split, however, no break has so far occurred in the international continuity; and in 1976, the parties of Eastern and Western Europe met together in Berlin. Palmiro Togliatti, who, together with Dimitrov, was the ablest and most prestigious of the old Comintern cadres, gave a powerful impetus to the critical stance of most West European parties when he wrote his testamentary Yalta memorandum in connection with a last-minute attempt to bridge the Sino-Soviet rift. Although, here and there, various forces are probably moving towards new splits and excommunications, the main tendency hitherto has rather been one of frank debate. Carrillo's latest book, which contains a bitter and vehement critique of the USSR, elicited a vitriolic Soviet reply. But it was soon emphasized that no condemnation had been intended. There may be some immediate domestic advantage to be reaped from excommunication or secession, but the development of socialism in the world will benefit from neither. The Soviet leadership certainly has nothing to gain from a situation where it would have to relate only to bourgeois enemies in the West. As for the Western parties, they will draw much strength from democratic change in the socialist countries, and would mainly contribute to preservation of the *status quo* if they were to cut themselves off from the parties in the East. The Sino-Soviet conflict has been of profit only to the United States.

We may now synthesize the general line of development of the democratic-socialist strategy in the advanced capitalist countries by distinguishing *four decisive stages*. It should be emphasized from the outset that this summary only highlights the most crucial turns and greatly simplifies the complex historical process. In particular, it leaves out of account the internal debates and oscillations within the Second International – those which involved figures like Bernstein, Kautsky, Luxemburg and Pannekoek. Nor does it refer to the debate on the Russian 1905–8; the evolution of inter-war Austrian Social Democracy; the changes and schisms of the Comintern; the present-day differences between the PCI and PCF; or the various contributions of left-wing Socialism. With all these qualifications, however, such a perspective may provide a useful correction to the fashionable and superficial image of 'Eurocommunism', which is projected in a generally quite unhistorical manner by the Western media.

A number of elements are common to all the strategies: the determinant role of the inner contradictions of capitalism and of the class struggle; the basic definition of socialism; the necessity of revolution in the sense of a conquest of state power by the working class, as distinct both from seizure of power by a group of revolutionaries and from conciliation with the bourgeoisie. The strategies differ principally in the way they conceive of *six aspects*: a) the character of the revolution, b) working-class organization, c) the relationship of the working class to classes other than the main enemy, d) the enemy class, e) the character of the state, f) the main route to state power.

1. The classical strategy of the Second International

a) The revolution may in principle take many forms and arise out of many concrete situations, but it is above all a *natural historical process*, following from the development of capitalism and the growth of the proletariat. This conception had its polemical edge against Anarchism and the pre-Marxist revolutionaries, bourgeois or socialist, who issued from the radical wing of the French Revolution. 'Social Democracy is a revolutionary party, but not a party which makes revolutions. We know that our goals can only be reached through a revolution [a conquest of political power] but we know also that it is as little in our power to make this revolution as it is in that of our adversaries to prevent it. Therefore, it does not come to our mind to instigate or prepare a revolution.'[8] These lines were

[8] K. Kautsky, *The Road to Power*.

written by Kautsky in 1893 and quoted by himself in *The Road to Power* – that work which is, together with the Erfurt Programme of the SPD, the key text of the classical strategy. Revolutions, then, are not made; they *come*.

b) The proletariat has to organize itself, in trade unions and other special organizations, but above all in a *class-conscious political party*. The essential preparatory task is to build this up into a large mass party, and to keep it free of bourgeois influences.

c) In relation to the working class – unproblematically defined so as to include salaried employees – all other classes tend to form a single 'reactionary mass'. The proletariat constitutes the great majority of the population, and class alliances are excluded in a socialist transformation of society.

d) The enemy is *the bourgeoisie as a whole*, together with its aristocratic allies.

e) The state is an instrument of class rule, but its *class character* derives from its *governmental and legislative apparatus alone*. If the latter is conquered, the whole state apparatus falls without difficulty into the hands of the working class.

f) The main route to power is the fight for equal and universal suffrage and elected government. Once these are achieved, or very soon after, the proletariat will tranquilly *elect* the workers' party into power. The bourgeoisie may resort to violence. But the massive weight of the working class ensures that it will suffer at the most a very brief setback.

The fatal defects of this strategy, even in its best formulations, were its passive expectation of the revolution; its cavalier treatment of the state apparatus; and its failure to envisage the possibility of bourgeois class rule in democratic forms.

2. The Bolshevik strategy of the early Comintern

In 1917, the Bolsheviks developed in practice a new strategy, which was later explicated in Lenin's *Left-Wing Communism – An Infantile Disorder* and in the resolutions of the first Comintern congresses.

a) The socialist revolution is now seen as a *concrete political task*, something which quite definitely has to be prepared, organized and undertaken. However, it can be made only under certain objective conditions and only with the support of the majority of the working class.

b) From this novel conception of the revolution follows a novel conception of the working-class party. The aim of the latter is still to organize the workers politically and to rally the majority behind itself. What is new is the emphasis on the party as a *combat unit* able to make a revolution. The requirements of a combative revolutionary party are formulated in the 21 Theses specifying the conditions of admission to the Comintern.

c) The combative strategy is coupled with a certain flexibility of tactics. Thus, *class alliances* may become part of revolutionary strategy, as they did in 1917 when the Bolsheviks supported land seizures by the peasantry for individual family use.

d) The enemy is still *the bourgeoisie as a whole*.

e) Stress is laid upon the specificity of the class character of the state apparatus and on its irreducibility to the legal arrangements of the governmental and legislative apparatus. From this stems the goal of *'smashing' the state apparatus* and erecting a distinct proletarian state: the dictatorship of the proletariat. This 'dictatorship' is a democracy in that it is envisaged as the rule of the overwhelming majority of the population. Denial of voting rights to the bourgeoisie and the banning of all opposition – measures which were gradually introduced in the USSR – are explicitly presented as the result of special Russian conditions.

f) Although other possibilities may exist, *armed insurrection* is regarded as the main route to state power. The act of insurrection is dependent upon the entry of the old order into a profound political crisis, one aspect of which is the commitment of a majority of the working class to the revolution and the party of revolution.

3. The Popular Front strategy

The experience of Fascism brought the development of strategy to a third stage. The unexpected and unprecedentedly savage explosion of bourgeois violence revived for a short period the socialist goal of a non-bourgeois society within certain social-democratic parties. But it made its most significant and lasting mark upon the Communist parties. Although the Popular Front was at first a defensive alliance, it developed into a new strategy for socialism in those cases where Fascism had already succeeded. Immediately after the war, this became the general strategy of the CPs. The Leninist view of revolution as a concrete task was changed, while on the other points the lessons of the first two decades of the Comintern gave rise to alterations and fresh specifications.

b) The persistence of non-Communist workers' parties led to a reorientation of early Comintern positions, which had insisted upon the sharpest possible demarcation of the revolutionary party from Social Democracy. There arose instead a policy of *party unification*. But it was asserted at the same time that the united party would have to be of an essentially Leninist type – that is to say, based upon disciplined revolutionary organization, a Leninist view of the class character of the state, and acknowledgment of the decisive historical role of the October Revolution and the USSR.

c) From the redefinition of the immediate enemy (see point d. below) flowed a broader notion of class alliances. However, another specification was of greater importance for the relationship between democracy and socialism. The class alliance was now seen as also involving *an organizational alliance*, or strategic coalition, with the independent parties and other organizations of the allied classes. The leadership of the strategic coalition of the Popular Front should be firmly invested with the unified workers' party (by contrast to the defensive Popular Front of the thirties, in which the Communists remained a minor partner, even though they had usually taken the initiative in its formation).

d) The immediate enemy was no longer the bourgeoisie as a whole, but *monopoly capital*. In the *two-stage* strategy that was advanced, the first stage aimed only at destruction of the power and positions of monopoly capital and at the establishment of a new democracy.

e) Lenin's view of the class character of the state was preserved. But now *a clear distinction was made between democratic and terroristic forms of bourgeois dictatorship* or class rule. The smashing of the old state apparatus and the creation of a new one was adapted to the conception of two stages. In the early post-war period, opinions differed over whether the socialist state would have to be a dictatorship of the proletariat, although no clear alternative was presented. Quite soon, the traditional goal of proletarian dictatorship was reaffirmed.

f) Once successful, Fascism could only be crushed by violence. But it was envisaged that a new democracy could then be established by peaceful means; and that the main road forward to socialism was one of *peaceful development*, based on the strategic coalition.

The post-war constellation of power in the world made realization of this strategy possible only in Eastern Europe. If any one of the post-war elaborations of a national road to socialism in the West

were to be given especial mention, it would probably be the one
expressed in the political practice and numerous speeches and
articles of Palmiro Togliatti, the leader of the PCI.[9]

4. The fourth strategy

For want of a better name, I shall provisionally call this the fourth
strategy. It would be fashionable, but wrong, to term it the 'Euro-
communist' strategy, because it is neither all-European nor confined to that continent. It is not even of European origin. For the
first real elaboration and practical application was made by the
Chilean Communist Party – the chief architect of *Unidad Popular*
and of its victory at the polls in 1970.[10] This new strategy is being
developed through continuous debate on the entire Left. Nevertheless, it is a striking fact that the CPs were once again the initiators
of the process.

The originality of this strategy lies in the further specifications
made to points b) to f).

b) The objective of working class party unification is now abandoned as unattainable and replaced by one of *co-operation* between
equal and independent *parties*.

c) The organizational class alliance is no longer conceived as a
bloc under the more or less institutionalized leadership of the unified
working-class party. It is rather *a coalition of equal and independent
partners*, of which the co-operating workers' parties form the core.

d) The immediate enemy is still *monopoly capital*, and most parties
continue to advance a *two-stage* strategy. (The first stage is a parliamentary or presidential democracy which breaks the dominating
power of monopoly capital.) But there are some variations. The PCI
projects the intermediate goal of a 'historical compromise' with
Christian Democracy, yet it does not foresee a distinct social stage

[9] Cf. the sympathetic theoretical analysis by G. Vacca, *Saggio su Togliatti*, Bari
1974. A serious and well-documented study of PCI policies in the immediate
post-war period, written from a non-Marxist standpoint, is H. Hamrin, *Between
Bolshevism and Revisionism*, Stockholm 1975.

[10] The best introduction to the thought of the Chilean party leadership is the
frank and well-conducted series of interviews published as E. Labarca, *Corvalán
27 Horas*, Santiago de Chile 1972. (I have consulted the West German translation:
Corvalán–Labarca, *Kommunistische Politik in Chile*, West Berlin 1973. Cf. the
French collection: L. Corvalán, *Chili, les communistes dans la marche au socialisme*,
Paris 1972.) For a solid review, seasoned with leftist evaluations, of the experience
and background of *Unidad Popular*, see I. Roxborough et al., *Chile: The State and
Revolution*, London and Basingstoke, 1977.

on the gradual road of socialist transformation. Similarly, the immediate strategic objective of the Swedish CP is to break the hold of monopoly capital (or 'big finance', as the party calls it). But it does not conceive of a discrete anti-monopoly stage of society.

e) A number of specifications have been made concerning the class character of the state. There is a tendency to *de-emphasize*, in my opinion seriously to underestimate, *the class character of the non-repressive state apparatuses*. The talk is now of 'democratizing', rather than 'smashing', the bourgeois state apparatus. The *institutional arrangements necessary for democracy to operate as a continuous process* – the conditions of opinion-making, elections, and so on – are now described *in concrete detail*. Except in the case of the Chilean CP, this has been accompanied by explicit criticisms of the lack, or malfunctioning, of such institutions in the existing socialist countries. In order to end all ambiguity about the democratic character of the socialist state, the concept of the dictatorship of the proletariat has been abandoned.

f) Advance towards both the intermediary stage and the further one of socialism are now located principally on the road of *parliamentary elections*, to be fought separately by the parties of the strategic coalition. Greater emphasis is also placed on the role of non-violent *mass struggle* at all levels of society.

The Chilean CP adhered to its democratic socialist strategy throughout the difficult years of 1972 and 1973. But it would be wrong to say that the fourth strategy was applied, and bloodily defeated, under the Allende regime in Chile. *Unidad Popular* also contained strong leftist elements, which gained the upper hand in the Socialist Party and MAPU. As a result, the *Unidad Popular* had no coherent strategy and tactics in its later period. It zig-zagged between efforts to avoid total polarization – which would have pushed more than half the population into opposition – and displays of fiery rhetoric and new strides forward that could not be consolidated with the existing forces.

It is virtually impossible to say whether the strategy of the CP and Allende would have been successful if it could have been consistently applied. Afterwards, the CP self-critically admitted its lack of an adequate military policy (see below). At present, the most highly elaborated conception of the fourth strategy is the Common Programme of the French Union of the Left and the documents of the 22nd Congress of the PCF, *Le socialisme pour la France* (Paris 1976).

Finally, the range of the present democratic-socialist perspective should be delineated. The most advanced experience so far took place in a peripheral and relatively underdeveloped country, Chile, and it now lies crushed in blood. After the fall of the dictatorships in Greece, Portugal and Spain, the strong underground Communist parties were overtaken by superior bourgeois and social-democratic forces. The political weakness of the Portuguese bourgeoisie made possible major socialist and democratic gains, but their social base was too narrow to permit a revolutionary breakthrough. Having been carried away in 1975 by the extreme radicalism of vanguard sectors of the working class and army, the PCP has since had to entrench itself in a tenacious defence of past gains against a mounting Social Democratic attempt, under international blackmail, to bring about the more or less total restoration of capitalism. Hitherto, the latter policy of the Communist Party has met with considerable success. But it is France and Italy that hold out real prospects of short-term advance. They are important capitalist countries, but they are not the most crucial ones, and their current political crisis is of a rather special nature.

The notables format of bourgeois political representation in the Fourth Republic was a very archaic mode of rule, particularly given the existence of a relatively strong labour movement. The Fifth Republic held together, in a peculiar combination, a plebiscitary president, installed in power through a kind of coup d'etat, a new party format and the old notables system. The strength of the social explosion detonated in May by the student movement was in part due to the fact that moderate sectors of the middle strata, the petty bourgeoisie and even the bourgeoisie proper did not immediately identify the Gaullist regime either with themselves or with the state of law and order. At the moment of truth they rallied to de Gaulle, but he soon disappeared and died, followed quickly by his successor, Pompidou. As a result, the Fifth Republic entered a crisis of division and disarray, which, coming on top of deeper economic, social and political convulsions, has endangered bourgeois rule itself. Merely to point to the governmental instability of the Fifth Republic is, of course, to touch only the surface of the political scene. But it is precisely there that the most profound social forces fight out their struggle for power. That was one of Lenin's most precious teachings on political crises.

The crisis in Italy is largely one of pre-capitalist politics and is driven forward by the weakening of the political hold of the

Catholic Church – an institution which pre-dates even the feudal epoch but which is a central component of the Christian Democratic party format. The crisis is also fuelled by a parasitic and blatantly inefficient *sottogoverno* – in reality, a commodity form of feudal clientelism – and by the recent drying up, through migration and industrialization, of large reservoirs of captive populations in southern Italy.

Democratic and socialist advances in France and Italy will have very wide repercussions on the whole of the advanced capitalist world, affecting particularly the Mediterranean, and probably also influencing developments in Eastern Europe. But the current situation in France and Italy does not signal a general political crisis of developed capitalism; nor is it highly probable that progress in these two countries will bring one about in the short run.[11] Despite the remarkable capacity of the Liberal Democrats to preserve their extraordinarily corrupt clientele system, it is in Japan that the next major political upheaval of developed capitalism seems most likely to occur. By contrast, the two other main pillars of capitalism, the United States and West Germany, appear extremely stable. The West Germans are increasingly taking over the American role of gendarme of Western Europe, operating both through the state apparatus and with funds accumulated from secret sources and channelled through the Social Democratic *Friedrich-Ebert-Stiftung*.

We should also stress the limitations of what will be achieved, even if the Left wins the French elections of 1978, even if its Common Programme is fully implemented, and even if the still distant and less far-reaching Historical Compromise is realized in Italy. Profound social and political changes will occur, but in neither case will they bring about a society of developed, democratic socialism.

---

[11] The political crises in France and Italy are thus rather more concrete and specific than the 'crisis of the state' of contemporary capitalism, or the 'crisis of state monopoly capitalism'. It is remarkable that, among the eleven essays contained in the very interesting book *La crise de l'Etat* (ed. Nicos Poulantzas, Paris 1976), not one deals with the crisis of Gaullism and the Fifth Republic. In reviewing this work, a Communist writer counterposes to the focus expressed in its title the notion of a crisis of state monopoly capitalism; but the only thing he has to say about the differences between France and Italy and the rest of the advanced capitalist world is 'to note the decisive role of the "subjective moment" as the moment of self-organization of the working class'. (J. Lojkine, '"Crise de l'Etat" et "crise du capitalisme monopoliste d'état"', *La Pensée* No. 193, June 1977, p. 125.) Neither Gaullism nor Italian Christian Democracy seems to have been the subject of a full-scale Marxist study.

As is made more or less explicit by both the PCI and the left-wing parties in France, capitalism will remain. An important new stage will have been reached, but fresh setbacks may also be inflicted before the advent of socialism. Moreover, even a socialist society is not yet classless, communist society. In France and Italy, too, Communists and Socialists are still only at the beginning of a long march.

2.

The Future as History

Democratic socialism is a prospect of the future, and hardly the most immediate future, in Western Europe, North America, Japan and Australia. If it is to become a reality, then the struggles for, and achievement of that goal will be part of future history. In the current state of discussion on socialism and democracy, this point is unfortunately not quite as banal as it sounds. For what is involved in the statement that the struggle for socialism will have to be part of future history in order to have real significance? Above all, the road to socialism cannot be treated only or mainly in terms of ideals, hopes and dreams, as a glowing utopia – although this too is necessary. It will have to be based on the realities of the past and present, and will be as full of contradictions, ironies, paradoxes, defeats, victories, compromises, errors and surprises as all the rest of human history. Lessons can be, and should be, drawn from the past and the present, but neither can be remade or abolished by the powers of thought.

Let us now briefly indicate a number of realities and problems that socialist struggle as future history has to take into account. We shall not attempt to present an exhaustive list – which would be an impossible task – nor even mention all the most urgent problems. Our discussion will simply focus on a few questions raised by the preceding essays and by my reading of the current debate on the Left.

One obvious aspect of the future as history is the fact that it has to be based on the forces of the present, in this case the labour movement. The latter has developed and changed in the past; and so it will, no doubt, in the future. But realities cannot be thought away or ignored, even if they appear unpleasant. Thus, in North-West

Europe and in Australia and New Zealand, no socialist strategy is realistic which does not explicitly try to come to grips with Social Democracy, and explain how it can be transformed; how it can be involved in co-operative alliances; and how the relations of strength within the labour movement can be altered. Not even the grim SPD, with its dire record stretching from Gustav Noske to Helmut Schmidt, can be wished out of existence. Moreover, in order to reckon seriously with Social Democracy, it is necessary to treat it as an organization, rather than evasively reduce it to the general form of 'Socialist Democratic workers'.

In the Latin countries, where the balance of power on the Left is fairly even, that kind of wishful thinking is much less attractive. However, when we referred above to the forces of the present, we intended the word 'forces' to be taken in a strong sense. Not only adherents of the status quo but also sincere socialists are clamouring that the Communist parties should distance themselves 'once and for all' from their past. Indeed, such a demand may well find a certain echo among the many new recruits, who are more likely to have heard of the wrongs than of the merits of the Communist past. Now, one of the great sources of strength of Communism lies in its long experience and record of combat, endurance and discipline. It is true that these qualities were not infrequently deployed on the wrong occasion or in support of issues which were not fully correct; and some of these parties do seem to need a development of internal democracy, an unfolding of their inner dialectic. But if the road to socialism is to be a history of class struggles, and not a walk towards the sun, then the experience and combativity of the Communist parties will be an enormous asset for the Left as a whole. Were they to become conglomerates of intellectual-led factions like the Socialist parties, the whole labour movement in these countries would be weakened.

The combative revolutionary is associated with the theory and practice of Lenin – that *bête noire* of Social Democrats and non-Communist Socialists. However, the latter would be wrong to close their eyes to the contemporary and future relevance of Lenin: to his view of the socialist revolution as a concrete political task; his concepts of political crisis and revolutionary situation; his stress on the importance of the class character of the state apparatus; his combination of flexible tactics and broad alliances with a steadfast strategic commitment; his analysis of the tasks and possibilities of the labour movement in a definite international context of imperialism. Much may even be learned from his arguments, crude and summary though they were, that democratic institutions can function to reproduce bourgeois power and exploitation. The France of the Common Programme will undoubtedly have to face up to that reality. The Communists are much more interested in their partners' future commitment to a socialist strategy, than in their renunciation of past practices. But Communists have to admit that positive contributions have also been made by other sections of the Left. Social Democracy was from the beginning aware of the enormous difference between democratic and dictatorial forms of bourgeois class rule; and a large part of its criticism of Stalinism was on the mark. Moreover, the intellectual volatility of the contemporary Socialist parties is, when placed alongside the solidity and resoluteness of the Communist parties, a prophylactic asset against rigidity and ossification.

The contrast between the behaviour of the Second International in 1914 and that of the Comintern in 1939 highlights another problem of socialist history, whether past, present or future, namely, *the contradictions of nationalism and internationalism*. On the one hand, the independence of the national Communist parties has increased their sensitivity to the concrete problems and traditions of the formation in which they work. Such fine attunement is clearly an essential part of the capacity to direct a socialist revolution. (The quite special circumstances of post-war Eastern Europe constitute a partial exception, but a high price has had to be paid for it.) On the other hand, independence also generates tendencies towards national integration, that is, absorption into the existing bourgeois social framework. The national road to socialism is a long one, and it may turn, and has turned, into a national halt at the stage of reformed capitalism.

Internationalism is an equally contradictory phenomenon. In order to function as a material force, it must involve participation in the common struggle of an international movement, and not just feelings and proclamations of solidarity with the oppressed and exploited of all lands. But internationalism has also bred subservience to abstract directives and alien models – not very successful ones at that. The internationalist road to socialism may turn, and has turned, into a ghetto lying outside both national socialism and national capitalism. Nowhere did the sections of the Comintern, or indeed those of the Second International, ever accomplish a socialist revolution. These contradictions form part of a reality which has to be faced, lived and mastered, rather than a Gordian knot which may be cut by the sword of the national road or that of proletarian internationalism.

We must now consider a further lesson of the experience of the Second and Third Internationals – as well as of the short-lived left-Social Democratic Two-and-a-Half International which was set up in the early twenties under the leadership of the Austrians. In all those countries where the possibility of democratic socialist advance is now opening, or was opening in the early seventies (i.e., Chile), classical Social Democracy has been a weak force. In other words, there are no strong historical roots of *labour reformism*. The predominantly maximalist tradition of Italian Socialism involves passive expectation of the conditions in which the maximum (socialist) programme can be realized. The Chilean Socialist Party was built upon the traditions of Third World military progressivism (Marmaduke Grove) and on dissident left-wing communism of a Trotskisant, and later Fidelista, inspiration. Beneath the humanist rhetoric of Léon Blum and above the rather insignificant minority of leftists lay the real bedrock of the French SFIO: torpid bourgeois parliamentarism and municipalism, directed by political manoeuverers and local mayor-notables. The new Socialist Party did not have its origins in a working-class movement: the transformation of the SFIO was conducted from a base in a number of left-wing technocratic and intellectual socialist clubs, from which François Mitterand emerged as the leader.

The opposition between Social Democratic reformism and Communism and Socialism cannot be obliterated by the sort of cheap cliché, very fashionable among Swedish Social Democrats for instance, according to which the forces of the Left are currently engaged in a repetition of the classical reformist evolution. The tremendous differences between the Swedish party of Branting and Per Albin Hansson, which was early converted to Bernstein's revisionism, and the party of Gramsci, Togliatti, Longo and Berlinguer – differences in both theoretical maturity and fighting experience – should be obvious to anyone not blinded by ideological spectacles. The contrast between the French Common Pogramme and the current policy of any Scandinavian Social Democratic party is, of course, even more evident. True, the perspective of the Union of the Left is not altogether unlike that of the British Labour Party in 1945; but, again, the party of Attlee, Bevin and Morrison was part of a different world from the one inhabited by the tough French Communist Party.

However, it should be acknowledged that, as working class parties embarking upon a gradual strategy of socialist transformation, the French and Italian Communist Parties will be confronted with a major problem: labour reformism. Neither their own history nor that of their partners and competitors provides them with direct experience of this obstacle (though, of course, certain lessons may be drawn from the 1945–47 period). What is to be done then? Well, our first task is to study very carefully the various concrete experiences of labour reformism: the development and achievements of Swedish Social Democracy between 1932 and 1976 (on which the present writer is directing a research project in Sweden); the swift transformation in the 1930s of the Norwegian Labour Party from a maximalist party – which, after a brief entry *en bloc* into the Comintern, remained for another decade a mass party with an explicitly revolutionary programme – into a Social Democratic party committed to administration of a reformed capitalist society; the British Labour government of 1945–1951; and the Nordic equivalent of the Historical Compromise, namely, the 1966 Finnish coalition government, which comprised a strong Communist Party, an even stronger Social Democracy and the Agrarians, but which reached an impasse after only a couple of years.[12] There exists no international leading

[12] At least for an outside observer with no knowledge of the Finnish language, there is a striking contrast between the strategic impasse and unimaginativeness of the third largest Communist party in Western Europe, and the initiative and advances of the French and Italian parties. Since the mid-sixties, the Finnish party has been divided from top to bottom, roughly in the proportion of 60 to 40, between a more pragmatic and moderate majority and a more orthodox and radical minority. First appearing with the adoption of a new party programme in 1965 and a generational change of leadership, the divergence has since broadened under the impact of the disappointments of the coalition government, which was in principle supported by both tendencies. The whole party is deeply attached to the USSR, though the minority is the more dedicated wing. (The CPSU has apparently played a key role in keeping the party together.) In general, the minority's criticisms of the majority resemble somewhat Chinese polemics of the early sixties against the PCI, and those of the first Maoist groups against the 'revisionist' Communist parties. Like the Chinese, it invokes in its support the documents of the international party conferences of 1957 and 1960. (See T. Sinisalo, *En kommunist har ordet*, Helsinki 1976). These positions are probably one reason why left-wing Marxist intellectuals have rallied more or less *en bloc* to the minority since the late sixties; there they have been preoccupied with a large-scale project

centre of the revolutionary labour movement, and nor should there be one. But it appears absolutely crucial to report and analyse the various national experiences in more continuous and searching forms than brief meetings and joint communiqués of intent.

We have said that *socialism* may be part of future history. It will, then, be not a programmatic ideality but a real society, marked by contradictions, difficulties, deficiencies and struggles, and manifested in a number of different forms. Whether socialism is part of present history is an empirical question, which I am convinced must be answered in the affirmative. But the reply naturally depends on how the question is put. Now, if socialism is that which socialists are fighting to realize in history, is it very meaningful to *define* it as the summation of all our ideals? No society has ever actually expressed all the ideals of its protagonists. Of course, ideals have played an important role both as goals of endeavour and as guides for criticism. But according to a fundamental thesis of the materialist view of history, neither apologetic nor utopian ideas provide much insight into the functioning and evolution of history. Consequently, an idealist conception would not help us to understand and realize the development of socialism as part of future history.

We have presented above a number of quite distinct variants of bourgeois rule. Any scientific theory of socialism must elaborate a similar analysis of existing and possible forms of socialism and their modes of operation.

Little has been said so far of the repressive apparatuses and the problems of reactionary *violence*, of whose existence Communists and left-wing Socialists have long been aware. Here again, a real contradiction is involved – one which cannot be conjured away by pious declarations of faith in the peaceful road or sloganeering on the necessity to arm the workers. The repressive apparatuses are no paper tigers: they are real, and they are on their guard. As the experience of Chile hammered home, the worst possible course is to issue violent verbiage from the roof-tops when it cannot be supported by material force. That is a contradiction between words and deeds. But there is a deeper one.

---

of economic studies on Finnish state monopoly capitalism – a project of which rather little has so far been realized. In this quite unique context, radicalization on orthodox positions can be combined with membership in a mass working-class party – although a price has had to be paid, in terms of both inflexible relations between the two factions and stagnation of the party's role in society.

On the one hand, the best defence against bourgeois violence, where an unarmed population faces a vigilant repressive apparatus, is undoubtedly a broad and firm popular alliance. When they were considering the viability of a military take-over in the early 1930s, the strategists of the German Reichswehr bore in mind the experience of the general strike against the 1920 Kapp-Luttwitz putsch. They soon came to the conclusion that it would be too difficult to run the country against the opposition of the overwhelming majority of the population.[13] However, the construction of a broad popular alliance tends to require total abnegation of dual tactics and vanguardist revolutionary violence. This is expressed by Luigi Longo, a Communist leader with long and varied experience of parliamentary legality and underground work, civil war (Spain), and armed resistance. His opinion is endorsed by Enrico Berlinguer in his reflections on Chile: 'As Comrade Longo has said, the possibility that reaction may resort to violence "must not lead to a duality in our prospect and practical preparation".'[14]

On the other hand, the history of ferocious bourgeois violence is an undeniable fact, which makes it necessary to prepare for a violent reaction. It has often been stated that a characteristic of Communist parties is their ability to engage in drastic switches of line and tactics. This was indeed part of Lenin's teachings, and it may to some extent be verified in the history of the Comintern. But, in modern times, it is in fact the bourgeois state which has proved capable of the most rapid switches, again and again taking the Communist parties by surprise. This is illustrated not only by the completely unexpected ferocity of Fascism, the Kuomintang, and the Indonesian and Chilean armies. It has also been expressed in less bloody forms: the expulsion of the Communists from the French and Italian governments in spring 1947 and in Chile somewhat later; de Gaulle's coup of 1958 and his reassertion of power on 30 May 1968 (although in the latter case the PCF, alone on the French Left, was aware of the possibilities open to him); and the carefully staged provocation in Portugal on 25 November 1975.

For these reasons we should also listen very attentively to another experienced Communist leader, the Chilean Volodia Teitelboim,

---

[13] F. Carsten, *Reichswehr and Politics 1918–1923*, Oxford 1966, p. 403.
[14] E. Berlinguer, 'Reflections after the Events in Chile', *Marxism Today*, February 1974, p. 42.

whose party was the first to develop and put into practice a gradualist democratic strategy for socialism: 'Of course, a peaceful transition deserves its name only to the extent that it rules out civil war. However, through the numerous vicissitudes and sudden changes of its course, it does not escape from the law that "violence is the mid-wife of history". We must continually keep this truth before us, even though the very act of changing course presupposes that the rider has another horse available for his advance through history. It is always difficult to change horses in mid-stream, and much more difficult when the relief mount has not been prepared in advance. The possibility and capacity of effecting such a change must exist, quite apart from a clear perception of its necessity. The matter is not only decided at the moment when the change is made; it presupposes that considerable work has already been performed . . .'[15]

Once more, this is a genuine contradiction which must be faced and mastered. But the task cannot be accomplished from a writing-desk in Lund, Sweden, nor, it would seem, from any other desk or rostrum; it can be handled only in political practice.

In the preceding essays, we have paid more attention to the other state apparatuses, which have hitherto been the subject of greater neglect. Thus, we have contrasted the cadre administration of existing socialist states to the *bureaucracy* and *technocracy* of the bourgeois states. In order to function effectively as instruments of collective working class supremacy, the cadres must simultaneously belong to a labour movement independent of the state and exercise powers of non-commanding direction over bureaucrats and mana-gers. Recent Western strategic formulations have emphasized only the first aspect. But the advanced democratic and socialist state will also need to employ political and ideological weapons against bureaucratic-managerial reproduction of the subordination of the workers. Some of the political cadre functions may be fulfilled by unions of state employees, such as those already developed in the monopoly capitalist state, and through devolution of central powers to elected regional and local assemblies. However, state bureaucrats

[15] V. Teitelboim, 'Reflexiones sobre los "mil dias" del gobierno de Unidad Popular en Chile', *Materiales*, Barcelona, No. 3 1977, p. 27. This article was originally published in the international CP journal *Problems of Peace and Socialism (World Marxist Review)*, No. 1 1977. The editors have recently carried a whole series of valuable reflections on the Chilean experience, of which the most notable so far is probably that of Jorge Insunza in No. 5 1977.

and managers will not thereby disappear, and problems of popular control will remain. Under Social Democratic and liberal pressure, the present conceptions of socialist democracy have largely evaded the serious and complicated questions of bureaucracy and technocracy. In the end, sweeping theses on *autogestion* (or self-management) may prove as misleadingly utopian as the picture of the dictatorship of the proletariat drawn in *State and Revolution*.

A related problem concerns the politicization or *socialization of private life*. The democratic socialist strategy is committed to pluralism, both within the strategic coalition and in society as a whole. Now, pluralism is no doubt an important part of democracy as a process. But in the present bourgeois societies, it also increasingly involves atomization of the population – isolation, insecurity, humiliation, degradation, self-disdain and self-destruction. The notion of alienation expresses but poorly these sombre aspects of life in modern bourgeois society, particularly in the big cities and their suburbs. Although present in every capitalist society, they are more pronounced in the highly developed ones of the United States and Scandinavia than in, for example, France or Italy. Clearly, no socialism can be built upon this kind of 'pluralism', which reproduces on an expanding scale the subordination of the working class. In part, these problems will be solved by the unfolding of mass struggles for social transformation, in which normally atomized people, who feel they are 'no good', will be drawn into the life of society and regain their human value and dignity. But a solution also presupposes that the democratic-socialist coalition will consciously go beyond existing bourgeois conceptions and practices of 'pluralism' to organize social collectivities at all levels and in all parts of society. (PCI writers have correctly argued that, in this respect, socialism has a greater affinity with Catholicism than with liberalism.[16])

The strategic conception of a broad anti-monopoly alliance, in its variegated formulations, embraces a number of analytical and material contradictions, which are rarely made explicit. The struggle for such an alliance, expressed in concrete organizational and programmatic practices, involves acknowledgment of a very

[16] Togliatti himself pointed to the affinity of Christian and Communist-Socialist 'solidarism'. (Cf. Vacca, op. cit., p. 283.) For a recent statement see, for example, Achille Occhetto's contribution to N. Bobbio et al., *Il marxismo e lo stato*, Rome 1976, p. 94.

important reality: namely, *the mass base of current bourgeois power* and the strategic necessity to win that base away from the ruling class. But to strive for something through hard work implies that it does not yet exist, or that it exists only incompletely. The attempt to show the middle strata and petty bourgeoisie that there is a material basis for common struggle with the working class is not assisted by analyses which ignore the *de facto* ability of monopoly capital to rally large sections of these layers behind itself. Indeed, the success of such a strategy depends upon an understanding of how this has happened. Much valuable work has already been done, both in economic analysis of 'the state of the monopolies' or the state as 'total capitalist', and in cultural study of 'hegemony' and 'legitimation'. We have presented above a by no means finished set of tools with which to undertake deeper analysis of the modalities of bourgeois rule – processes and mechanisms of reproduction; different modes of ideological interpellation; multiple determinants of state power; formats of representation and their functioning; and processes of state mediation of the rule of the ruling class. Much more work needs to be done on these questions.

A further analytical problem of the anti-monopoly strategy should be mentioned at this point. Are conflicts between monopoly and non-monopoly sectors of the bourgeoisie so serious and deep-rooted that significant groups of the latter can realistically be expected to ally themselves with the working class? As for the petty bourgeoisie, its strategic weight varies greatly from country to country, according to its size and political tradition; it thus plays a much more important role in France and Italy than in Britain or Sweden. These questions should be tackled with instruments of scientific analysis, freed from both *ouvrieriste* prejudice and wishful thinking. Nor should they be overloaded with heated ideological polemic. Strategically, the decisive aspect of the anti-monopoly conception is *the concrete attempt to unblock a non-revolutionary situation, characterized by ongoing administration of capitalism,* through a broad democratic alliance for major social and political change. This will not of itself bring about socialism, but it may set the wheels of history moving in a socialist direction.

Deep analytical contradictions arise when the difficulties of this strategic endeavour are not adequately confronted. But the concept of *anti-monopoly society* also involves *contradictions in reality,* investigation of which constitutes a central task of Marxist economic and political analysis. Here we shall merely indicate a few of the most obvious problems.

Modern monopoly capital is not predominantly based on parasitic *rentier* layers, but on the most dynamic and efficient fraction of the bourgeoisie. In the great majority of cases, the big corporations pay higher wages and provide better working conditions and union rights than small and medium-size enterprises. Socialization of these monopoly sectors will clearly give direction and dynamism to the whole economy. But how will it be possible to unite the various partners of the anti-monopoly alliance? How can workers' demands for equal wages, improved working conditions and broader union rights be reconciled with the quest of less efficient, non-monopolistic capital for higher profits and increased authority?

The power of a democratic government will depend to a great extent on its capacity to maintain living standards and levels of employment. However, capitalist competition generates new monopolies, new 'commanding heights' of the economy, thus reproducing monopoly capital once more. The process may be checked by further socialization and discriminatory taxation; but in anticipation of such measures, the capitalist dynamic will slow down, giving rise to flight of capital, factory closures, and rising unemployment. In order to sustain itself and continue the advance to its socialist goals, the government will rely heavily on the development of the initiatives and struggles of the masses themselves. But this too will tend to alienate moderate sectors of the class alliance.

A society of anti-monopoly democracy is one in which the domination of national monopoly capital has been more or less completely broken. However, a large part of the power of monopoly capital is *international*, located both in the notorious multinational corporations and in the international agencies of finance capital such as the World Bank, the International Monetary Fund, and the club of national banks of the leading capitalist states. The government may nationalize that part of the multinational corporations which is based on its own territory. But what should be done with the external holdings of native multinationals? If they too are expropriated, the resulting socialized multinationals will continue to be run on more or less capitalist lines. If they are relinquished, then problems of foreign trade and the balance of payments will have to be solved before the whole economy can be restructured on a planned socialist basis. Even if we disregard this particular dilemma, the new enterprises, no longer dominated by big capital, will probably encounter serious difficulties in their search for export markets and foreign credit. It may be possible to escape international blackmail, of the kind that was applied to Chile and Portugal, by turning to the socialist countries. The Soviet Union, for example, has given considerable support to Cuba and Vietnam without threatening their national independence.

These and many other contradictions and problems still have to be overcome – and they will be overcome one way or another. But in order to tackle them in the right way, it is far better to prepare for them in advance.

In the end, however, the history of the future cannot be written. It has to be made.

INDEX OF NAMES

Printed in the United States
By Bookmasters